The Best of
the
Doll Reader

Volume IV

Article Reprints — 1982 to 1989
Compiled and Edited by Virginia Ann Heyerdahl

Published by Hobby House Press   Cumberland, Maryland 21502

Additional copies of this book may be purchased at $14.95
from
Hobby House Press, Inc.
900 Frederick Street
Cumberland, Maryland 21502-1298
or from your favorite bookstore or dealer.
Please add $3.30 per copy for postage.

Introduction

Following the success of **Volumes I, II** and **III** of **The Best of the Doll Reader**, Hobby House Press, Inc., is pleased to publish **The Best of the Doll Reader, Volume IV**, a compilation of 52 of the most interesting and well-researched articles appearing in previous issues of **Doll Reader** magazine. We feel these enlightening articles will interest you as well as aid you in all facets of your doll collecting hobby.

This volume is divided into two chapters: Antique and Collectible. The Antique section focuses on such dolls as pincushion half-dolls, chinas, automata, papier-mâchés, woodens, bisques, metal-headed dolls and others. Included also are several articles on dolls with unusual hair styles.

The Collectible section features articles on such diverse subjects as *Charmin' Chatty*, *Muffie*, *Chuckles*, *Sweet Sue*, *Toni*, *Dy-Dee*, *Tiny Tears*, *Betsy Wetsy*, *Crissy*, *Peggy*, *Kiddie Pal Dolly* and, of course, the ever-popular *Barbie* and her friends, to name just a few. As an added bonus for collectors, Toy Fair articles from 1986 through 1988 feature the new dolls debuting each year.

We feel this well-rounded collection of articles is sure to please the most discriminate doll collector and it is our hope that you will continue to enjoy the articles that appear in **Doll Reader** magazine. If you do not already subscribe, we invite you to do so in order to further the enjoyment of your hobby of collecting dolls.

Virginia Ann Heyerdahl
Editor — April 1991

Gary R. Ruddell
Publisher — April 1991

TABLE OF CONTENTS

Page 12

Page 23

Automata —
A Living History

by **Dana Hawkes**, Department Head, Collectibles,
Sotheby's, New York City

All photographs courtesy of **Sotheby's,** New York City.

Nowadays, in our self-conciously sophisticated world, it is difficult for us to imagine the effect early automata had on their audiences. Like magic, these animated figural machines amazed an ignorant public by their many naturalistic movements. One Victorian automaton, known as the *The Smoker*, even inhaled and exhaled smoke from a cigarette.

The Smoker was made during the heyday of the automaton, the second half of the 19th century, but sophisticated machines were being made at least a century earlier. In 1770, a brilliant Hungarian, Wolfang von Kemplen, created a fascinating automaton called the *Chess Player*. The life-size figure, dressed in Turkish attire, would invite any one in his audience to challenge him to a game of chess. However, before the game began, the doors to the base of the figure were opened, allowing the public to look for any hidden accomplices in the mechanism. Having satisfied the audience, the figure would begin his game, moving the magnetic chess pieces with his right hand. Needless to say, he won every time — even Napoleon was defeated. As we know today, machines do not have a mind of their own, so how was this possible?

The most likely explanation seems to be that a midget, who was also a chess master, was concealed somewhere under the figure and he operated the mechanism. Unfortunately, the secret of the *Chess Player* was lost when it was destroyed in a fire at the Chinese Museum in Philadelphia in 1854.

A true automaton, without the aid of human manipulation, was built by Jaquet-Droz in 1774. A little boy sits behind a mahogany table and, as Alfred Chapuis and Edmond Droz describe the movement in their book, *Les Automates*, "the boy dips his quill in an inkwell on his right, shakes it twice, puts his hand at the top of the page and then pauses. Further pressure on a lever sets the automaton moving, and the boy begins to write. He forms his letters carefully, distinguishing between the light and the heavy strokes. (It is worth noting that he is the only automaton writer who does this.) He also leaves spaces between the words and changes over from one line to the next as required. After the last letter of his text, this hard-working scholar puts a final full-stop and then finishes." Other automata created by the Jaquet-Droz brothers include the *Draughtsman* and the *Lady Musician*, both of which can now be seen in the Historical Museum in Neuchatel, Switzerland.

All through the 18th century and right into the 19th, magicians and showmen used automata as part of their performances. However, by the 1860s in France, the market was ripe for small luxury animated toys. Traveling exhibitions of

Illustration 1. The *Magic Cupboard*, depicting a boy seated on top of a cupboard, is shown with other automata.

Illustration 2. *Pierrot*, who sits at a desk writing a letter by the light of a lamp.

life-size automata, such as the *Chess Player*, had created a demand for similar performing figures on a smaller scale which could be enjoyed at home. The middle classes now had more and more money to spend on anything novel, like automata, while rich visitors from abroad provided a ready market for souvenirs such as toys and singing birds. This was the golden age of French toy making and it saw the emergence of a number of famous workshops, such as Vichy, Leopold Lambert, Roullet et Decamps, Phalibois, Renou and Theroude.

The first and foremost of these French makers was Gustave Pierre Vichy, who flourished in the 1860s and 1870s. He created a variety of automata including magicians, acrobats and musicians. The musical mechanisms and the many cams (the cams trigger the rods that activate each movement of the figure) are concealed either within the body or in the base. The most readily identifiable characteristic of Vichy automata is the acorn-shaped knob of the start/stop mechanism. The heads were usually made of composition, finely molded with individual facial details and then painted. In order to allow realistic movement of the eyes and mouth, he used kidskin, which, unfortunately, has usually dried out and has to be repaired. The heads will nod and turn — usually in time to music — while the hands move. Sotheby's has sold several Vichy automata in recent years, but the most fascinating by far is the *Magic Cupboard*, shown in **Illustration 1**, which depicts a boy seated on top of a cupboard. He turns and reaches toward the cupboard door, which suddenly opens and a fly flies out. Failing to catch the fly, the boy catches sight of a pot of his grandmother's gooseberry jam. He hesitates before reaching in for it, when suddenly the pot spins around to reveal his grandmother's face on the other side. Her spectacles rise and her jaw drops in alarm as the boy steps back in alarm. He gestures with a biscuit in his left hand, nods his head and sticks out his tongue. The cupboard door closes and a mouse runs up a block of cheese on the counter. The extraordinary piece sold at Sotheby's recently for $23,600.

Another amusing automata by Vichy is the *Pierrot*, shown in **Illustration 2**. The figure sits at a desk writing a letter by the light of a lamp. As he writes, his head follows his hand as it

Illustration 3. The *Smoking Dandy* who actually smokes a lit cigarette which is placed in his cigarette holder.

moves across the page. Gradually, he begins to feel sleepy and gradually lowers his head. His eyes start to close and the light slowly dims. Then, realizing that he has fallen asleep, he awakens and turns up the lamp and continues writing. An example sold recently at Sotheby's, even though the clothes and lamp were replaced, for $9,900.

Another important French automata workshop was that of Leopold Lambert. Lambert made most of his figures with bisque heads made for him by Jumeau, the famous French doll manufacturers. The key to the mechanism usually has the initials "LB," which often get incorrectly ascribed to Lucien Bontems. His most popular pieces are those representing women participating in daily activities such as selling fruit, having dancing lessons or playing with marionettes.

Another popular one is the *Smoking Dandy*, shown in **Illustration 3**, which always creates a lot of enthusiasm because he actually smokes. A lit cigarette is placed in his cigarette holder and elegantly he brings it to his mouth. From the movement of the bellows within his body, he inhales and exhales. Unfortunately many times I have found the bellows dried out and not working — usually as a result of too much smoking.

The automaton of the *Lady Playing the Tambourine*, shown in **Illustration 4**, is another example by Leopold Lambert. The elegant figure, wearing a green silk dress with lace overlay and a pair of ballet slippers, who sits on a square base covered in green velvet, turns her head side to side as her right hand shakes a tambourine and her left hand brings the mask up to her face while she crosses her legs. All her actions are done in time to music.

Animated animals, like rabbits popping out of cabbages or playing musical instruments, were the favorite subject of the Roullet et Decamps workshop. The business began with Ernst Decamps in the latter part of the 19th century and was passed on to his son-in-law, Jean Roullet in the early 1900s. Like the other French automata workshops, they also made examples of people doing everyday activities. One piece in particular was the *Photographer*, shown in **illustration 5**. A pensive lady stands on an old trunk and peers through her camera lens at a dog, whose tail wags in anticipation of having his photograph taken. Suddenly a bird pops out of the camera and cockoos and the dog, surprised by the sudden activity, jumps up and turns his head toward the camera. This fun piece sold for $17,500 in June 1986 at Sotheby's.

Over the last five years enthusiasm for automata has grown considerably and the original examples are becoming more and more difficult to find. So many have been destroyed over the years because of their delicate nature. Automata continue to be made today, but they do not have the same charm, or indeed the intricate movements of earlier examples. Michel Bertrand in Switzerland continues to make elaborate automata using original parts from old Vichy examples. He worked with the Vichy workshop as a small boy and has spent most of his lifetime with automata. Early automata, evocative as they are of past customs and all-but-forgotten craftsmanship, are precious examples of "living history." Their study is a fascinating one and, added to the excitement of the thrill of the chase, makes collecting them a rewarding hobby. □

Illustration 4. The *Lady Playing the Tambourine* whose actions are all done in time to music.

Illustration 5. The *Photographer* in the act of taking a photograph of a dog.

Suggested Reference Books
on the Subject

1. Battaini, A. and Bordeau, A. *The Mechanical Dolls of Monte Carlo,* New York, 1985
2. Beyer, Annette, *Faszinierende Welt der Automaten,* Callwey Verlag Munchen, 1983
3. Chapuis A. and Droz, E. *Les Automates,* Neuchatel, 1949
4. Hillier, Mary, *Automata & Mechanical Toys,* London, 1976
5. Prasteau, Jean, *Les Automates,* Paris, 1968
6. Ryder, Steve, *Animated Androids-A Brief History of Automata,* London, 1978
7. Weiss-Stauffacher, H. and Bruhn, R., *Automates et Instruments de Musique Mecaniques,* Office de Livre, 1976

Collecting Antique Dolls

by **Dorothy S. & Evelyn Jane Coleman**

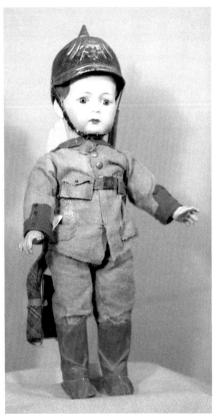

Illustration 1. 14in (36cm) bisque-headed doll that, like so many other dolls' heads of the period just before World War I, resembles the Vatican sculpture by François Duquesnois. No mark has been found on this doll on either the body or the head. It has flocked hair, glass eyes, a closed mouth and a jointed composition body. The original clothes and accessories represent a German soldier of the early 1900s. *Jean Lusby Collection.*

Illustration 2. 10in (25cm) china shoulder head wearing its original commercial dress trimmed with ribbons. The petticoat with a pinked edge is revealed under the gauze dress. The doll is on a commercial body with leather arms. There is a molded snood with a cluster of blue grapes at the top of the head. Much of the original gold luster remains on the snood. The eyes are painted blue while the hair is black. Unusual china head dolls are among the many dolls about which one day we hope to know more.

Since you are reading this issue of the **Doll Reader**® it can be assumed that you are a collector of dolls. To most collectors their greatest pleasure is finding a long sought-after doll and adding it to their collection. Then the pleasure is increased by studying about the doll and learning about its origins and history. Webster's *Dictionary* tells us that "collect" means "gather together for a hobby, to accumulate," but, actually, collecting dolls is much more than this at the present time.

One can scarcely keep up with all the doll books, doll shows and doll auctions around the world. The interest in collecting antique dolls has indeed become international. More and more books on dolls are appearing on the market. The number of collectors increases phenomenally. What is so intriguing about collecting dolls? And why is the hobby growing so rapidly? The collecting of fine art such as paintings and sculptures are often beyond the financial reach of the average

pocketbook. Coins, stamps, decoys and other popular collectible objects lack the multiplicity of interests that are inherent in antique dolls.

People have been collecting dolls for over a century, but their place as works of art has only recently become generally appreciated to any extent. Collectors will be amazed at the tremendous number of renowned artists listed in our new *Collector's Encyclopedia of Dolls, Volume Two.* The number of different dolls and the great number of people and companies engaged in the production of dolls in the past is also staggering. When Volume One first appeared nearly 20 years ago, some collectors complained that it contained all the information about dolls and left no room for further information to be found by others. How wrong they were is demonstrated very clearly by the new Volume Two which is nearly twice the size of Volume One and contains all new information; almost all of it on dolls produced before 1931. Moreover there is still a vast amount of information to be discovered, recorded and analyzed by knowledgeable researchers and collectors. This is as true today as it was many years ago. In the U.F.D.C. (United Federation of Doll Clubs, Inc.) 25th Anniversary special silver commemorative booklet, published in 1974, page 13, the article entitled "Twenty-five Years Ago" by Doris Frank Ludwig stated:

"Everyone [at the first U.F.D.C. Convention in 1950] traveled by car —to the home of Janet Johl and the opportunity to see her outstanding doll collection, even more thrilling was the chance to discuss her books, exchange information and hear her plans for future research. She made it quite clear that she did not consider herself an authority in any way, but just a beginner in the field of doll research, and that time would continually bring new information to light, and repudiate long-established ideas held by collectors at that time." By 1950, Janet Johl had

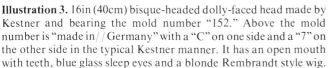

Illustration 3. 16in (40cm) bisque-headed dolly-faced head made by Kestner and bearing the mold number "152." Above the mold number is "made in// Germany" with a "C" on one side and a "7" on the other side in the typical Kestner manner. It has an open mouth with teeth, blue glass sleep eyes and a blonde Rembrandt style wig.

RIGHT: Illustration 4. 14in (36cm) bisque-headed baby doll also bearing the mold number "152." However, this head was made by Hertel, Schwab & Co. Sometimes heads with this number just have the mold number and the size number, while others have "made in Germany" and still others have "L. W. & Co.," which would mean that the head had been made specifically for Louis Wolf & Co. This bisque-headed baby on a five-piece bent-limb composition baby body has a short cropped blonde wig, blue glass sleep eyes and an open mouth with teeth. It wears its original romper suit made shortly after it was purchased in the early summer of 1914 in Düsseldorf, Germany.

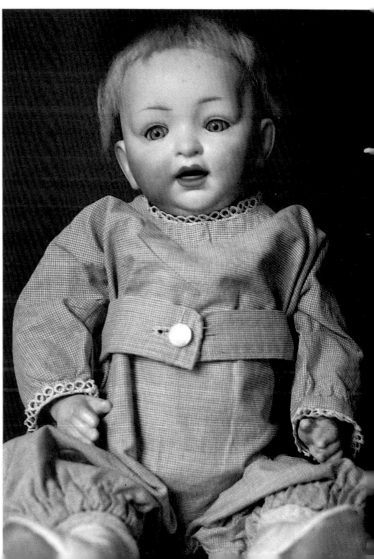

TOP RIGHT: Illustration 5. 15in (38cm) doll believed to be made by Jumeau. It has a red stamp "5" with a white place above the "5" where the mark has been removed. In the Bébé Jumeau size-height relationship table of the *Collector's Encyclopedia of Dolls, Volume Two*, size 5 is the correct size number for Jumeau dolls that are 15in (38cm) tall and were made when they were pouring the heads in 1894 to 1913. In several of the accounts about the Jumeau factory during the 1890s it was recorded that they did not mark all of their dolls because they were seconds. There is a slight warping of the head of this doll. It has its original blonde wig, brown glass stationary eyes and is on a ball-jointed composition body with jointed wrists. It is wearing its original clothes. *Jean Lusby Collection.*

Illustration 6. 17in (43cm) bisque-headed doll with a cloth body and leather arms. At first glance the doll might be called a "French Fashion lady type." Its head certainly resembles dolls that are often categorized as "French Fashion types." However, on examination, the doll appears to be a German doll; certainly the body is made in a German manner. The original clothes represent a young girl rather than a lady. Details must be studied to properly identify dolls.

already published her first two books. Today we know how true her prophecy became and that it still holds true for the future.

A new collector can be overwhelmed by the tremendous number of dolls and the vast number of books on dolls and doll related subjects. However anxious collectors may be to own dolls, they should acquire and study some of the reliable books on the subject in order to obtain their greatest pleasure. Time and money spent on books can be most rewarding in helping collectors to achieve a worthwhile collection of dolls. Often a well researched doll has extra value not only for its greater appreciation but also for its monetary importance. Dolls that are identifiable as to makers, dates and origins are of greater value than those about which the collector has little knowledge.

Some books, including ours, have a section on "How to use this book." It is most important to study this section carefully. Indexes are of tremendous help as well as the cross references. The

new Volume Two has many tables, charts and illustrations of marks not previously recorded that enable the collectors to identify their dolls with greater speed and accuracy. This is also true for the over 3000 dolls, many of them in original clothes, that are shown in the book. Let us suppose that you have just purchased a darling character baby doll with a bisque head and a jointed five-piece composition baby body. The only mark on the doll is "152" and "Made in Germany" incised on the back of the head. You have heard that 152 is a Kestner number and this fact is verified in Volume One. However, turning to the Kestner entry of Volume One, Illustration 962, you find that Kestner mold 152 was different from your doll. Then you go to the numeral index in Volume Two and find that Hertel, Schwab & Co. and Simon & Halbig also made bisque heads for dolls with a mold number 152. After studying all the references to 152 in the numeral index you decide that your doll fits the description of the Hertel, Schwab & Co. mold number

152 doll's head. Thus you begin to find information about this particular bisque head. Are the wig, sleep eyes and open mouth with teeth typical or is your doll an unusual head? Of course the hand painting, the handmade wig and hand-blown glass eyes make your doll look just a little bit different from any other doll even though it was made in the same mold. What about the body? Who used the Hertel Schwab & Co. bisque heads on their baby bodies?

Collectors will find the answers to innumerable questions about their dolls in the many text pages and illustrations in *The Collector's Encyclopedia of Dolls, Volume Two.* In what years were dolls of the size of a particular doll made? How much did it cost originally? How does the original price, adjusted for inflation through the years, relate to the present day value of the doll? The size number on a doll is generally in code, but at last many of these codes have been studied and the relationship between the size number and the height of the doll may be found in one of the many size-height relationship tables. These tables help to identify the maker of the doll, to detect whether the body is original to the head, to discover whether the head is a reproduction and, in a few cases, such as the Bébé Jumeau, to learn the approximate date of the doll.

Now the collector comes to the clothes and here the many catalog pages illustrated in Volume Two of the *Encyclopedia* plus the pictures of dolls in original clothes give accurate examples of how your doll should be dressed. *The Collector's Book of Dolls' Clothes* also provides valuable information regarding the correct costume. One of the catalog pages that was contemporary with your doll may perhaps show exactly what your doll originally wore. Small changes in a doll's clothes were frequently made by the manufacturers especially to keep the garments in the latest style. If your doll wears clothes that were recently made and are inappropriate or it has no clothes at all, *The Collector's Book of Dolls' Clothes* will provide patterns that will be suitable for making clothes for your doll. The size of your doll will probably necessitate adapting the pattern to fit the particular size of your doll. Once again it is necessary to read the directions carefully to learn just how easy it is to change the patterns so that they will fit your doll. It has been found that if the height and date of an old doll

Illustration 7. 16½in (42cm) Kämmer & Reinhardt bisque-headed doll, mold number 126, one of the *Mein Liebling* series of dolls. This doll has flirting and sleep eyes that also have the naughty mechanism, an open mouth with two teeth and a bent-limb baby composition body.

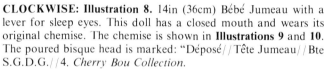

CLOCKWISE: Illustration 8. 14in (36cm) Bébé Jumeau with a lever for sleep eyes. This doll has a closed mouth and wears its original chemise. The chemise is shown in **Illustrations 9** and **10**. The poured bisque head is marked: "Déposé//Tête Jumeau//Bte S.G.D.G.//4. *Cherry Bou Collection.*

Illustration 9. Front view of the original chemise on the bisque-headed Jumeau doll shown in **Illustration 8**. This chemise dates the doll as early 1890s before the flowered print chemises were made. The ribbon belt is a replacement. *Cherry Bou Collection.*

Illustration 10. Back view of the Bébé Jumeau doll shown in **Illustration 8**. Note how much plainer the back of the chemise is than the front shown in **Illustration 9**. Bébé Jumeau dolls had shoes and stockings when they were sold in chemises after 1889. *Cherry Bou Collection.*

Illustration 11. Close-up of the hand and jointed wrist of the 14in (36cm) Bébé Jumeau shown in **Illustration 8**. The size of doll is 4. This size-height relationship tallies with the size-height table in *The Collector's Encyclopedia of Dolls, Volume Two*, which was based on the size-height relationship tables as given in the French store catalogs of the period when they were advertising Jumeau dolls. *Cherry Bou Collection.*

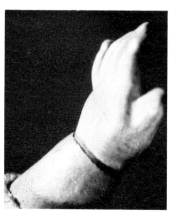

matches those of the old clothes the costume will fit perfectly.

You must read Volume Two of *The Collector's Encyclopedia of Dolls* carefully even though you have been collecting and studying dolls for a long period of time. There is still a tremendous amount of new information for you to discover and learn. You may have thought the only K★R 117 was called *Mein Liebling*. However, Mein Liebling was a line of dolls and included dolls with mold numbers other than 117. In fact there are many names associated with dolls that are the names of a line of dolls rather than just the name of a specific mold for a doll. Collectors should begin to learn to differentiate between the names for the various lines of dolls and names for specific dolls.

Did you realize that the *Rock-A-Bye Baby* dolls with newborn infant bisque heads made by Armand Marseille were products of Cuno & Otto Dressel, who used the trade name for both the open and closed mouth versions? (See **Illustration 21** in the article "Carved, Stuffed, and Molded Dolls — Highlights of The Doll Treasures at the Chester County, Pennsylvania, Historical Society, November 29, 1985, to August 5, 1986" in the December 1985/ January 1986 **Doll Reader®**, page 95.) Several other names were given to dolls with these same Armand Marseille heads. The distinction in name between the open-and the closed-mouth versions appears to be only a modern misnomer. How many bébés made by Jumeau had names other than Bébé Jumeau? Can you date a Bébé Jumeau by its original chemise? Were the shoes on your doll made in America or in Europe? Are dolls currently advertised as "authentically dressed" really in original clothes? Are they in clothes contemporary with the doll? Or are they in clothes made recently by someone who has studied early dolls' clothes or by someone who really knows very little about dolls' costumes of the past? If you can differentiate between poured and pressed dolls' heads, do you know what this difference signifies, especially with those dolls made in France?

The study necessary for the complete identification of your doll probably seems like a lengthy task but it is truly worth all the effort. To be a true collector of dolls today, one must know what marks and especially mold numbers mean. They must be familiar with the names of the dolls, and their

TOP TO BOTTOM: Illustration 12. Close-up of an 18in (46cm) molded felt doll bearing the later large round metal button which identifies the doll as being made by Lenci. These metal buttons were used to attach the paper identification tag to the doll's garments. Later these tags were simply sewn to an undergarment. Note the round white and brown highlights in the iris of the eyes. The lower lip is of a lighter color than the upper lip. There are two dots on the lower lip. This series 110 doll wearing its original orange felt coat and matching dress was purchased from Gladys H. Hilsdorf.

Illustration 13. 16in (41cm) molded felt face doll bearing the cloth label of Alma, an Italian firm. Like the 300 series Lenci dolls, this doll has a molded hollow torso made of felt. Note the eyes are less round than those of the Lenci doll seen in **Illustration 12**. This Alma doll wears a multicolored pieced jumper with a plain white felt blouse and a blue tie which matches the hair bow.

Illustration 14. 12½in (32cm) Simon & Halbig bisque socket head, mold number 949 on a ball-jointed composition and wood body.. The bisque head has a solid dome crown except for three small holes used for stringing. The doll wears all original clothes of pink satin and lace for the dress, pink felt for the high crown hat, with a pink ostrich plume and pink shoes and socks.

makers, especially those that they are anxious to collect.

A knowledgeable collector of antique dolls should be able to recognize whether a porcelain head is poured or pressed, whether the size number corresponds with the height of the doll, whether a doll wears its original clothes or not and the significance of other details. As other collectors increase their knowledge of dolls and prices rise ever higher and higher, the collecting of dolls becomes a more varied, comprehensive and demanding subject. No longer will some of the fanciful fairy tales about dolls suffice for the modern collectors. It is necessary to study our dolls themselves more thoroughly and to learn where, when and how they were actually made. Dolls may be children's playthings but old dolls are now historical artifacts for adult collectors. A curator at the Metropolitan Museum Art in a recent telecast defined "Art" as including objects that had a true sense of time and place. Certainly antique dolls in original clothes, which includes those wearing clothes made for the doll during the period when the doll was first being played with, can be considered perfect examples of "Art" according to this definition. Congratu- lations should go to all of you who have appreciated already the many worthwhile facets of doll collecting and are enjoying the artistic pleasure and knowledge that can be attributed to your collection of dolls. □

Hair Styles in Bisque
Circa 1860 to 1880

by **Estelle Johnston**
Photographs by **Estelle Johnston**

Untinted and tinted bisque shoulder head dolls (referred to as parian) with molded hair were made in a profusion of styles from the girlishly simple to the elaborately sophisticated. In addition these heads were designed with or without pierced ears, or occasionally with molded earrings; with painted blue eyes — in some models painting of the highest quality — or inset blue glass eyes with painted eyelashes; many shades of blonde hair to occasional glazed black hair or very rare dark brown glazed hair; glazed or lustre-fired decorations on head and/or shoulders, often in conjunction with molded collar or bodice; and occasionally with swivel neck. The difficulty of inserting glass eyes in a swivel head represents the ultimate in technical expertise.

Development of hair styles very naturally followed that of the fashionable ladies of Europe during the 1860s and 1870s. In the early 1860s hair was still often arranged from a center part in relatively simple forms following the natural lines of the head, and snoods were popularly used in many ways for back hair. For evening, long curls were favored, often decorated with pearls, flowers, feathers or a draped silk scarf and, of course, any combinations thereof. The use of artificial hair to augment the natural led to larger plaited or coiled rolls of hair known as chignons, and by the mid-1860s these chignons extended directly back from the head, balancing the movement of the skirt shape from a full circle to a form of ellipse with sweeping train. Artificial hair was increasingly available; frisette for the forehead, switch to be arranged by the wearer, coils, braids, curls, waterfall, for example, in keeping with milady's needs. Photographs of the period attest to excesses which the makers of these dolls had the good taste to avoid. By the 1870s hair rose from the forehead to height and fullness at the back of the crown and from there cascaded to the back of the neck or shoulders in a wealth of luxuriant plaits, curls and/or rolls — echoing the bustle and complex drapings of the back of the skirt. Combs and coronet-like combs were fashionable as well as ribbon ornaments and hair formed in bow shapes.

OPPOSITE PAGE: Illustration 3. Two lady dolls with hair styles of the mid 1860s. Doll on left has drawn back from center part with featherstroking of hair on temples and softly waved wings, all hair drawn up to back of crown and falling in loose ringlets topped with two glazed roses and their lustre-tipped leaves, pierced earlobes, blue glass eyes and rare slightly open mouth, white bisque. Doll on right has hair drawn back in similar wings with more puffing above forehead and caught at back to form chignon of massed curls, painted blue eyes, pierced earlobes, rare flat swivel neck, white bisque.

LEFT TO RIGHT: Illustration 1. Mid 1870s. Doll showing the style seen in *Illustration 27* translated into bisque, black and gold comb and bow at front of ruffled and decorated collar, painted decoration on front of bodice, pierced-in ears, very pale tinted bisque.

Illustration 2. Back view of doll shown in *Illustration 1*.

 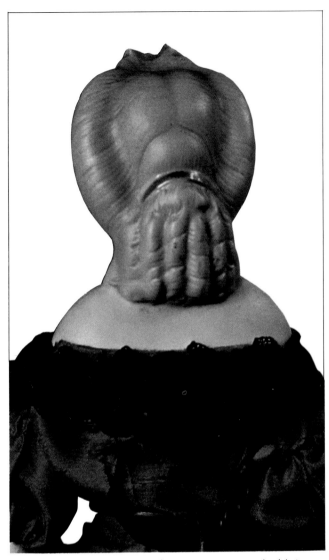

LEFT TO RIGHT: Illustration 4. Mid 1860s. Blonde hair poufed and rolled around face with butterfly over rose decoration at center top, back hair parted in center and then separated in a pouf caught with a gold lustre comb at the nape of the neck and ending in massed ringlets on the back of the shoulders, molded gold lustre earrings, white bisque.

Illustration 5. Back view of the hair style shown on the doll in *Illustration 4.*

LEFT TO RIGHT: Illustration 6. Two variations of a style from the late 1860s with clustered curls on the top of the forehead. Left to right: sides swept back in poufs marked by two glazed black side combs and caught at the back with a larger glazed black comb above massed ringlets on the neck, the curls on the forehead topped with a small bow of hair and the ears pierced through the lobes, white bisque; finest molding and painting of eyes with striation in the blue irises, upper and lower lashes, stroked brows — even in small sizes of this head, molded guimpe with gold lustre buttons, white bisque.

Illustration 7. Back view of the hair styles on the dolls shown in *Illustration 6.* Note the hair arranged in puffs with braids outlining the top puff on the doll on the right.

OPPOSITE PAGE: Illustration 8. Mid 1870s. Blonde center-parted hair lifted at sides to cover high coronet of braids at back of crown, molded white guimpe with blue ribbons, molded black necklace with red and white glazed stone or locket, pierced-in ears, tinted bisque.

Illustration 9. A group of simpler hair styles of the early 1860s. Clockwise from lower left: center-parted blonde hair rolled in poufs framing the face, black snood stretched smoothly over back of head, ends of hair in three smooth rolls, molded shirtwaist with glazed white collar, white bisque; blonde center-parted hair curled and caught at each temple with gold lustre clip or comb, molded shirtwaist with decorated bow and seams, pale tinted bisque; young girl style with center-parted blonde hair waved back from temples into two braids caught together with black bow at back of crown, short curls, pale tinted bisque; young lady style with center part and short blonde curls held by black ribbon band edged with gold lustre, molded gold lustre earrings, molded black ribbon necklace with gold lustre cross, fine eye painting with shading across top of pupils and long upper and lower lashes, pale tinted bisque.

BELOW: Illustration 10. Back view showing varied uses of the snood, early to mid 1860s. Left to right: glazed black hair with center part, crown held by gold lustre snood finished with pink-edged ruffle, lower hair in smooth back roll; (front) center-parted blonde hair rolled in poufs framing face, black snood stretched smoothly over back of head, ends of hair in three smooth rolls; "Empress Eugenie" style with lustre scarf and glazed white feather (an evening headdress) with green snood holding blonde hair in smooth back roll.

The fine bisque of these dolls allowed much freedom of modeling in both hair and additional decorations and these exquisite ladies are found in white bisque and in tinted shades from barely discernible off-white to full flesh tones. Approximate dating of some hair styles is offered for costuming clues but, of course, does not imply the date of any given doll. The variety of heads is so extensive that I continue, after more than 20 years of studying and collecting, to see new examples. This is just a part of their fascination. □

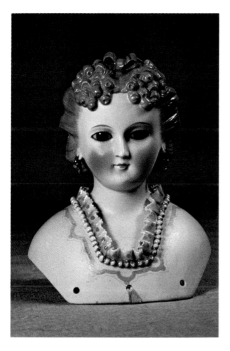  

TOP ROW LEFT TO RIGHT: Illustration 11. Late 1860s. Fancy doll with clusters of curls on each temple topped by a rose lustre bow over the center part, hair falling in soft short curls at the back, blue glass eyes, pierced earlobes, painted and glazed neckline with molded ruffle and beads, white bisque.

Illustration 12. Back views showing the variations of curls covering the back of the head. Left to right: the back of the doll shown in *Illustration 13;* (front) the back of the doll shown in *Illustration 11;* doll with gold-edged rose lustre ribbon over top of head, pierced-in ears, molded locket on black ribbon necklace.

Illustration 13. Late 1860s. Another fancy lady with clustered curls across top of forehead and backed by gold-edged blue lustre ribbon with rosette at top and smaller bows above each ear, hair caught with rose lustre curved flat comb at back of crown and falling in loose curls over back of head, molded and glazed ruffle and gold lustre bead neckline, pierced-into-head ears, very pale tinted bisque.

BOTTOM ROW LEFT TO RIGHT: Illustration 14. Late 1866 to 1867, repeated again in the late 1870s. Blonde hair drawn back from the face in soft waves and caught at the back of the crown with comb and ribbon, the back arranged in a large chignon topped with two small ringlets, one smaller curl escaping at the nape of the neck, molded, painted and glazed neckline with ruffle, gold lustre beads and inner gold-edged and laced guimpe, pierced-in ears, white bisque.

Illustration 15. Back views, left to right: doll shown in *Illustration 16;* (front) doll shown in the front in cover photo; doll shown in *Illustration 14;* doll shown in *Illustration 19.*

Illustration 16. Mid 1870s. Very fancy lady doll with small curls over forehead banded with gold lustre beads (suggesting artificial curls woven with beaded edge), back of head encircled with full braid below which small ringlets fall on back of neck, hair on back of head twisted and poufed into the beginning of the full braid, gold-edged blue molded necklace, molded and painted fancy neckline, blue glass eyes, pierced earlobes, pale tinted bisque.

Illustration 17. Early 1870s. 19in (48.3cm) complete doll with molded tawny center-parted hair featherstroked at temples and rolled back over full braid which circles entire head, black and gold coronet-like comb supports braid at top of head as well as the controlled arrangement of two large and two smaller center vertical rolls of hair over the back of the head, original linen-weave silk dress, overskirt and jacket trimmed with rose velvet ribbon and scalloped blue silk, enameled butterfly stickpin and matching earrings in pierced earlobes, white bisque, cloth body with tan leather arms.

Illustration 18. Mid 1870s. 16½in (41.9cm) full-length doll with blonde center-parted hair crimped with sides drawn up over very thick braid which circles head, a variation of the hair style shown in *Illustration 17*, evening headdress of net and flowers not molded, silk evening dress with fine lace panel in a style several years earlier than the hair, glass eyes, swivel neck, pierced-in ears, flesh-tinted bisque, cloth body with fine bisque arms and legs.

Illustration 20. Back views showing the doll in *Illustration 4* on the left with hair twisted and poufed asymmetrically while the doll on the right shows a very large braid vertically covering the back of the head.

LEFT: Illustration 19. Mid 1870s. Blonde hair rises from the face in waves and poufs to a chignon at the crown covered with small falling curls and caught around the bottom with a braid from which tendril curls escape on the neck, molded and glazed "jewel" hangs from blue ribbon molded necklace, molded gold lustre earrings, white bisque.

LEFT TO RIGHT: **Illustration 21.** Late 1870s. Two variations of hair bows which would have been artificial and pinned to the head, as shown in *Illustration 26*. Doll on left has front hair center-parted and looped around a black comb with gold beads, back hair soft loose curls topped by bow of hair, blue glass eyes, pierced-in ears, tinted bisque, molded white glazed jewel with black necklace. Doll on right has short blonde curls massed above forehead and framing the face, caught around top of head by black ribbon and at the back by a bow of hair, pierced-in ears, tinted bisque.

Illustration 22. Back view of the dolls shown in *Illustration 21*.

Illustration 23. *The Englishwoman's Domestic Magazine*; a plate of 1866, page 48, showing a variety of popular hair styles which are echoed in molded bisque dolls.

Illustration 24. *The Englishwoman's Magazine*, page 40, volume 8, January 1870, showing the arrangements of braids and curls on the back of the head.

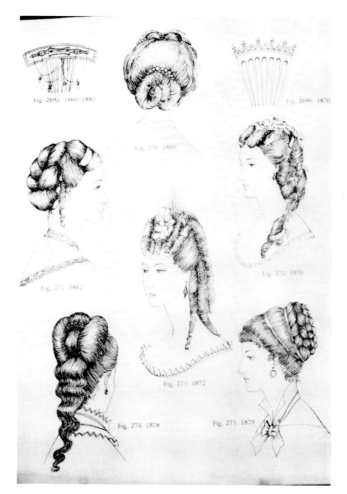

CLOCKWISE: Illustration 25. *The Englishwoman's Domestic Magazine*, page 257, volume 20, May 1876, showing the treatment of masses of hair piled at the crown and creating back interest.

Illustration 26. *Women's Headdress and Hairstyles*, page 125, "Mid-Victorian Hair Styles 1860 - 1880," showing some of the more popular styles which resemble those in molded bisque.

Illustration 27. *The Englishwoman's Domestic Magazine*, page 86, volume 14, 1873, showing combs and the high coronet-like braid at the back of the crown as shown in *Illustrations 1* and *2*.

BIBLIOGRAPHY

The Englishwoman's Domestic Magazine, London, Ward, Lock & Tyler, Warwick House, Paternoster Row., Volumes II, VIII, XIV, and XX. 1866 - 1876.

English Women's Clothing in the Nineteenth Century, C. Willett Cunnington, Faber and Faber Ltd., 24 Russell Square, London. 1937.

Fashions in Hair, Richard Corson, Peter Owen, London. 1971.

Victorian & Edwardian Fashion - A Photographic Survey, Alison Gernsheim, Dover Publications, Inc., New York. 1963, 1981.

Women's Headdress and Hairstyles, Georgine de Coutais, B. T. Batsford Ltd., London, 1973.

The Engaging Charm of Leather Dolls

by LaVada Spicer

Although dolls have been made of many different materials and strange items like ivory, wishbones, bread and so forth, perhaps the strangest material to date is leather. We do know kid-bodied dolls were made throughout the 19th century and well up into the early part of the 1900s, but few people realize that whole dolls, heads, half arms and legs were made of leather.

In Philadelphia, advertisements for all-leather dolls could be found as early as the 1820s, and kid-leather heads on all-wood bodies have been dated from the 1840s.

History tells us that during 1866, two men simultaneously obtained patents for an all-leather doll and a leather doll's head. The man who received a patent for the all-leather doll was Pierre Clement of France; the other man was Franklin Darrow, in the United States. Other all-leather dolls were patented in America in 1903, with some patents being granted as late as 1917. The very homeliness of some of these early leather dolls are what gives them part of their engaging charm.

There has not been all that much written about leather or rawhide dolls to help in identifying particular types one might run across sometime and one hardly knows where to begin in trying to date clothing that is usually found on these dolls. Time, and the rough treatment children and animals have bestowed upon these dolls, have contributed to all but obscuring the facial features on the leather and cloth doll in the illustration, but one may

still see the value of having such a doll in one's collection.

The dress this doll would have worn for the period would be made of a cotton print, with a low rounded neckline and short full-spread sleeves trimmed with a similar darker fabric around the hem. The back of the dress would be closed with two or more safety pins on the real doll. The underwear for our primitive leather

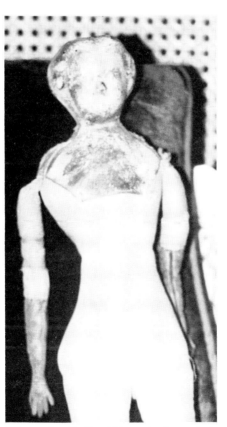

Illustration 1. *Rawhide or leather primitive doll.*

doll would consist of a white cotton petticoat and lace-trimmed cotton chemise extending to the crotch. She would also wear striped cotton knit socks, leather shoes with no heels and a small rounded apron bound in white and pinned or buttoned in back which covers the skirt of the dress and completes the costume.

The doll has a molded shoulder head and half arms made of leather. The rest of the body is cloth stuffed firmly and is very shapely, almost like a lady body. The facial features have all but been worn off by time or cleaning, but the character of the doll can still be seen.

The Eskimos and American Indians still make good quality authentic style leather dolls today, but collectors may have to look hard for these, as there are cheaply made souvenir type dolls abounding all over. The really good dolls are always harder to find.

A few small all-leather dolls have surfaced lately. They are usually labeled "Made in France" and are very outstanding dolls. Made in the very small size of from 4in (10cm) to 6in (15cm), they have been found dressed in original clothes, in excellent condition. It has been assumed they were made in the 1920s by an unknown French maker who made babies and children types. If one is lucky enough to own one they do indeed have an expensive doll. The price range for these in a 1982 price guide was $400.00 to $500.00. Sure makes one appreciate them all the more. □

Illustration 1. An elegant 17in (43cm) Parisienne whose trunk contains a wealth of fashionable clothes and accessories. Note especially the white ermine-lined cape (top center) and delicate feather collar (lower right).

Dolls with Original Wardrobes — 1830 to 1960

by **Lorna Lieberman,** Curator of Dolls, Wenham Historical Association and Museum, Inc.

Photographs by **Dorothy McGonagle**

"Dressed to Kill," in a devastating rather than life-threatening sense, is a special exhibit at the Wenham Museum which will chronicle two basic types of historic dolls: those sold with commercially produced clothing and accessories, and those so adored by their owners that entire wardrobes were created for them by loving-hands-at-home. Over 35 dolls and their original wardrobes will be on view in the East Gallery of the Wenham Museum from June 3 through September 6, 1987. The majority of them have been loaned from private collections throughout the country and include extremely rare

and wonderful examples of doll art and miniature couture. Dolls from France, Germany, England and America will be represented. They are made of bisque, cloth, china, composition, paper, plastic, wax and wood.

Dolls in original clothing have come to be appreciated by today's collectors, who value a more complete history of their dolls. When a doll retains not only its original clothing but a trunk full of wearing apparel and all manner of tiny accessories, we are indeed fortunate, for then much is revealed about the life and times of the doll. We are privileged to peek at the fashions of the

day and, in addition, sense the social, cultural, economic and moral values of its first owner's family.

The earliest example to be shown is a 20in (51cm) French papier-mâché, owned by the Museum, whose beautifully sewn wardrobe dates from 1828 to 1843. Another early doll is a 9in (23cm) papier-mâché of 1840, still tied into her original box, with several changes of clothing. A slim-faced wigged china, sold as a Sanitary Fair doll in the early 1860s, will stand majestically amid her extensive finery.

A Bru-to-melt-your-heart and her four commercial French costumes will

Illustration 2. "Rosie," a 16in (41cm) Jumeau doll whose head is incised "5," with her wardrobe of homemade clothing which includes a brown plush coat, two silk and velvet dresses, a brown wool tweed suit, batiste blouse, plush bonnet and satin face mask.

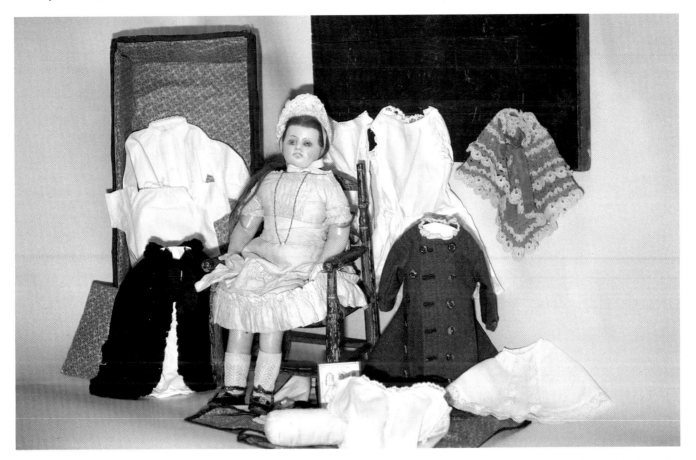

Illustration 3. 24in (61cm) "Eliza Uzielli Jeaffreson," whose name and date, 1882, are written in black script on the lid of her original wooden box. She is a poured wax doll from England and is surrounded by her bedding, nursing bottle, ivory rattle, handkerchief, capes, coats, nightgown and beautifully sewn underwear.

be on view, as well as a pair of Huret bébés, sisters actually, who were purchased in Paris along with their small wardrobe of dresses, bonnets and accessories.

Bisque fashion dolls from France will be displayed in profusion, with literally hundreds of the minute treasures found in their traveling trunks. Mysterious and amazing baubles are discovered in the trunks of these Parisiennes, some defying identification. It seems that nothing was too precious for a French doll to own. A fashion-type bride and groom will proudly share their trousseau with us — he with *one* change of clothing, and she with too many to count.

Two sweet-faced Kestners with homesewn wardrobes, one from England and the other from Boston, will charm the viewer. Homemade clothing, often by the child owner, is a sure sign of a loved doll.

Bringing us up to a more modern era will be a Dorothy Heizer cloth fashion-type doll, believed to be a portrait of Wallis Simpson, Duchess of Windsor. She is accompanied by her marvelous valise and Heizer-made wardrobe and tiny accessories.

Completing our time line will be *Ginny, Barbie*® and *Crissy*, whose extensive and expensive wardrobes delighted little girls in the post-World War II days.

ABOVE LEFT: Illustration 4. 19in (48cm) turned-head German child of the 1890s with her finely sewn wardrobe. Boston provenance.

LEFT: Illustration 5. 5½in (14cm) French-type all-bisque with a marvelous array of stylish dresses and hats.

These are just a few of the many delights awaiting you at Wenham Museum this summer. In addition to the special exhibit, over 1000 antique dolls plus dolls' houses, miniatures, toys and games from the Museum's permanent collection may be viewed.

The Museum is open to the public Monday through Friday, 11:00 a.m. to 4:00 p.m., Saturday, 1:00 p.m. to 4:00 p.m. and Sunday, 2:00 p.m. to 5:00 p.m. It is located 40 minutes north of Boston by train, or by car take exit 20N off route 128 to 132 Main Street (Route 1A) in Wenham, Massachusetts. The admission fee is $1.50 for adults and 50¢ for children ages six through 14. □

Illustration 6. The elegance of this swivel-neck glass-eyed 15in (38cm) Parian bisque lady is somewhat at odds with her simple homesewn wardrobe.

Illustration 7. 7in (18cm) sweet-faced German all-bisque with molded long black stockings, surrounded by her many homemade dresses, hats, capes and coats. An extra special possession: her red crocheted hammock.

China Celebrates Heritage

by **Mona Borger**

Photographs by **Ken Borger**

The extraordinary costume worn by this china doll intrigued me from the start. It was first seen in the doll cabinet of the previous owner, who had been told the costume represented a Lapland bride. The veil, then covering the doll's face, had been misunderstood as bridal in nature. Though the description seemed questionable, I knew the doll's costume was very special. It was perfectly hand-sewn, skillfully embroidered and exactingly detailed throughout. The ominous black figure was outstanding among other wonderments wearing pretty silk pastels, lace and bows. On each visit to my friend's home, a quick glance assured it was still there; it had become my anticipated treat. I never **really saw** any other doll in that cabinet. The owner was sympathetic to my smitten condition, and eventually allowed us to acquire the doll. No doubt, it had become increasingly difficult to converse with a gaping guest whose nose was pressed against the glass cabinet. The doll has resided with us for six or seven years; the costume intact and still intriguing, its origin still unconfirmed.

So, interest falters and revives again when nudged. Dorothy and Evelyn Jane Coleman nudged me with their article, *"The Neglected Dolls"* in the *UFDC (United Federation of Doll Clubs, Inc.)1984 Souvenir Journal* for San Antonio, Texas (Coincidently, 1984's UFDC Competitive Exhibit/ Antiques offered the first class for China Doll in Regional Costume since the New York, New York, convention, resulting in four fine entries, but precluded previous blue ribbon winners. This doll wears a UFDC National Blue Ribbon awarded at Chicago, Illinois, in 1966 and did not qualify to enter.) National competition, where additional costume theories might be gathered, is an annual nudge. Any house call by a doll collector thought to have a keen interest in costume is always a nudge. Costume books and albums have been consulted when available, and as time allowed. No suggestions have resulted; hope for information had begun to run out. The doll in its curious costume was not neglected, but was intermittently set aside.

Recently, Estelle Johnston's beautifully photographed two-part essay, *"Cherishable China Dolls,"* **Doll Reader**®, (February/ March 1985, pages 98 to 102 and April 1985, pages 121 to 126) not only nudged, but pushed me into action. Her generous words on my book's behalf were gratefully received, and stimulating. Time was allotted to look through every costume book at our local library, one shelf, one book, one page at a time. A single picture can sometimes be rewarding. Into the second afternoon, absorbed and enjoying it, a page turned to reveal a photograph of a woman, circa 1860, wearing a costume like MY CHINA DRESSED IN BLACK! The book, *The Folk Dress of Europe* by James Snowden, and I had never been at that shelf simultaneously. What I read was hard to believe and what I saw was unmistakable.

LEFT: Illustration 1. 20½in (52.1cm) glazed china shoulder head doll.

RIGHT: Illustration 2. Women's national costume of Iceland, circa 1860, designed by Sigurdur Gudmundson. *Photograph courtesy of W. H. Smith Publishing, Inc.*

COSTUME ORIGIN REVEALED

It was a designer's costume! In 1860 Sigurdur Gudmundson (1833 to 1874), an Icelandic artist and antiquarian, designed the costume shown in the reprint of the old photograph. Gudmundson, the first significant painter in Iceland's modern history, founded in 1863, The National Museum of Iceland, which still exists. He was definitely not your average dolly-dressmaker. His costume design for women was one small part of a large overall attempt to revitalize much-needed hope and spirit among the people of Iceland. The country's problems were nearly devastating: the harsh glacier makeup and volcanic action of the island resulted in a serious lack of population, and prevented forming new communities. Only 25 percent of the island was ever habitable, and they had been dominated by other countries, most often Denmark, since the 11th century. Through the 1900s, Icelanders conducted vigorous efforts for political change, intent on survival and eventual independence. Gudmundson was among the leaders of those efforts.

The usual manner by which regional costumes develop — a natural growth in number of people, separation of one group from another, and a desire to display that difference through clothing — had never occurred in Iceland. (Of necessity, they had stuck together to survive.) There was, instead, a **national** tradition of dress evolved from ancient times, not regional at all. Their cultural heritage from 9th century beginnings is rich in literature and arts, and that past was revered and preserved by the people. The 1860 costume by purposeful design was expected to become Iceland's national folk dress, meant to be worn on appropriate occasions of festival as a symbol of pride in their heritage, survival and country. Gudmundson's design project was successful and durable. The costume, and occasional variations are still worn annually in Iceland on June 17 to celebrate the Anniversary of The Establishment of The Republic, now called National Day. Iceland's independence was finalized in 1944.

WOMAN'S COSTUME DESCRIPTION

Iceland's national folk dress, complete with headdress, worn by the woman shown in *Illustration 2* features symbols plucked from antiquities, but incorporates clothing worn by middle-class women of the 1860s. According to Gudmundson's plan, the dress, usually practical-black, was an intentionally wearable garment to encourage its use, and reflected Icelander's skills at wool weaving, embroidery, lace making, metalwork and silversmithing.

The jacket, or bodice, and skirt were separates worn hooked together; the center front, meant to gape slightly exposing a panel of white embroidery, was closed at the top with a brooch. The neck, front closing and cuffs appear to have borders of contrasting texture, embroidered in gold metallic thread; a narrow, white lace ruffle edges the neck; a double row of gold rimmed the armholes. The skirt bottom also shows a border of contrasting texture with the gold design embroidered above on the skirt fabric. The belt, or girdle, was either of metal links, or embroidery. The headdress was derived from ancient times: a complicated wrapping and pinning of cloth-over-padding wound about a tall cone curving toward the face (similar to a turban) became simplified. The cloth wrapping was eliminated and replaced in the 1860 version, by waist-length sheer veiling draped down the back. (The doll's veil was meant to be in the back!) The tall curved cone of the woman's headdress was held in place by a metallic circlet, remaining ancient in character. Illustrations in Snowden's book show several headdress variations, circa 1771, and stars bordering garment fronts, circa 1810; all examples shown have decoration of interest, but are left to our imagination as to meaning. The stars and their number (11 on the doll's headdress) are undoubtedly significant to Icelanders, much as 13 stars represent our original states, used when we revel in American history.

DOLL'S ATTIRE

''The realization that you are the first person to know a certain fact about some doll and can share this information with countless others is indeed a tremendous thrill,'' wrote Dorothy Coleman in 1977.

Seldom does a china doll enthusiast have that opportunity. Unmarked dolls, comparing sculpting and painting styles, and much serious speculation are the usual available clues among china dolls. While this costume discovery is a precious (and thrilling) morsel to me, one should also understand that the origin of this china doll head and body remain unknown. (It is possible Denmark may be the country of the doll's origin, as trade existed between Iceland and Denmark. That, again, is speculation.) To have found the dated Iceland costume photograph, duplicating the costume of a very old china doll, was totally unexpected. To find **anything definite** in regard to old china dolls, is highly unusual.

The doll's outer garment is black wool, the gold embroidered on applied dark brown velvet borders; the jacket was indeed finished as a separate garment with skirt pleats basted to it. The jacket front is snugly hooked; the armholes, shoulder and back seams have applied black velvet ribbon edged with gold cord. Underneath, there is a long-sleeved knee-length white linen chemise with a narrow white lace ruffle at the neck. Unlike the brooch mentioned on the woman's jacket, the doll wears a metal necklace with a circular pendant of filigree and star design. The belt, **both** metallic-linked **and** gold-embroidered, opens behind the central round link, and is lined with red silk. The jacket embroidery is gold metallic cord, each leaf worked over an individual stiff foundation; the threads at the neck are tarnished by the abrasion of the necklace. The skirt embellishment differs in design from the garment in the old photograph, but is gold metallic cord, looped to conform to the repeat design, and applied with hidden stitches, worked **over** the only seam at center back. Matching cord, used at the top of the brown velvet skirt border, also curves through the leaves of jacket and belt, and edges the black velvet ribbon on the jacket seams. A cotton print, one dark color printed on tan background, discolored by age, hemfaces the skirt for 3in (7.6cm) and lines the jacket.

BELOW: Illustration 5. Doll's metallic-linked and gold-embroidered belt or girdle.

ABOVE: Illustration 4. Necklace with star pendant of oxidized base metal worn by the doll.

LEFT: Illustration 3. Gold-embroidered motif bordering hem of doll's garment.

The doll is a glazed china shoulder head on a stiff-legged all-leather body; the shoulder head measures 4½in (11.5cm), the doll's total height is 20½in (52.1cm). The headdres is linen with 11 metal eyelet-backed stars sewn to a white silk band, ending in a bow at the back; the net veil, edged with 1/2in (1.3cm) lace, is attached by linen tape. There are two petticoats: one of heavy diagonally-woven cream wool, pleated into a linen waistband, sewn closed, mid-calf length, worn over the chemise; the other, of white (now darkened) linen, tightly gathered into a 1/2in (1.3cm) wide linen waistband, tied closed with 3/16in (.45cm) wide linen tapes, is ankle-length with a 3/4in (2cm) hem. There are no drawers. All pieces are so perfectly stitched you wonder if thread counting was employed. The linen fabrics and tapes match throughout all garments. Black stockings are knit-to-shape, not seamed, and tied up at the knees in square knots by braid, woven in lengthwise stripes of brown, rose and yellow with 2in (5.1cm) long loose ends. The shoes are a simple construction of hide; seamed at the toes, to form a point, and at the heel, then drawn up about the foot with linen tape insertions, with no additional sole or heel. The shoes are the only items remotely describable as crudely made. The doll's attire so closely resembles that of woman in photograph it is almost eerie.

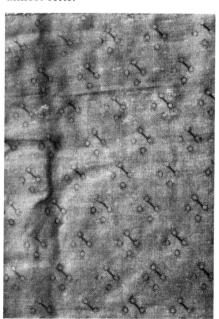

LEFT: Illustration 6. China head doll in Iceland's national costume, circa 1860.

ABOVE: Illustration 7. Cotton print of hem facing and bodice lining of doll's garment.

Illustration 8. Doll's back view showing the bodice construction and cuff openings.

Illustration 9. Doll's petticoats, stockings, knee-ties and simple hide shoes.

EDUCATIONAL VALUE

This account is to demonstrate that certain dolls in original clothing are, or could be, a valuable source of information to costume, textile and cultural studies, whether from historic or current aspects. For instance: had this doll, displaying a combination of the three subjects and more, been available to the author before publication of *The Folk Dress of Europe,* considerable information could have been added to the Iceland chapter.

As collectors and interim caretakers, we must knowledgeably decide which, if any, of our dolls are in this category. Respect them, and remain wary of the temptation to remove, replace or tamper with important garments or condition. Our creative instincts should be confined to other dolls "in need" of this attention.

Snowden's book provides an informative basis for understanding national, regional, festival or folk costumes for people in its "Introduction, The Nature of Folk Dress." Collectors currently owning, or considering dolls in such costumes would find the book extremely helpful. □

Bibliography
Article:
THE NEGLECTED DOLLS, Dorothy and Evelyn Jane Coleman, UFDC 1984 Souvenir Journal - dolls in regional costumes.
Article:
CHERISHABLE CHINA DOLLS, Part 1, Part 2, Estelle Johnston, Doll Reader®, February/March and April, 1985 - renewed inspiration.
Book:
THE FOLK DRESS OF EUROPE, James Snowden. ISBN: 0-8317-3422-1. (Copyright 1979 - price $12.95) First published in England, Mills and Boon, London. U.S. publication, Mayflower Books, Inc., W. H. Smith Publishing, Inc. New York City - for permission to reprint photograph.
Book:
CHINAS/DOLLS FOR STUDY AND ADMIRATION, Mona Borger, Borger Publications, San Francisco, Ca. - for further description of doll, page 27.
Encyclopedia:
ACADEMIC AMERICAN, and COLLIERS' - historical background, Iceland.
Museum:
THE NATIONAL MUSEUM OF ICELAND, Thjodminjasatn, P.O.B. 1439, Sudurgata 41, Reykjavik, Iceland -Director, Thor Magnusson. State Antiquary. Icelandic antiquities; collection of art and coins, textiles, costumes, native crafts. Founded in 1863.

Kate Jordan's *Happifats*

by **Susan Brown Nicholson**

During the same time the *Kewpie* doll was bombarding the world, the small all-bisque creature call a *Happifat* was created by Kate Jordan. Patented in 1914, they are hollow bisque dolls in two sizes and three styles. *Happifats* in the 3½in (9cm) and 4½in (11cm) sizes were either boys or girls. A baby *Happifat* also appeared in the 3½in (9cm) size.

In the 1914 Butler Brothers catalog, they sold for $2.25 for an assorted DOZEN, wholesale! Or, you could purchase a 4in (10cm) size pair for 39¢. While this seems like a dream to collectors today, I am sure we do not want to trade today's wages for those of 1914.

The *Happifats* surely were named for their big smiles and equally big tummies. Their little movable arms are foreshortened. While standing, our arms at rest can nearly reach our knees. The *Happifats* can barely reach their waists.

As appealing as they are to collectors, they have a hair style only a mother could love with one large curl in front and two swags in the back on an otherwise bald head. The eyes are quite large with a hint of eyelashes but no eyebrows. The molded mouth and teeth are puckered in such a way as to indicate an overbite, but "Oh, what a face."

The girl is dressed in pink with a blue sash and shoes or in blue with a pink sash and shoes. The boy usually is seen with brown trousers and a hunter green jacket. Some dolls are marked with a copyright "C," others with paper labels. The dolls were made both in Germany and Japan. The quality of bisque is better on the German-made products. The Japanese dolls are marked "NiPPON."

Besides the dolls, Kate Jordan designed and signed a set of six postcards published by the Edward Gross Company. The postcards are very scarce and command prices as high as the dolls. The set consists of: (1) Sweets to the Sweet, (2) Kick out the Grouch, (3) Cultivate Repose, (4) Turn your Back on Care, (5) Gather Ye Rosebuds while Ye may and (6) To Bring You Luck. The six cards are each individually numbered. The heavy olive green postcard stock is the same stock used to print a set of rare Kewpie postcards published by Gross. They are marked on the back: " 🅖 ."

Happifat children's dishes consist of a teapot, creamer, sugar and cups with lunch plates. The cups and plates feature several different Happifat motifs.

Keep looking for these adorable creatures in a number of places, doll shows, postcard shows and with the children's dishes at shops and shows. On a gloomy day, they can bring a giggle to your heart. □

Illustration 1. *Three pieces from a child's tea set decorated with drawings of Happifats. Shown are a 5½in (14cm) teapot, a 2½in (6cm) creamer and a 2½in (6cm) by 4in (10cm) sugar bowl. The set also includes six 2in (5cm) tall cups and six 5¼in (13cm) diameter plates. Each piece is marked: "Ruddlstadt Made in Germany."*

LEFT: Illustration 2. *4in (10cm) Happifats girl in a pink dress with a blue ribbon from trim which gathers in a large bow in the back. The shoes match the blue ribbon which is molded.*

RIGHT: Illustration 3. *Back view of 4in (10cm) Happifats girl, seen in Illustration 2, showing the interesting hair and the bow in the back of the dress.*

RIGHT: Illustration 4. *Close-up of the back view of the 4in (10cm) Happifats girl, seen, in Illustrations 2 and 3, showing the detail of the marking "NiP-PON" and the bow on the back of the dress.*

BELOW: Illustration 6. *Back view of 3½in (9cm) Happifats boy, seen in Illustration 5, showing the tails of the jacket and the interesting hair.*

LEFT: Illustration 5. *3½in (9cm) Happifats boy in brown trousers with a dark green jacket with tails. The shoes are a matching green.*

LEFT: Illustration 7. One of a set of six postcards designed by Kate Jordan and featuring her drawings of the Happifats, published by the Edward Gross Company. Each of the cards in the series is individually numbered and signed with the printed signature of Kate Jordan. This one is "Kick out the Grouch" and is marked on the front: "© EDWARD GROSS CO."

ABOVE: Illustration 8. Another of the six postcards designed by Kate Jordan and featuring her drawings of the Happifats. This one is "Turn your Back on Care" and is marked on the front: "© EDWARD GROSS CO."

LEFT: Illustration 9. Another of the six postcards designed by Kate Jordan and featuring her drawings of the Happifats. This one is "Cultivate Repose" and is marked on the front: "© EDWARD GROSS CO."

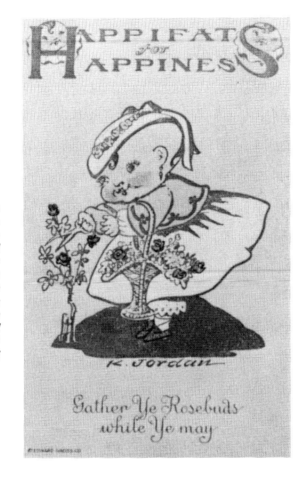

RIGHT: Illustration 10. *Another of the six postcards designed by Kate Jordan and featuring her drawings of the Happifats. This one is "Gather Ye Rosebuds while Ye may" and is marked on the front: "© EDWARD GROSS CO."*

LEFT: Illustration 11. *Another of the six postcards designed by Kate Jordan and featuring her drawings of the Happifats. This one is "To bring You Luck" and is marked on the front: "© EDWARD GROSS CO."*

Metal Head Dolls —
Plentiful, Collectible, Reasonable

by **Dian Zillner**

Photographs by **Suzanne Zillner Silverthorn**

As the popularity of bisque and desirable hard plastic dolls continues to rise, the prices keep pace, reach new heights and make doll collecting a very costly hobby. New collectors may become discouraged because of these high prices and decide to settle for a less interesting hobby because they cannot afford the beautiful bisque dolls they see displayed for sale at antique shows.

However, there are many types of dolls that are still affordable to the average collector. When composition, celluloid or metal has been used for a doll head, the price falls considerably and gives the average beginning collector a type of doll to purchase and enjoy that she (or he) can afford. Metal head dolls, in particular, seem to have been overlooked by doll enthusiasts. These dolls can provide an interesting and varied collection to a hobbiest at a reasonable cost. Metal head dolls have had a long life and some of the oldest are now nearly 100 years old.

The first metal doll heads were patented in France in 1861 by René Poulin but the metal heads increased in popularity when German companies began making the heads around 1890. The most famous firms used the trademarks "Diana," "Juno" and "Minerva."

The "Minerva" heads were made by Buschow & Beck beginning in 1894. These heads were distributed in the United States by Alfred Vischer & Co. The German company of Alfred Heller was responsible for the heads marked "Diana." They were produced from 1902 until 1908. The "Juno" heads were made by Karl Standfuss beginning in 1904 and they were distributed by Geo. Borgfeldt & Co. in the United States.

The heads were made of several

Illustration 1. 12in (30cm) to 16in (41cm) early metal shoulder heads with kid bodies, composition or celluloid lower arms; painted eyes and hair; no marks on heads; date from early 1900.

kinds of metal including tin, brass, lead, copper, zinc, pewter and even aluminum. The early heads were shoulder heads which had molded hair and painted eyes. By 1900 as styles changed, wigs and glass eyes were added. The heads can be found with closed painted mouths or with open mouths with teeth. The bodies were usually kid with hands of bisque, celluloid or composition. Some heads were sold alone so many dolls were made up at home and placed on homemade cloth bodies. The general sizes of these dolls ranged from about 10in (25cm) to 22in (56cm) in height.

Because the doll heads were unbreakable, there are still many

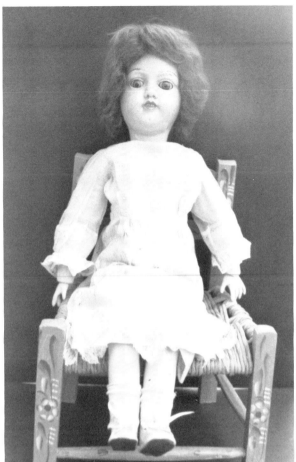

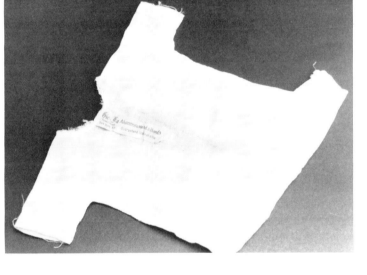

ABOVE LEFT: Illustration 2. 16in (41cm) metal shoulder heads on kid bodies with bisque lower arms; wigs, glass eyes, open mouths with teeth; no marks on heads; date from around 1920.

ABOVE RIGHT: Illustration 3. 25in (63cm) aluminum socket head by the Giebeler-Falk Doll Corporation on ball-jointed body with aluminum hands; mohair wig, tin eyes; head marked with a star with the letter "G" inside it and the number "25" and the letters "US Pat.;" dates from 1919.

RIGHT: Illustration 4. Original tagged chemise worn by the aluminum head doll, shown in **Illustration 3**, made by the Giebeler-Falk Doll Corporation. The tag reads: "Gie-Fa Aluminum Head and Hands, Guaranteed Unbreakable, New York, N.Y."

available. The only major problem found in these dolls is the poor condition of the paint on many examples. There are still enough dolls in good condition at reasonable prices that a discerning collector should purchase only the best. A metal shoulder head doll of average size and in good condition is currently available for around $75 to $85. A similar doll with wig and glass eyes should cost between $100 to $125.

Fewer metal dolls were made during this period with socket heads but **Illustration 3** shows a large 25in (63cm) tall doll with aluminum metal socket head on a beautiful ball-jointed body with aluminum hands. She was made in 1919 in New York City by the Giebeler-Falk Doll Corporation. The back of her head has a star with a "G" inside it and the number "25" along with the letters "US Pat." She also still has her original chemise as shown in

Illustration 4. The label reads: "Gie-Fa Aluminum Head and Hands, Guaranteed Unbreakable, New York, N.Y." She wears a mohair wig, has metal sleep eyes and an open mouth with painted teeth. A doll of this type will be more expensive and could cost $200 or more.

As the 20th century progressed, baby dolls became popular and the United States firms added new metal head models to meet the new demand.

Illustration 5. 12in (30cm) and 14in (36cm) baby dolls with metal heads on cloth bodies with composition arms and legs; sleep eyes. The doll on the right has a shoulder head and the other has a socket head. There are no marks on either head.

Illustration 6. 20in (51cm) toddler doll with mohair wig, sleep eyes, open mouth with teeth; cloth body with crier, composition arms and legs; dates from the late 1920s or early 1930s.

Illustration 7. 18in (46cm) metal shoulder heads on replaced bodies of cloth and kid; painted molded hair, painted eyes; both marked "Minerva" on the front of the head. The doll on the right has an open mouth with teeth.

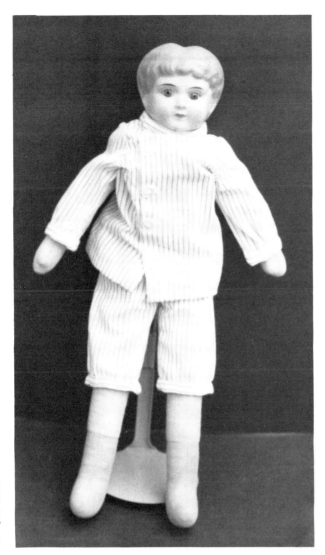

Illustration 8. 12in (30cm) metal shoulder head on all-cloth body; glass eyes; head marked "Minerva" on front; dressed as a boy.

Some companies even manufactured a doll that was made all of metal with a wig and sleep eyes. The Atlas Doll & Toy Co. in New York City made these dolls from 1917 until 1925. The Art Metal Works company from New Jersey also made a similar doll of brass with movable joints in 1919. The more usual model used only a head made of metal combined with a cloth body and composition arms and legs. The Amor Metal Toy Stamping Co. in New Jersey made this type of doll in 1922. These dolls are still available from many dealers for $50 to $75 depending on size and condition. The all-metal dolls are not plentiful and therefore would be much more expensive.

By the later 1920s, several companies were making a toddler doll with a metal head, wig and tin sleep eyes mounted on a cloth body with composition arms and legs. These dolls also had a crier box then popular in many dolls. The toddler should be priced at about the same price as the baby dolls that are similar.

As the 1930s progressed, composition dolls such as the Ideal *Shirley Temple* and the Effanbee *Patsy* gained popularity and the old metal heads went out of fashion.

Although the type of doll that was made of metal changed with the years, the material did retain a place in the doll world for over half a century. Because of the many years of metal doll manufacturing and the unbreakable quality of the material, there are excellent examples of these dolls still available to the collector. The quality will range from the common painted hair and eyes shoulder head on a homemade body to a mint head with glass eyes to the beautiful as a bisque head shown in **Illustration 9** which came on a kid body with bisque arms, glass eyes and wig.

The collector should discriminate and look for fine examples at reasonable prices. This is one type of doll in which the supply currently outpaces the demand. The time is right to begin investigating metal head dolls which are presently plentiful, collectible and reasonable. □

Author's Note: For additional information on metal head dolls, readers should refer to *The Collector's Encyclopedia of Dolls* by Dorothy S., Elizabeth A. and Evelyn J. Coleman and the *German Doll Encyclopedia 1800-1939* by Jürgen and Marianne Cieslik.

Illustration 9. 21in (53cm) metal shoulder head on kid body with bisque lower arms; glass eyes, open mouth with teeth; head marked "6" on the back and an unclear trademark is stamped on the front; dates from the early 1900s.

45

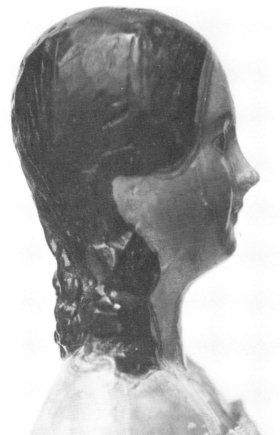
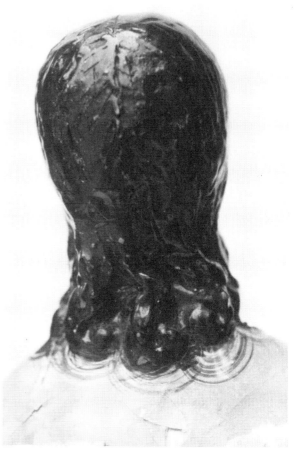

Molded Coiffure Papier-mâché Ladies, Part I

by Sybill McFadden

All photographs by the **author**
All dolls from **Sybill's Museum of Antique Dolls and Toys.**

ABOVE LEFT: Illustration 5. 21in (53cm) "Milliners' Model" man, seldom found among the molded hair papier-mâché dolls. He is all original and provides valuable information about male attire in the 1830 to 1850 period. He wears a brown cashmere wool jacket with a black velvet collar, tight fitting black trousers, a black silk cravat and a black silk vest which, unfortunately, is disintegrating. He was purchased with the 18in (46cm) molded hair papier-mâché lady, seen in **Illustrations 1** through **4**, as a pair. **ABOVE RIGHT: Illustration 6.** Close-up of the 21in (53cm) "Milliners' Model" man, seen in **Illustration 5**, showing the detail of his hair and face. His hair style is of the period, center-parted. He has unusual brown painted eyes under gray feathered eyebrows. **BOTTOM RIGHT: Illustration 7.** Back view of the 21in (53cm) "Milliners' Model" man, seen in **Illustrations 5** and **6**, showing the molded comb marks in his short hair.

OPPOSITE PAGE:
ABOVE LEFT: Illustration 1. 18in (46cm) molded hair papier-mâché lady wearing a two-piece blue polished cotton skirt and bodice. The bodice is topped with a net and lace overblouse which, while old, looks to have been added along the way. Her hands have carved fingers. She wears net pantaloons with bows which peek out below the skirt. **ABOVE RIGHT: Illustration 2.** Close-up of the 18in (46cm) molded hair papier-mâché lady, seen in **Illustration 1**, showing the detail of her head and face. Her center-parted black painted hair falls to the cheekbones where it loops over her ears and becomes long curls. Her face is well painted. She has blue painted eyes and rosy cheeks. **BOTTOM LEFT: Illustration 3.** Side view of the 18in (46cm) molded hair papier-mâché lady, seen in **Illustrations 1** and **2**, showing the detail of her hair. **BOTTOM RIGHT: Illustration 4.** Back view of the 18in (46cm) molded hair papier-mâché lady, seen in **Illustrations 1, 2** and **3**, showing the black painted hair as it drops from a smooth crown to long curls at the back and sides. There are painted gray strokes around the face and under the curls on the back of the neck.

Facing the world with sober mien, she is a small, reticent doll whose amazing hairdo rivets instant attention. She is a molded hair papier-mâché of the early 1800s.

Her hallmark is an understated simplicity and grace of form contrasted by an elaborate, sometimes towering, molded coiffure.

Prized by today's collectors, the dolls are ladies and an occasional rare man doll, which most of us call "Milliners' Models." It is, however, an inept term with no historical veracity, as it is generally believed that the dolls were conceived as playthings for children. The proper term by popular vote in the U.F.D.C. (United Federation of Dolls Clubs, Inc.) *Glossary* is "molded hair papier-mâché." It is correct and descriptive, but even the most exacting among us agree it seems a bit lengthy and involved when talking informally about these dolls. Thus, the term "Milliners' Model" persists for lack of a succinct, better name. In this article, then, perhaps you will forgive us if, for variety's sake, we use both terms.

Eccentric and beautiful, the dolls are a reflection of the contradictory era in which they appeared. In the early 1800s the beginning of industrialization and an emerging new middle class was converging on the elegance and sophistication of a no longer reigning aristocracy. This contradiction can be seen clearly in the contrast between the elaborate and sophisticated coiffures of the so-called Milliners' Model and the simplicity of the self-effacing little gowns they wore. Finding one today without clothing, the natural inclination might be to costume her in an elegant gown in keeping with her hair style. Originally, it was seldom done that way. Here, then, we see once more, the doll becoming the mirror of social realities.

Until the early 1800s dolls were for the wealthy and as such, were gowned and coiffed to appeal to the aristocracy. We are seldom told or shown, nor do we have extant examples today of what the less fortunate child played with. She, we must surmise, contented herself with homemade rag or wood babies, or with the cheaply made dolls bought for pennies at the summer fairs of the day, none of which were destined to last beyond childhood's few years of play.

Industrialization and the new middle class changed all that. Technology was now applied to doll making, with the resultant rapid improvement in the quality of dolls. We see the height of this art being reached in the 1860s and continuing through the next 40 years, as Germany and France vied for top honors at the annual fairs and top place in the world's markets with their fine china ladies and gorgeous bisque dolls. The final wind down of that glorious 40 years arrived, ironically, while still at the peak of their prowess with the real child-inspired, amazingly lifelike character dolls at the beginning of the devastating World War I.

In the early 1830s, however, the molded hair papier-mâché doll takes her place as one of the first to benefit from the new technology of mass production. Made in Germany, their elaborate heads of pressed papier-mâché were made in quantity, their wooden arms and legs turned by machines, and their quality kid bodies, though still hand-sewn and stuffed with wood sawdust and bran, were also made in quantities sufficient for export. The finished doll was now a product.

Until this time, fine wooden and papier-mache dolls had been created, but were often one-of-a-kind or one of only a small number, produced mostly by hand. True, Germany's home cottage industry had been producing large quantities of peg-woodens, parts of these dolls turned on home lathes, and England was making wax dolls at the time, also. However, the so-called Milliners' Models were among the first dolls to reflect the true beginning of improved technology in doll making.

Combining three materials — papier-mâché, kid leather and wood — the final result became a doll, elongated, slim, spare and elegantly constructed.

The heads on the Milliners' Models are, of course, their fascination. Coiffure and face were pressed in the same molding to become a hollow papier-mâché head. The hair styles are many and varied, as illustrated by a comment in the 1940s of Mrs. Emma Clear who ran the then-famous "Humpty-Dumpty Doll Hospital" in Redondo Beach, California. She said, "We have had as many as 24 of these little dolls come for repairs in a single day and not two of them had the same style of hairdo." While there is still a variety of hair styles, these coiffure dolls, alas, are no longer so plentiful!

The faces are almost never beautiful, and the coiffures sometimes verge on the grotesque. Others are less elaborate. The original gowns were usually of simple cloth and unadorned. However plain of face and dress, the dolls, nonetheless, present an aura of gentility and refinement. The necks are slender, the shoulders sloping and on some there is a suggestion of a bosom. These were the standards of beauty of those times.

The wasp-waisted kid leather bodies were made of two pieces cut front and back, then stitched down the middle and firmly stuffed, resulting in the simplest of classic body styles. Graceful arms and legs of wood, turned on lathes, were inserted in the lower half of the limbs, and secured with colored bands of red or blue paper, just above the elbows and knees. The turned wooden legs terminate in pointed slippers nearly always painted in red or green, sometimes tan or black, now all faded to rose and pastel shades. They were without heels in the style of the day. The dolls were made in many sizes ranging from 6in (15cm) to 8in (20cm) to a very large 38in (96cm).

Some collectors still ponder the function of these unique dolls, wondering if they were designed as fashion figures. Some of them have been found wearing original high-crowned bonnets over their coiffures, which may have given rise by early collectors to the "Milliners' Model" concept. As hard as it is to visualize these stiff, inarticulated dolls as childrens' playthings — they **do** seem so "unplayable" by today's standards — we must return again to the early doll making when childrens' dolls were far from ideal. Most were lady dolls and many were too large, too heavy or too stiff for small girls. Yet play with them they did, as documented in paintings, drawings and old photographs.

In the 1830s through the 1850s, the period of the molded hair papier-mâché dolls, playthings were considered satisfactory for children only if they were educational. It was part and parcel of the Victorian concept, and was a long time dying. The Milliners' Models, then, would have proved apt dolls for the education of small would-be seamstresses for whom learning the art of "sewing a fine seam" was a womanly necessity.

Times change. In today's modern world even the darning of a sock is a lost art, and children's play is very different.

However, though the molded hair papier-mâché doll may not have been

LEFT: Illustration 8. 9½in (24cm) all original molded hair papier-mâché lady wearing a flower printed and striped pink cotton voile dress with matching pantaloons. It is hand-sewn and well made but typically understated. **TOP RIGHT: Illustration 9.** Close-up of the 9½in (24cm) molded hair papier-mâché lady, seen in **Illustration 8**, showing her unusual and elaborate coiffure with black curls placed in diagonals toward the face and rising toward the center. Wisps of hair are painted around the face in double lines outlining the hair. **BOTTOM RIGHT: Illustration 10.** Side view of the 9½in (24cm) molded hair papier-mâché lady, seen in **Illustrations 8** and **9**, showing how all her hair at the back is pulled up into the high hairdo which results in an equally strange appearance from the sides.

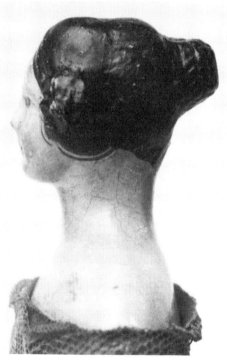

LEFT: Illustration 11. 11in (28cm) molded hair papier-mâché lady from the 1830s, wearing a blue polished cotton underdress with embroidered net over it. Faded blue ribbons decorate the off-the-shoulder gown and are sashed around the waist with beige satin ribbon. She also wears net covered blue pantaloons which show beneath the hem of disintegrating hairpin lace. Her dress is rather more elegant than the norm. Note her broad deep shoulder plate which is typical of these dolls. **TOP RIGHT: Illustration 12.** Close-up of 11in (28cm) molded hair papier-mâché lady, seen in **Illustration 11.** Her black painted center-parted hair displays clusters of side curls and a triple braid bun at the back. She has blue eyes and smiles slightly. **BOTTOM RIGHT: Illustration 13.** Side view of the 11in (28cm) molded hair papier-mâché lady, seen in **Illustrations 11** and **12,** showing the hair which is drawn from the crown into a braided bun at the back and the painted single strokes outlining the front and sides of the hair which is typical on all of these dolls.

the child's ideal play doll in her time, she takes her place in the ongoing transitional history of doll making, and comes to fortunate collectors today as a unique treasure from a long ago time, now only to be imagined in our fast paced modern world. □

China Character Dolls

by **Yolande Mezey Harrison**

Photographs by the **author**

Illustration 1. Close-up of 9in (23cm) china googly whistler boy. Note the incised inverted eyebrows and open mouth puckered into a whistle.

Illustration 2. Close-up of 9in (23cm) Dutch girl showing the lace design on her hat and the detailed modeling in her face.

Pleasant and stately ladies are the visions conjured by many as a stereotype of china dolls and the majority of chinas do place in this stereotype. However, there are exceptions. China characters do exist though are rarely found. For those who love china dolls, the search for the unusual can be rewarded with a scarce find. The two pairs described and illustrated here reveal interesting characters departing from the usual, proof that china dolls continue to surprise and delight us.

A delightful character boy who displays many lovely features (see **Illustration 1**) is unusual in several respects. He is a golden brown eye googly and has a completely open mouth puckered into a whistle. His eyebrows are incised and inverted. His molded hat appears to be Dutch and he has brown hair above his prominent ears. He is pink toned and is a socket head, not a shoulder head for he does not have a shoulder plate. He is marked: "Germany 16518." His body is cloth over wire with leather hands. His clothing is all original, made from wool felt and he wears wooden Sabot shoes.

His companion (see **Illustration 2**) is a serious face girl with a decorated Dutch hat. She is marked "16519" and is also pink toned and a socket head. Her body construction is identical to her partner's. She, however, has

Illustration 3. Close-up view of 12in (30cm) black china young man showing the prominent features of eyes and mouth and the stand-up collar and knotted tie. *Zona Sutherland Collection.*

Illustration 4. Silhouette profile view of 12in (30cm) black china young man. *Zona Sutherland Collection.*

intaglio eyes and dark blonde hair. Her clothing is made of wool and silk material and she wears wooden Sabot shoes. The maker of this pair has not been identifed. The era of manufacture is the first quarter of this century.

It is with fascination that we examine the dark brown china characters. The young man's face displays distinctive modeling of ethnic features and his shoulder has a molded shirt with a stand-up collar and red tie (see **Illustrations 3** and **4**). He is not visibly marked and the inside of his shoulder was not examined. He is on a cloth body with dark china hands and brown china boots. He has molded ears and a special hair treatment done in a dull matte finish which provides a nice

contrast. His large painted eyes, wide nose and mouth are dominate features in his narrow youthful face. Interesting modeling detail was done by the manufacturer to his neck for an "Adam's apple" and contour muscles in the back of his neck. He is redressed in a dark green two-piece suit with pearl buttons.

His companion (see **Illustrations 5, 6** and **7**), looks like his sister because the facial features and face shape are similar. She has large eyes and mouth which dominate her face and an undecorated shoulder plate. Her hair is molded short and curly with a dull matte finish. She does not have exposed ears. Her long neck and proportions give her a youthful lady appearance. She, too, has dark brown china hands

and legs, with red heeled molded boots. She is wearing an old dress of blue and white print cotton which has three layers of ruffles and is tied with an old red ribbon. She, too, has no visible identification marks and also the inside of her shoulder plate was not inspected.

When these black character chinas were manufactured and where is not known. Based on their modeling and their boot wear, they are placed in the last quarter of the 19th century.

These delightful china characters add interest to a china doll collection and are a treasure to seek. For collectors who had added china characters to their "want" lists — happy hunting!

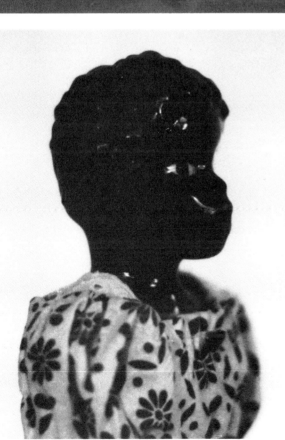

ABOVE: Illustration 6. Close-up of 11½in (29cm) black china young lady, seen in **Illustration 5**, showing prominent features of her eyes and mouth and very strong family resemblance to the young man seen in **Illustration 3**. *Zona Sutherland Collection.*

LEFT: Illustration 7. Profile view of 11½in (29cm) black china young lady, seen in **Illustrations 5** and **6**, showing distinct modeling. *Zona Sutherland Collection.*

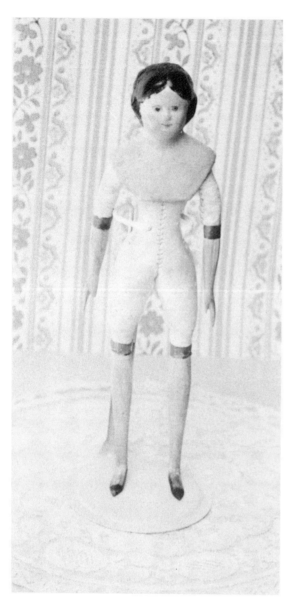

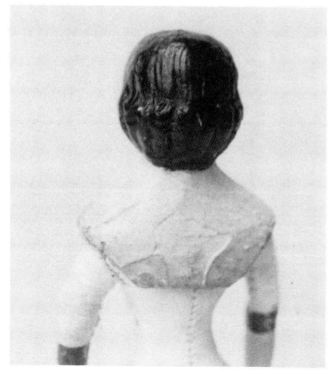

Molded Coiffure Papier-mâché Ladies, Part II

by **Sybill McFadden**

All photographs by the **author**

All dolls from Sybill's Museum of Antique Dolls and Toys

18   19

Illustration 14. 8½in (22cm) doll with hand-pressed papier-mâché shoulder plate on neat kid leather body which is entirely hand-sewn and firmly stuffed with sawdust, seamed front and back with waist seams only (to create the wasp waist), as the body is patterned in two pieces. The blue bands of polished paper secure the wooden limbs, which have been delicated turned on lathes, to the kid leather. The hands are mitt type with separate thumbs. The legs terminate in feet with pointed-toe slippers painted in rose, green, brown or black. The feet are attached to the legs at the ankles in a separate operation. This all results in a well-made, slim, trim body of the type used on all these dolls.

Illustration 15. Close-up of the 8½in (22cm) hand-pressed papier-mâché shoulder plate lady, seen in **Illustration 14**, showing the wide shoulder plate attached to the neatly hand-sewn kid body common to all these dolls. Note the roughness of the hand-pressed papier-mâché.

Illustration 16. Back view of the 8½in (22cm) hand-pressed papier-mâché shoulder plate lady, seen in **Illustrations 14** and **15**, showing the simple hair style. The black painted short hair shows the comb marks, culminating in many narrow curls around the bottom. Note the wide shoulder plate and the roughness of the hand-pressed operation. Note also the wasp waist of the kid leather body and the paper bands which attach the wood forearms to the leather upper arms.

Illustration 17. 11in (28cm) molded hair papier-mâché lady wearing her all original gown of pink and white checked gingham, all hand-stitched. Matching pantaloons show beneath the skirt.

Illustration 18. Close-up of 11in (28cm) molded hair papier-mâché lady, seen in **Illustration 17**, showing her black painted hair in soft side puffs which are pulled into side wings and tucked under a bun of small bunched curls at the back. She has blue painted eyes.

Illustration 19. Side view of 11in (28cm) molded hair papier-mâché lady, seen in **Illustrations 17** and **18**, showing the curls which are clustered at the back. The hair in front and on the sides is outlined with a painted gray line.

The following are additional examples of the molded hair papier-mâché ladies discussed in the first part of this article.

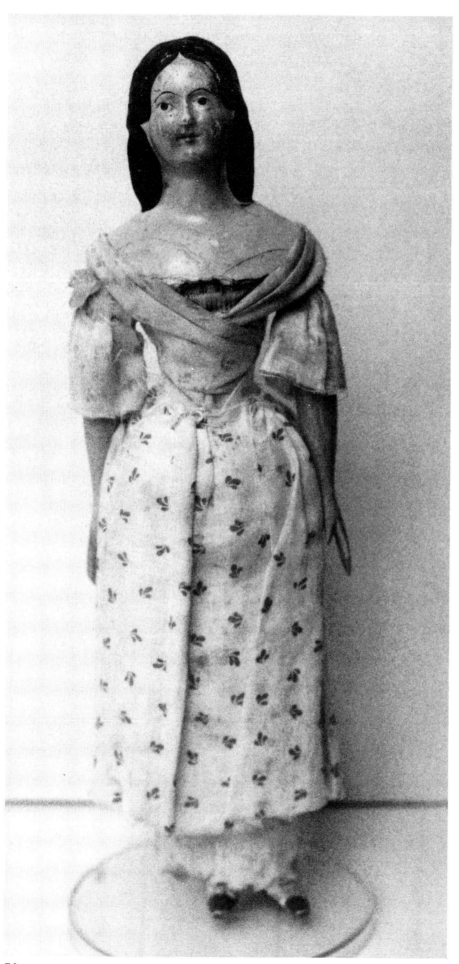

Illustration 20. 8½in (22cm) molded hair papier-mâché lady wearing a printed cotton gown with a leaf figure in red on the skirt and blue on the bodice. A band of trim is tucked in the bodice top. She wears white percale pantaloons under her gown. This dress is less well-made than the norm.

21

22

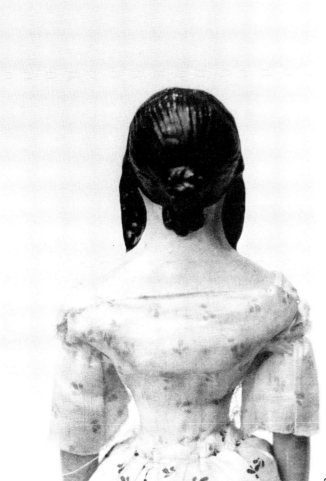

Illustration 21. Close-up of 8½in (22cm) molded hair papier-mâché lady, seen in **Illustration 20**, with her hair curving from a center part and looped back at the cheekbones where it falls to the shoulders in double braids, exposing a bit of each ear.

Illustration 22. Side view of 8½in (22cm) molded hair papier-mâché lady, seen in **Illustrations 20** and **21**, showing the double shoulder-length braids and the remainder of the hair drawn back into a bun of curls.

Illustration 23. Back view of 8½in (22cm) molded hair papier-mâché lady, seen in **Illustrations 20, 21** and **22**, showing the hair which is drawn back tightly from the crown, with molded comb marks, into a bun of curls from which three small curls escape on the nape of the neck. This coiffure is more intricate than it is possible to depict in the illustration.

23

Illustration 25. Close-up of 12½in (32cm) molded hair papier-mâché lady, seen in **Illustration 24**, showing the detail of her hair style, known as the Apollo's Knot, which was popular in the 1830s. There were many variations, but in this one the center-parted hair is drawn tightly from the back and crown, braided in many braids and drawn upward over a hair form into a braided topknot. Curls are clustered at either side of the face. Note the painted single strokes outlining the hair around the face, typical of these dolls. The doll is nicely painted, well varnished, has blue eyes and rosy cheeks.

Illustration 24. 12½in (32cm) molded hair papier-mâché lady with a towering coiffure. She wears her all original yellow multi-print cotton dress with large puffed sleeves. Despite the elaborate hairdo, the dress is simple. She wears white cotton pantaloons and a petticoat under the gown. Her shoes are painted a soft rose and rose paper bands secure her wooden arms to the kid forearms.

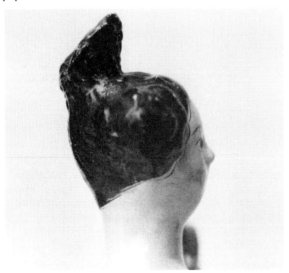

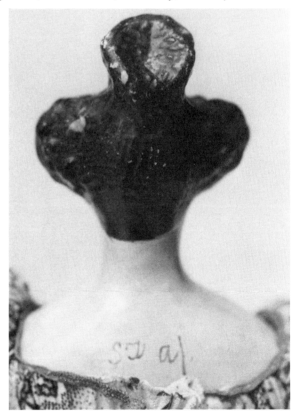

Illustration 26. Side view of 12½in (32cm) molded hair papier-mâché lady, seen in **Illustrations 24** and **25**, showing the Apollo's Knot, a fanciful hair style which appears both odd and amusing.

Illustration 27. Back view of 12½in (32cm) molded hair papier-mâché lady, seen in **Illustrations 24, 25** and **26**, showing the Apollo's Knot with the hair drawn tightly upward and the braided ends tucked into the topknot creating a concave center. The letters seen on the shoulder plate are in faded brown ink and are a mystery.

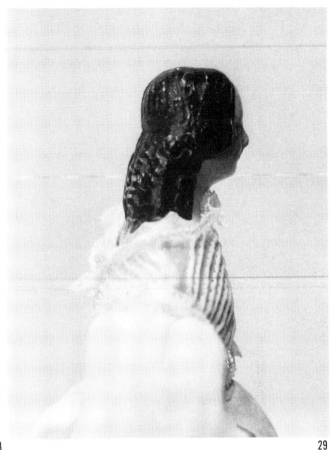

28

29

Illustration 28. Close-up of 8in (20cm) molded hair papier-mâché lady showing the delicate painting. Her painted black center-parted hair is caught up in side loops at the cheeks. She has blue eyes and the rosy cheeks of a very young girl. Her dress is a replacement.

Illustration 29. Side views of 8in (20cm) molded hair papier-mâché lady, seen in **Illustration 29**, showing the hair looped back at both sides which falls into long curls around the sides and back.

Illustration 30. Back view of 8in (20cm) molded hair papier-mâché lady, seen in **Illustrations 28** and **29**, showing the long black curls which fall beneath a black ribbon which is painted on the back of the head.

30

The First European Dolls in America

by **Dorothy S. & Evelyn Jane Coleman**

Illustration 1. Drawing by John White, a member of the British Sir Walter Raleigh expedition that came to Virginia (now Roanoke Island, North Carolina) in 1585. This expedition to the New World brought English dolls to the Indians and it was stated, "They are greatlye Dilighted with puppetts and babes which wear brought oute of England." The writing in dark brown ink at the top of this picture reads, "A chiefe Herowars wyfe of Pomeoc//and her daughter of the age of .8. or//.10. yeares." The girl holds a doll dressed as an Elizabethan lady. The original picture is in the British Museum and is described there as "Black, various shades of grey and brown water-colours, touched with white and crimson body-colours, over black lead;" and measures 26cm (10⅜in) by 15cm (5⅞in). *Courtesy of the Smithsonian Institution, photograph no. 18725.*

John White, an artist and an important member of the Roanoke Island expedition, was the grandfather of Virginia Dare, the first white baby born in what was to become the United States. Being an artist, John White recorded in pictures the events of this expedition in 1585 to the New World sponsored by Sir Walter Raleigh. Among John White's important drawings was a picture of a little Indian girl holding a doll dressed in Elizabethan European costume. The doll had obviously been given to the little girl by a member of the Sir Walter Raleigh expedition. John White, the artist who came with this expedition, returned to England and later came back only to find that the original colony had disappeared. Fortunately John White's pictures provide an important record of the Indians found on what was later to be known as Roanoke Island, off Dare County, North Carolina. The contrast is striking between the nearly naked Indians and the doll dressed in Elizabethan style with a stiff ruff.

The original rendition of this picture is in the British Museum in London, while a copy is in the Smithsonian Institution in Washington, D.C. This picture has appeared in several books including *The Doll, Collectors of America, Inc, 1940 Manual*. This Manual shows the picture by John White of a little Indian girl holding the Elizabethan doll and quotes from "The Story of Dolls Tells the Story of Mankind," an article by Dr. Walter Hough, Head Curator of Anthropology at the Smithsonian Institution. The article was read by Dr. Hough before the American Association for the Advancement of Science, and also published in the *New York Times Magazine*, March 6, 1927. The article reads, in part, as follows:

"The first doll that ever came to America was given to a little Virginia Indian girl in 1607 by someone belonging to the expedition of Sir Walter Raleigh commanded by the redoubtable Captain John Smith. It is fortunate that John White, the artist of the expedition, recorded this event in one of his pictures, giving us some inkling of the joy of the dusky little maid, perhaps Pocahontas herself over her Elizabethan doll with its stiff neck ruff. The quaint old book which describes the Indians of Virginia in 1607 says of the little girls: "They are greatlye Dilighted with puppetts and babes which wear brought oute of England."

There seems to be some confusion in Dr. Hough's account of the John White picture. It does represent the first European doll in America, a doll that was given to a little Virginia Indian girl in 1585 not 1607. John White was on the 1585 expedition sponsored by Sir Walter Raleigh. When James I came to the throne in 1603, Raleigh was charged with treason and lanquished in the Tower of London until his release in 1616. It is doubtful that he had anything to do with the 1607 expedition on which Captain John Smith came to Virginia. John Smith had come to America on earlier expeditions but since he was not born

until 1580 he would not have been old enough to command an expedition at age five in 1585 when John White came to America on Sir Walter Raleigh's expedition. Presumably the quotation from a "quaint old book" could have been written by Captain John Smith about his trip to America in 1607. Captain Smith was a voluminous writer and might be called a "Romantic." "Puppetts and babes" would have referred to dolls in that era. Of course "wear" is an old spelling of "were."

A somewhat similar contemporary doll was shown in the 1577 portrait painting of Arabella Stewart (aged 23 months), a cousin of Queen Elizabeth. This painting now hangs in Hardwick Hall, England.

Apparently dolls were brought to the Indians in Virginia from England on both the 1585 Raleigh expedition and the 1607 John Smith expedition. The entire eastern coast was called "Virginia" at that time, even our present Massachusetts area was called

"Virginia." One can well imagine the delight of the little Indian girls to whom the English dolls were given. We are greatly indebted to John White for providing a lasting record in his picture of one of these very early dolls. □

Illustration 2. Theodor de Bry made an engraving based somewhat on the figures in the John White drawing. This engraving was published in 1590 in a volume named *America.* It can readily be seen that the drawing by a person who had actually seen the American Indians in 1585 differed from the engraving made about five years later by de Bry in England. However, the costume on the doll is shown in much greater detail in the 1590 engraving than in the 1585 drawing and together with the English rattle is probably representative of the toys in England at that time. This engraving, also in the British Museum, was published by de Bry in a volume titled *America,* part I, plate VIII. It is 15cm (5⅞in) by 22cm (8½in). *Courtesy of the Smithsonian Institution, photograph no. 57527.*

Nobilis Matrona Pomeioocenſis.   VIII

8

Fact and Fiction:
The Story of Letitia Penn

by **Ann Bahar**

Since 1960, The Historical Society of Pennsylvania has been home to the Letitia Penn doll, reputedly the oldest European survivor on the North American continent. So many legends surround this doll that when it was included in an exhibit called "Finding Philadelphia: Making and Collecting An American Past," the Society staff felt the time had come to verify the doll's credentials in an effort to separate fact from fiction. What followed was a unique adventure in doll research.

Thomas M. Gartner of the Museum Department told us that enquiries were sent "to experts at other museums, seeking their help in arriving at a more complete and accurate history of the Penn doll. In particular," he added, "we were trying to see if we could find any evidence in the genealogical record which either supported or discredited the familiar [William Penn] legend. We sought expert assistance to determine an accurate date for the Letitia Penn doll (the true date may not be consistent with the stories) and to determine the use for which it was originally made."

The Letitia Penn doll legend has its origin in a statement which a 19th century owner attached to her Will in August 1865. There, Mary B. Kirk wrote:

This doll was brought by William Penn from his daughter whose name it bears to a little girl in Philadelphia on his second visit to Pennsylvania in 1699.

It was given by one of her family to a Mrs. Prior of Philadelphia and presented by her to her friend Miss Ann Massey of that city. Miss Massey, afterward Mrs. Browne, when leaving Philadelphia with her husband to visit his family in England, left this doll with her intimate friend Mrs. Maher, . . . telling her if she never returned the doll was hers. Mrs. Browne died in England. Our friend Mrs. Maher gave the doll to me May 1858. She died the following August in the 75th year of her age.

Letitia is attired in "Court Dress" and just as William Penn brought her from England and in all these long years has been carefully preserved, save with the loss of one arm.

*OPPOSITE PAGE: **Illustration 1.** The Letitia Penn doll after extensive conservation and restoration more closely resembles her original self, a circa 1740 Georgian doll costumed in workbasket scraps and probably intended as a child's plaything, not a fashion doll as legend claims. The Historical Society of Pennsylvania.*

***Illustration 2.** Close-up of the restored face of the Letitia Penn doll. The Historical Society of Pennsylvania.*

*Illustration 3. Letitia Penn after restoration and conservation, her 1740 date finally established, stands proud. She retains her claim to being (probably) the oldest European survivor in North America and is glad that her costume, face and body have been treated and repaired. Note the new left arm, cleverly constructed to match the original one but **finished differently** to distinguish new from old. The doll stands approximately 20in (51cm) tall.* The Historical Society of Pennsylvania.

Wishing that some sketch might be handed down with her, I have written all our friend gave me of her history, which she knew to be perfectly reliable.

Mary B. Kirk

When Mary B. Kirk died in 1882, a relative added the following note to her 1865 statement:

A few days before Sister Mary's death which occurred on 3rd day the 12th of Dec. 1882. She gave me the "Doll" with the request that it should go to my son Mahlon when he is old enough to take care of it, and preserve it.

Mahlon Kirk

The legend went public in January 1902 when *The Ladies' Home Journal* published the article reproduced here, a story by Mary Towns-end Kirk entitled "A Doll Two Hundred Years Old." Instantly, Letitia became famous and her material value in the marketplace as well as her sentimental value as a significant relic skyrocketed. She passed through the hands of Izole Dorgan to take a prominent place in the famed Imogene Anderson Collection. She was displayed summer after summer at the State Historical Association in Ticonderoga, New York, with the old legend reiterated in 1937: That the doll had "been brought to Philadelphia from England in 1699 by William Penn for a friend of his little daughter. This doll is probably the oldest in America and the most famous individual doll in the Imogene Anderson Collection of Early American dolls."

The Penn doll's legend-ary history was further reinforced when well-known children's author and folk art historian Carolyn Sherwin Bailey published a best-seller called *Tops and Whistles* (New York, Viking, 1937), a compendium of fiction based on apocryphal tales from American history. Among these is "Letitia Penn Steps Out" which recounts the old story in sentimental detail. It concludes:

Little Miss Rankin of old Philadelphia grew up and then Letitia lost her, but the doll found other mothers. Her wooden body and her striped brocade and velvet dress lasted longer than did the Quaker bonnets and shawls. Letitia Penn saw Philadelphia grow from a small garden town to a great city. She saw sedan chairs and coaches give way to electric trains and airplanes. She broke an arm in her first two hundred years, and in her later life she went to live in a glass case in Connecticut. She has traveled to New York City to tell her adventures to large crowds who stood about her glass case in a great department store. Her hair has lost its brightness and her dress is faded but she knows more stories than any other American doll.

(pages 25 to 26)

That glass case belonged to Imogene Anderson; the department store was John Wanamaker's. By the 1980s the old stories were so deeply ingrained in the public's memory that even reputable historians were quick to publish the myth instead of applying their expertise to an

64

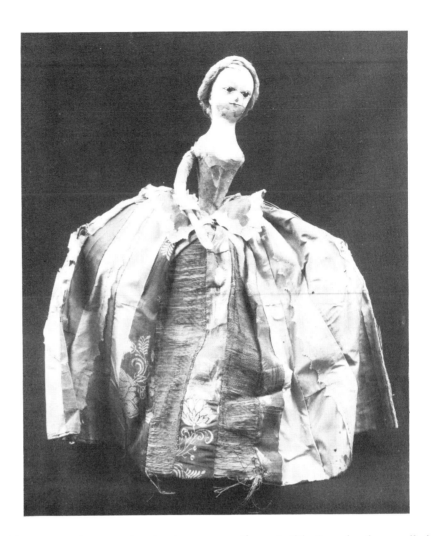

Illustration 4. *Letitia Penn before recent restoration and conservation. Note the condition of the fabric panels of her home-made costume, the missing arm and, most particularly, the broken and misaligned confusion of gesso on the doll's neck and face. This damage resulted from Letitia's wooden underbody shrinking over the years and required great care during restoration.* The Historical Society of Pennsylvania.

objective evaluation of the doll and its history. Of more than a dozen outstanding doll histories consulted during research for this article, only two — and those very hesitantly — suggested the old tales are suspect.

However, they **are** suspect. In fact, they are wrong. Everything depends on what Mrs. Maher recollected and recounted to Mary B. Kirk in 1858. Somewhere along the way the facts became muddled. If William Penn did indeed carry an English doll in his luggage the day the Canterbury docked in the port of Philadelphia in 1699, it was not the doll now called Letitia Penn. It could not have been, since **that** doll was made after 1720! The Letitia Penn doll may indeed be the oldest survivor among English dolls brought to America by the early colonists, but

she arrived at least a quarter of a century later than the legend says she did. And she did not arrive with William Penn.

Among the scholars to whom The Historical Society of Pennsylvania sent photographs and questions about the Penn doll were John Noble, Curator Emeritus at The Museum of The City of New York, Ann Coleman of The Brooklyn Museum, Caroline Goodfellow, Curator of Dolls and Toys at London's Bethnal Green Museum and Mrs. N. A. Marshall, Costume Curator at Bethnal Green. All agreed that the doll type as well as the costume date between 1720 to 1740, not earlier.

While letters were being exchanged and research was in progress in an effort to date the Penn doll objectively, the doll itself under-

went extensive conservation and restoration. As with other contemporary woodens, the old craftsman had coated Letitia's lathe-turned head and shoulders with a thin coat of gesso before painting her features. Large fragments of this gesso had come loose and early, probably amateur, efforts to reglue them only increased the damage. The conservation center repaired the cracked and broken gesso below the forehead and on the right cheek and chin. The doll was cleaned and given a new left arm, — a wooden forearm and hand and an upper arm "made of wound strips of polyester fiberfill. This arm was attached to the original 18th century shoulder hole with buttonhole twist, using a 4in (10cm) doll needle."

Since the 19th century,

Letitia Penn has been called a 20in (51cm) tall English **fashion** doll, but she is not a fashion doll. Her paneled skirt is a heterogeneous assemblage of workbasket scraps, a delightful mix of monochromatic silk and lush brocade panels familiar to doll historians but not to the historians of human costume. Dolls like this one with her full skirt stiffened by a brown paper lining were probably purchased as "naked babies," then dressed at home by their young owners, with considerable assistance from Nanny or Mother. Cloth was precious in the days when every inch of it had to be loomed by hand, and new yardage could not be purchased for Dollie. Instead, she wore "the memories of dozens of dresses," and surviving Georgian dolls so costumed have a very special quality and charm. For the collector, that is, not for the conservator, for whom the hodgepodge of fabrics and trimmings creates a nightmare experience in the laboratory. Dyes and threads in different cloths age differently, and each panel of a skirt like Letitia's must be analyzed separately and receive unique treatment.

The doll's clothing was cleaned gently with a microvacuum. The paper underskirt was repaired and repairs were made to silks where needed. To restore the skirt to its original fullness, the lab steamed the garment once a day for three days.

Using the middle color values from the old sleeve, a duplicate was created to clothe the new arm. Throughout the conservation process, interesting discoveries were made. Letitia's hair is cotton fiber attached to her head with glue and iron nails. Skirt detail formerly thought to be horsehair tested metallic and is probably silver. The paper lining inside the doll's skirt erased any lingering doubt about the costume being a genuine 18th century one. The lining is hand-molded paper made on a fabric screen. There are no watermarks, seams, lines or weave, features that appear with the advent of machined paper after 1803.

Recently, we had an opportunity to visit The Historical Society of Pennsylvania, see Letitia in her post-conservation glory and talk dolls with Curator Elizabeth F. Jarvis. Mrs. Jarvis explained that the metal stand which had supported the doll before conservation had caused considerable damage and had been discarded. A new permanent stand is being designed that will support the doll gently from underneath, permitting long skirts to hang freely below Letitia's very short legs.

We spent several precious hours with Mrs. Jarvis in the behind-the-scenes storerooms of The Historical Society of Pennsylvania, studying this famous doll that has played so many roles in history, — venerated icon, Kirk family treasure, prize in Imogene Anderson's collection, star of Carolyn Sherwin Bailey's book, respected and later questioned artifact in one of America's most revered collections of Americana. We discussed the stories. We looked at Letitia and Letitia's glass eyes stared back at us. It is unlikely that we shall ever learn the origin of the persistent legend which links this doll to William Penn's family history. What we **know**, however, is the "Letitia Penn" came to America very early in our nation's history and that she is a superb example of an English wooden of the Georgian period. These are facts, not fiction, and they must satisfy us. ☐

The Historical Society of Pennsylvania is located at 1300 Locust Street, Philadelphia, Pennsylvania 19107. Museum galleries are open Tuesday through Friday, 9:00 a.m. to 5:00 p.m. and Saturday, 10:00 a.m. to 3:00 p.m. The Society is closed Sundays, Mondays and most major holidays.

Illustration 5. *A closer look at the Letitia Penn doll before restoration shows the extent of damage and decay to fabric, paint and gesso. Note the doll's profile, typical of mid 18th century doll shapes, — also the crude spoon hands and dotted eyelashes and eyebrows, also typical of Georgian but not of William and Mary dolls. The Historical Society of Pennsylvania.*

Illustration 6. *In 1902,* The Ladies' Home Journal *published an article, shown here, by Mary Townsend Kirk. This feature in "Under The Evening Lamp" resulted in fame and fortune for the Letitia Penn doll whose legend (if one studies the records objectively) is totally dependent on what Mrs. Maher quite sincerely told Mary B. Kirk in 1858. One cannot help wondering whether there was* **another** *older doll that* **did** *arrive with William Penn in 1699! In any event,* **this** *doll was made at least 40 years after that docking in Philadelphia.*

UNDER THE EVENING LAMP

"Unto One of the Least of These"

By Franklin B. Wiley

I WAS at the height of the busy holiday season, only a few days before Christmas some years ago, that a large man stopped at a counter in one of the big stores in Boston to make a purchase. As he stood waiting for his parcel, many in the bustling, hurrying crowd, above which he towered head and shoulders, turned for another look at the massive figure and smooth-shaven, benevolent face, instinct with intellectual power. Just then, almost hidden by the jostling throng about her, a poorly dressed little girl came wandering by, crying bitterly. Instantly the faraway, meditative look in the big man's eyes changed to one of alert and sympathetic concern. Turning quickly, he stooped down and, stopping the child, asked her what the trouble was.

"I've lost my mamma, and I can't find her," she sobbed out.

Without a moment's hesitation he gently picked her up, and raising her carefully to his shoulder said: "Now, I am a very big man. You sit on my shoulder and you can see everybody in the room. In a few minutes you will either see your mamma, or she will see you."

Sure enough, in a short time the little one joyfully called out, "There's my mamma," and at the same moment a small, shabby woman came hurriedly pushing through the crowd toward them, her flushed face plainly showing the relief she felt.

"Oh, I thought I'd lost her!" she said with breathless eagerness as she came up. "I've hunted everywhere and couldn't find her."

She reached up her arms and took the child, hugging her close, too excited to remember to utter any thanks; but there was a look of gratitude in her tired eyes that spoke louder than words.

With a kindly smile Phillips Brooks picked up his parcel and walked away.

The Breakfast Face

By Flora C. Fagnani

SHE

OH! WHAT a bright face, my darling!
Tell me the secret, pray,
Of such a sweet face, come rain, come shine
At breakfast every day?

SHE

Why, dearest, just look at the bright side;
But, if you can see no bright,
Go to work with a will on the dark side
And polish with all your might!

Sang for Jenny Lind's Teacher

By Leigh Mitchell Hodges

THE good King Oscar, who has ruled so long and so wisely over Norway and Sweden, is a lover of music, and a good deal of a musician himself. When Emma Thursby, in the noontide of her fame as a soprano, was singing in Europe, she was received in Stockholm with great enthusiasm, and among her warmest admirers was the King. He was charmed with her voice, and often asked her to sing at the palace.

On one of these occasions he told her of an old singing-teacher whose life was drawing to a close under pathetic circumstances—Herr Berg, who in his palmy days had counted Jenny Lind among his pupils, and had trained that matchless voice, and followed its career with almost the pride of a mother. Now, for fifteen years, he had been confined to a little room in an old building in Stockholm, unable to get around by reason of an affliction, and cared for by a few faithful friends —among them the King himself.

King Oscar asked Miss Thursby if she would go and sing for the old teacher. One fine morning with her sister and her manager she hunted him up. When the singer stood before the aged master and lifted her clear, sweet voice in the "Bird Song," which Jenny Lind made immortal, his head fell on his breast, and he wept. One by one Miss Thursby sang the songs which were dearest to the Swedish Nightingale. As the last note of the last song died away he caught her hands and pressed them to his lips.

"You cannot know," he said, sobbing, "what you have given me. It is now so many years since I heard those songs that I taught her myself—and I had despaired of ever hearing them again. I cannot say how grateful I am."

Only a few years later the old man died. Perhaps, as the candle of his life flickered, the silvery measures of that morning's melodies lulled him peacefully into the Beyond.

A Doll Two Hundred Years Old

By Mary Townsend Kirk

IN 1699, when William Penn sailed from England in the good ship "Canterbury" —this being his second visit to his American Colony—he brought with him an English doll, of which, so far, scant notice has been taken, although it is believed to be to-day the sole surviving representative of that voyage across the Atlantic.

This doll, selected by William Penn's daughter Letitia, was sent by her to a little Miss Rankin, of Philadelphia.

Letitia Penn, the second, after two hundred eventful years, still retains, in a marked degree, much of the brightness and beauty of those early days when she was the pet of one little Quakeress after another. Her dress, not having changed with the changing fashions, is the Court dress of that period, and is made of striped and delicately tinted brocade and velvet; the skirt is very full and is distended over an enormous hoop. She is twenty inches in height, and her figure is long-waisted and slender, as are the pictures of Court beauties in those days. The full basque spreading out from the belt over the skirt enhances the slender effect. The hair is rolled away from the face much in the fashion of to-day.

Unfortunately, this doll had lost one of her arms before I knew her, but save for that she is in almost as perfect a condition as when she first landed in Philadelphia from her faraway home on the other side of the Atlantic.

Miss Rankin gave this doll to a Mrs. Prior, of Philadelphia, by whom she was presented to Miss Anne Massey of the same city. Miss Massey, afterward Mrs. Brown, on her departure for England, left the doll with her friend, Mrs. Maher, whose property she was to become should Mrs. Brown die while she was abroad. Mrs. Maher, formerly a Miss Burns, of Philadelphia, but for many years a resident of Maryland, thinking Letitia should return to her Quaker friends, in May, 1855, gave her to Miss Mary B. Kirk, of Sandy Spring, Montgomery County, Maryland.

On the death of Miss Kirk, in 1882, Letitia was left to Dr. Mahlon Kirk. She now lives in the retirement her great age demands, only being removed from her careful wrappings when strangers, whom her quiet fame has reached, come to make close acquaintance with this, the oldest doll in America.

My Sweet Brown Gal

By Paul Laurence Dunbar

WEN de clouds is hangin' heavy in de sky,
An' de win's a-tearin' moughty vig'rous by,
I don' go a-sighin' all erlong de way,
I des work a-waitin' fu' de close o' day.

Case I knows w'en evenin' draps huh shadders down,
I won' care a smidgeon fu' de weathah's frown;
Let de rain go splashin', let de thunder rub,
Dey's a happy sheltah, an' I's goin' dah.

Down in mid cabin w'en de evenin' closes,
Taters in de bah-lay'n shuck't,
No nig daih a-cross me, got to tek it jes'
But I's got de comp'ny o' my sweet brown gal!

So I spen' my evenin' listenin' to huh song,
Lak a blessed angel, how huh voice du ring;
Sweeter dan a bluebird flutterin' aroun',
W'en he sees de steamin' o' de new ploued groun'.

Den I hugs huh closah, closah to my breas'
Needn't sing, my da'lin', tek yo' honey res';
Does I mean Malindy, Mandy, Lize er Sal?
No, I means my fiddle—dat's my sweet brown gal!

Mother

By Virginia Woodward Cloud

THERE came a day when Cattle died
And every cropful filled beside,
And not a dollar left to these,
Then father said the plows must go
And all of us, we bitter know,
To go tell Mother.

Behind the barn, there we three stood
And wondered what none of us could.
Spare her the sight—we sure knew
But so our sorest need we locked in our
hearts, so she.

I spoke—I tried it, Brother's choice,
But Father said, "No, best be going,
Freckon I—" He gave a sighing.
"I choose 'tis my work that'll fall.
We'll need to tell Mother.

"Maybe a mortgage can be tried.
Here all her labor, worth, at need,
She loves each flower and field and bird—
I'll mortgage ere I'll say a word
To Mother!"

Upon his hands he bowed his head
And then a voice behind us said,
"Mortgage? And who's got to pay?
Now, Father, I've a better way!"—
And there, between the ricks of hay,
Stood Mother.

"I have been thinking," most a year,
We'd sell this place, and somewhere near
Just rent a cottage small and neat,
And raise enough for us to eat,"
Said Mother.

"There's trouble worse than loss of lands.
We've honest hearts and willing hands,
And not till earth and sea and river
Can rob of peace shall I be poor!
Can rob of peace shall I be poor!
She smiled. "And, I mean to say,
You all had better come to tea,"
Said Mother.

As through the sunset field to-day
We three went following after her,
The thrushes they sang everywhere,
Something had banished all our care
And we felt strong enough to bear
All things—with Mother.

And listen: Once there came a day
When troops returned from far away
And every one went up to meet
His own, within the village street;
But ere he reached our old milestone
I knew that Father came alone—
And not with Brother.

Then through the twilight, dense and gray,
All that our choking sobs could say
Was—"Who'll tell Mother?"

But waiting for us, by the wood,
Pale in the dusk, again she stood;
And then her arms round Father prest,
And drew his head upon her breast:

"The worst that comes is never Death,
For home lived while he drew breath!"
Said Mother.

Often, when some great deed is cried
Of one, by flood or flame, who died,
Of men who sought and won their fame,
While all the land rings with some name
Or other,

I think me of one warfare long,
Of Marah's water, bitter, strong,
Of sword and fire that pierced the heart,
Of all the dumb, unuttered part,
And say, with eyes grown more,
(Love's vision, that cannot forget),
"All heroes are not counted yet—
There's Mother."

A Story of a Father's Love

By a City Missionary

OLD Mr. —— has an only daughter. They are not well to rank, but he is honest and industrious. By trade he is a puddler in a foundry, and he earns four dollars and a half a day. Twenty years ago the wife and mother died, and the child of five became the old man's pet. Twelve years ago he sold his property and spent all his money in sending her abroad to study music. She came back two years ago a famous singer and a world's beauty, and refused to own her father. He has moved to the East Side in order that, by living on a pittance, he may have twenty dollars every week to give to her to buy clothes. Every week he sends it and every week she spends it, though she neither sees nor writes to him. Week after week he grows a little prouder and also a little sadder.

The Dated China Doll

by **Nancy & Pete Booz**

Photographs by **Pete Booz**

Illustration 1. 9½in (24cm) china head. Such a pleasant face! Note the typical details of red-orange eyeliner, black eyeliner, corner dots and outlined nostrils.

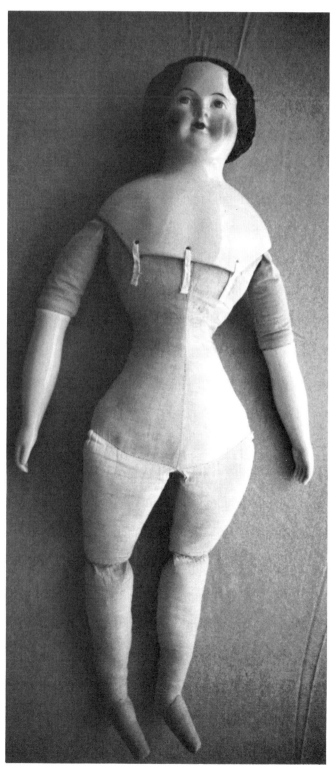

Illustration 2. Overall view of the head and body of the 31in (79cm) china doll. There are three sew holes in the front and three in the rear.

She was our first venture into the world of china dolls and turned into quite an adventure. We bought her because of her unusual size and overall good condition. We knew she was not particularly rare, being blue-eyed with black hair, but there was something serene about her expression and her clothing was nice.

Dating a china doll is usually based on the hair style as they are seldom marked. This doll was dated by the

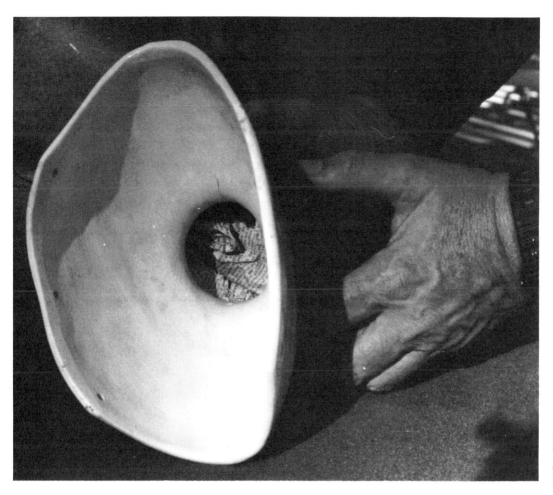

Illustration 3. Inner view of the china head showing the remaining newspaper left in the head.

BELOW: Illustration 4. The newspaper, *The Cincinnati Commercial* dated Saturday, December 1, 1866, found stuffed in the china dolls' head. Note the Associated Press byline.

newspaper found stuffed in her head and shoulders, *The Cincinnati Commercial* of December 1, 1866, in like-new condition. We speculated that the head, made in Germany, was part of a larger shipment which was broken down and repacked in Cincinnati using the local newspaper. Considering the date, she was probably a Christmas gift for some lucky little girl.

The head is on a commercial hair-stuffed body. When we bought the doll, the head was becoming detached and was removed completely at which time the paper was found. The only mark on the head is the number incised on the inner rear shoulder.

The newspaper is of heavier stock than today's newspapers and the ink does not smudge. We enjoyed reading the various articles and the ads for "cures." As recommended by an antique book dealer, the paper was pressed flat and the tears mended with magic tape. It appears the full sheet of paper was torn in two and we removed only the top half from the shoulders; the rest is stuffed in the head cavity where we left it.

This is a large china and awkward to handle with her heavy head (which probably accounts for her good condition), large china arms (possibly replacements) and lightweight body. The head is 9½in (24cm) tall, the doll's total length is 31in (79cm).

Her wardrobe consists of a machine-embroidered batiste dress, a comisole, petticoat, drawers and leather slippers — all beautifully handmade. The clothes were gently washed and the ribbon replaced.

We feel she is a charming addition to any collection and knowing something about her history is an added bonus. □

TOP TO BOTTOM: Illustration 5. Inside page of *The Cincinnati Commercial* which was found stuffed inside the china doll's head.

Illustration 6. The china doll put back together with her clothes.

Rabery & Delphieu Bébé Dolls

by Sylvia Tanner Pencosky

Photographs by Polly Judd

These dear little sisters with their creamy complexions, limpid eyes, flowing curls and chubby childlike bodies are French bébés. They are products of an opulent era often referred to as the golden age of doll production and were luxury toys intended for privileged children. These particular bébés were produced by Rabery & Delphieu. Research shows that the Parisian firm of Rabery & Delphieu conducted business from 1856 to 1898 and merged with S.F.B.J. in 1899. Early advertising indicates they sold a variety of cloth, kid and linen bodied dolls as well as marottes but they were advertising "jointed bébés" by 1881. The mark "R.D." was in use for the firm's bébés by 1890 and they were on exhibit at the Chicago World's Fair in 1893.

A square-shaped facial configuration is the most distinguishing characteristic of Rabery & Delphieu bébés. Earlier bébés generally have large almond-shaped paperweight eyes, lovely complexions and beautifully painted mouths, with the lips being nicely outlined and delicately tinted. The combination of a square face, large expressive eyes, widely arched eyebrows and a delicate mouth tends to give the R.D. bébé a very different "look." Their facial expression has been variously described as pensive, somber, aloof, haughty or serene. At any rate, it is not a face with universal appeal. I have heard more than one fancier of French bébés admit to the fact that on a personal level, R.D. bébés was an acquired taste.

It is probable that each bébé shown here was once treasured by a child long ago and in the case of the three earliest bébés — almost a century ago. Time brings change and these bébés have seen their share: a silk dress "melted," attic mice gnawed a cork pate, a composition finger was broken off, wigs dete-

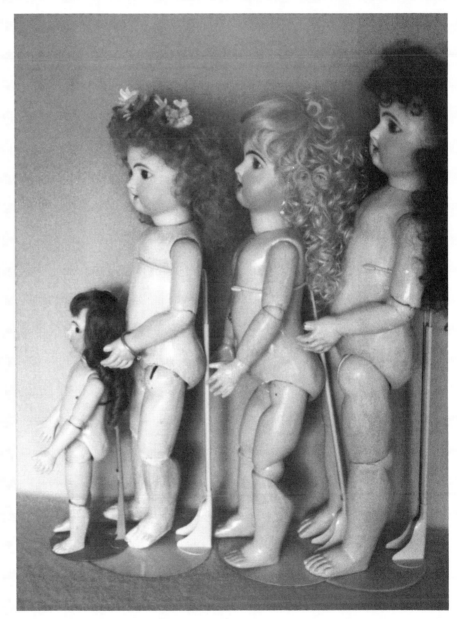

Illustration 1. Lineup of R.D. bébés, from left to right: 15in (38cm), 24in (61cm), 25in (63cm) and 28in (71cm), provides a good opportunity to compare size as well as body type. Note that the bodies of the 24in (61cm) and 28in (71cm) dolls are identical except for size. Their straight wrists and very large hands are typical of earlier French bébés. The 25in (63cm) bébé is considerably younger than her three sisters as evidenced not only by her open mouth with teeth but also by her jointed wrists and smaller hands. All four bébés have well modeled feet with nicely delineated toes. Interestingly, not one body bears the "BEBE-RABERY" stamp which is sometimes found on R.D. products.

ABOVE: Illustration 2. Leading a toy lamb, this Rabery & Delphieu bébé is believed to be wearing her original dress. The dropped waist, coat style sleeves and short skirt illustrate a style in which French bébés were frequently costumed. The matching bonnet and dress are pale pink wool trimmed with pink silk ribbon and cream cotton lace. Cream lace net on the bonnet frames the doll's face and is a good contrast to her dark brown paperweight eyes and her auburn human hair wig. Her dark brown leather shoes have pointed toes and lace up to tie well above her ankles. Each leather sole is impressed with the silhouette of a child. Just 15in (38cm), she is a lovely bébé. *Polly Judd Collection.*

Illustration 4. Close-up of mark incised on head of the doll shown in **Illustration 3.** This doll appears to be the oldest of the four R.D. bébés.

riorated, a shoe was lost, to name but a few. Furthermore, their present owners are probably considerably older and a lot less affluent than their first ones. Two things, however, have not changed. Their beauty has withstood the test of time and each bébé is even more highly treasured today.

Just as facial and figure characteristics vary among sisters in the human family, so do they vary among French bébés of the same family. Thus, comparative study noting differences and similarities among bébés is a good way to learn. First of all, we shall examine the obvious. All four bébés have good quality bisque heads with cork pates, pierced ears, paperweight eyes and French ball-jointed wood and composition bodies. Each bébé has the typical square face and the Rabery & Delphieu mark incised on the back of her head. Similarities seem to stop here and differences among the bébés are more interesting. Among these four little sisters are four body sizes ranging from 15in (38cm) to 28in (71cm), three different body types, three variations of the incised Rabery & Delphieu mark and three different eye colors. One bébé has an open mouth with six teeth while the other three have closed mouths.

The 15in (38cm) doll is the smallest of the bébés and has the most interesting body. The loose balls at shoulders, elbows, hips and knees sometimes tend to confuse beginning collectors who associate this method of articulation with German bodies. This is, however, not only an appropriate French body but an earlier and, therefore, more desirable one. The earliest body type is a good clue that this doll is probably the earliest of the four bébés. She is the only bébé believed to be wearing her original dress.

The 24in (61cm) and the 28in (71cm) bébés are earlier dolls as evidenced by their straight wrists, closed mouths and mauve eyeshadow. Their bodies and the marks incised on their heads are virtually identical except for size.

The youngest of the dolls is a good example of a late French bébé. Her deep paperweight eyes are a lovely shade of blue and her best feature. Her rosier cheeks, open mouth with teeth, jointed wrists and smaller hands are typical of her time and indicate she was probably produced after 1899 when Rabery & Delphieu was absorbed by S.F.B.J. or the Société Française de Fabrication de Bébés et Jouets.

Illustration 5. Poised with her hand on the back of a little chair, this 24in (61cm) bébé appears quite contented with the world. She has been redressed by her present owner in an old white dress of very fine cotton. The dress has white lace insertion on the yoke, very small bretelles at the shoulders and once belonged to a child. The bébé is also wearing slippers of pink fabric with leather soles. Their pointed toes are decorated with little metal buckles and pink silk ribbons. *George and Becky Nunnery Collection.* (The little kitten gazing up at the bébé is a Steiff. The small chair is circa 1890 and has a woven rush seat and back.)

Illustration 6. Incised mark of the doll shown in **Illustration 5.** The number "3" is a size number rather than a mold number. This is a rather small number for a 24in (61cm) doll.

(S.F.B.J. was a corporation composed of many French manufacturers who merged to fight off the impending economic disaster of German competition.)

Having seen these R.D. bébés with their different faces, perhaps you will choose to say, as I do: "Vive la différence!" If so, your search for an R.D. may be lengthy because, while Rabery & Delphieu bébés are not rare, neither are they plentiful. Be patient and one will eventually come your way, at which point, you should be in a position to realize one of their very nicest qualities. Current prices of Rabery & Delphieu bébés tend to be more reasonable than those of many of their more popular French sisters! □

Illustration 7. The largest of the four bébés, this doll is 28in (71cm) tall. Her white frock has a yoke and consists of multiple rows of tucks and lace inserts. The bonnet is made of old white straw and trimmed with many rows of lace. The doll's dark ecru shoes strap over the instep. Their rounded toes are decorated with small metal filigree butterflies and tattered silk ribbon. The leather soles are scuffed and worn, a sure sign that they were once worn by a child. "Serena," as she is called, does not seem to mind her second-hand shoes and proudly poses with her old lace net handkerchief and old metal mesh purse. The small table is oak and its full-sized version often held a large potted fern in the parlor around 1910.

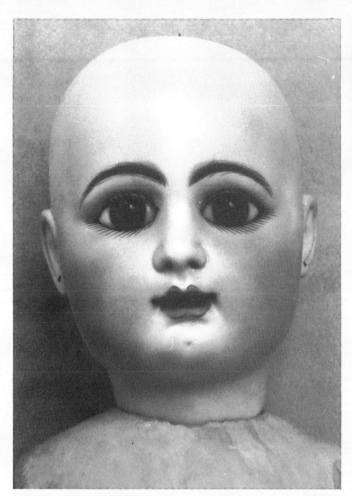

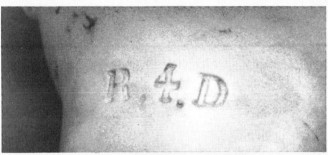

LEFT: **Illustration 8.** This is the same 28in (71cm) doll as shown in **Illustration 7**, but the distraction of her clothes, wig and cork pate has been removed. Here is a good illustration for the square face which is unique to R.D. bébés. Now is also a good time to study how eyelashes, eyebrows and mouth are painted. Note the darker coloring above the upper eyelashes. Collectors usually refer to this as "blushing." It is almost always the hallmark of an earlier bébé. Blushing is usually a very pale rose or light mauve tint and serves to highlight the eyes just as eyeshadow does for the modern woman.

ABOVE: Illustration 9. Incised mark of the 28in (71cm) bébé shown in **Illustrations 7** and **8**. The size number is "4." If you will compare the size number incised on each bébé's head with its height, you will note that all size numbers are very small when compared to the actual height of the dolls. The small size number to body height ratio is not common among French bébés so I find it very interesting.

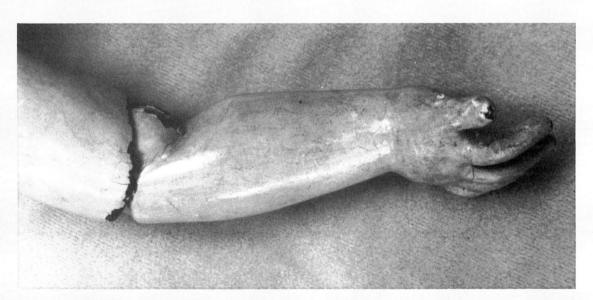

ABOVE: Illustration 10. Hand of the 28in (71cm) bébé seen in **Illustrations 7** and **8**. Hands of this bébé and the 24in (61cm) bébé are exactly alike except for size. Note the wooden ball attached to the forearm which is the most common method of articulation for French composition and wood bodies.

LEFT: **Illustration 11.** Incised mark of the 25in (63cm) bébé. The style of both the letters and size numbers varies from those of the other Rabery & Delphieu bébés. The incised mark is quite shallow which may mean that the mold was worn. This bébé has an open mouth with teeth and is the youngest of the four bébés.

Dolls Based on the Fiammingo Head

by **Jan Foulke**
Photographs by **Howard Foulke**

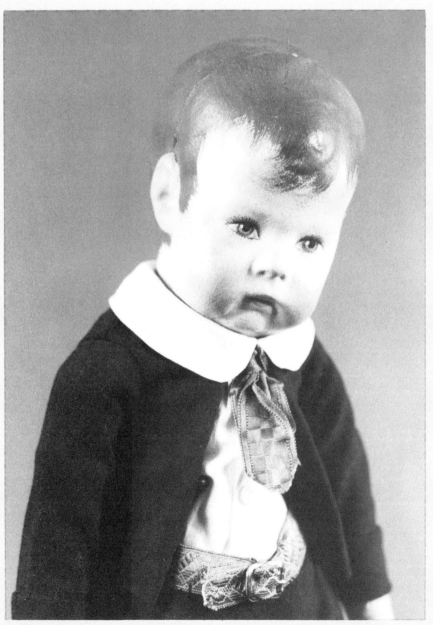

Illustration 1. *16in (41cm) Käthe Kruse* Doll I, *all cloth with painted features, painted hair, all original, circa 1910. These dolls were used as either boys or girls according to the clothing and the later dolls came wigged.* Private Collection.

In the June/July issue of **Doll Reader**®, page 110, in the "Dollars and Doll Sense" column, information was requested about a sculpture which is the head of a small child. That photograph prompted my reply, since this head, which is by the Flemish artist Francois Duquesnois (1594 to 1643), also known as Fiammingo, is very significant to doll collectors and the history of doll manufacturing, as it was used as the model for quite a large number of doll heads, both in Europe and the United States in the first quarter of this century.

One aspect of the Victorian sensibility of the last half of the 19th century was a love of ornamentation of their homes as well as themselves. Coupled with this was a deep interest in classical art, sculpture, music — anything which could be considered cultured. To satisfy the need for impressive-looking knickknacks, companies manufactured reproductions of classic sculptures. An example from such a catalog by August Gerber Arts, Cologne, Germany, is shown in the Ciesliks' *German Doll Encyclopedia*, on page 170. This firm was offering a copy of the Fiammingo head described as "Boy head, as bust, copy taken from the Paris original, in marble and bronze, Francois Duquesnois." With all of these classic pieces readily available, it is not surprising that doll designers, artists themselves who doubtless studied the masters of classic painting and sculpture, would turn to these pieces as sources of doll designs.

For quite a time, I have been assembling a file of photographs of dolls, which I feel are based on the

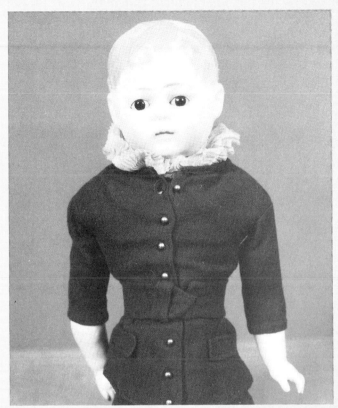
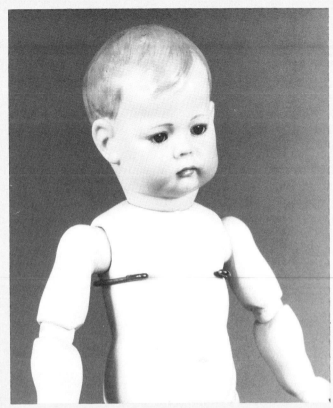

LEFT: Illustration 2. *The earliest doll (circa 1880) which appears to have been based on the Fiammingo head is a wax-over-composition boy with molded hair. The shoulder head is on a cloth body with papier-mâché limbs. He is 22in (56cm) tall.* H&J Foulke, Inc. **RIGHT: Illustration 3.** *The sharpness of the molding of this bisque head by Kämmer & Reinhardt, mold number 115, shows how closely the Fiammingo head was followed when compared to its photograph in the Ciesliks' German Doll Encyclopedia. He is 15in (38cm) tall. The doll also comes as mold number 115A with an open crown and wig as well as a celluloid version. It is circa 1911.* Carole Jean Stoessel Zvonar Collection.

Illustration 4. This 14in (35cm) bisque-headed doll by Armand Marseille is Fany, mold number 230, with molded hair. This face was also available with an open crown and wig as mold number 231 and came on either a baby or toddler body. It is circa 1912. Yvonne Baird Collection.

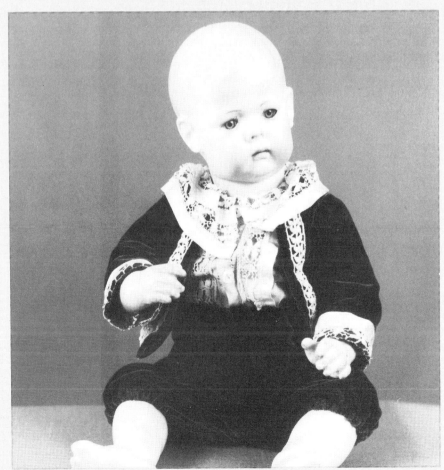

Fiammingo head. A copy of the Fiammingo head shown in Lydia Richter's *The Beloved Käthe-Kruse Dolls,* on page 28, started me on this project. Showing the head of this bust alongside a photograph of the Kruse *Doll I,* Mrs. Richter makes it evident that the doll was indeed modeled from the classic bust. Studying the bust also brought to mind other dolls which obviously also have their origins in the same face. There are doubtless others which have not come to my attention, but these are the ones I have gathered to date. Of course, this study also raises the question: Are these heads which follow actually based on the bust itself or on the Kruse *Doll I* which was copied from

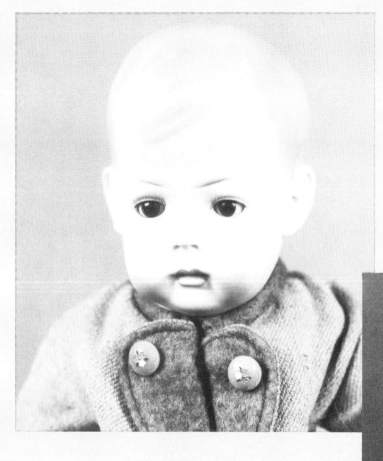

Illustration 5. The bisque head of this 14in (36cm) toddler boy was made by Hertel, Schwab & Co., mold number 154. Model number 157 has the same face with a cut head and wig. It is not surprising that Hertel, Schwab & Co. has such wonderful character faces, as the Ciesliks report that the founders were themselves sculptors. It is circa 1911. Carole Jean Stoessel Zvonar Collection.

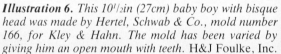

Illustration 6. This 10½in (27cm) baby boy with bisque head was made by Hertel, Schwab & Co., mold number 166, for Kley & Hahn. The mold has been varied by giving him an open mouth with teeth. H&J Foulke, Inc.

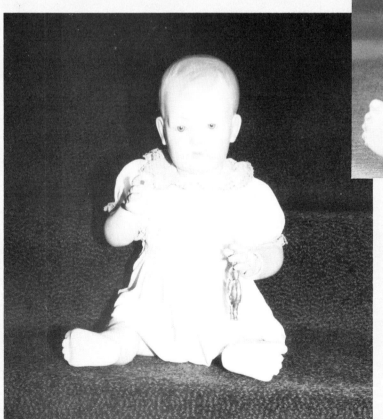

Illustration 7. The bisque head of this 19in (48cm) character baby was made by Bähr & Pröschild, mold number 2048, for Bruno Schmidt. Lesley Hurford Collection.

Illustration 8. *This 18in (46cm) character child has a bisque head, mold number 2072, made by Bähr & Pröschild for Bruno Schmidt. The face appears to be from the Fiammingo head with the addition of an open crown and wig. Richard Wright Antiques.*

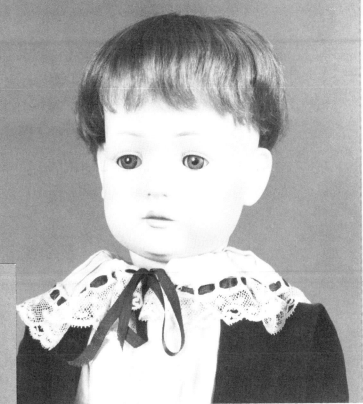

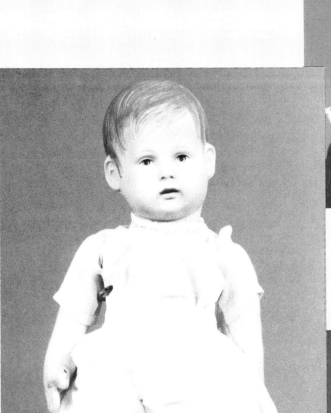

Illustration 9. *Character head of celluloid based on the Fiammingo head or the Kruse Doll I, by Rheinische Gummi und Celluloid Fabrik Co. (Schildkrote) with their trademark "turtle." It is 10in (25cm) tall with a stuffed cloth body. H&J Foulke, Inc.*

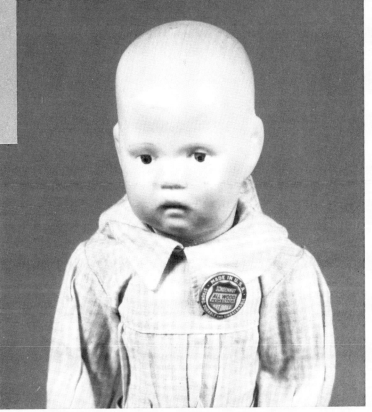

Illustration 10. *This 14in (36cm) Schoenhut doll is made entirely of wood, including the head, and shows some influence of the Fiammingo head, perhaps through the bisque-headed German characters, such as the Kämmer & Reinhardt 115, as it is known that Schoenhut made copies of the Kämmer & Reinhardt 101 and 114 models. However, Schoenhut heirs claim the head was modeled by Harry Schoenhut from one of the Schoenhut children. Collectors refer to this as the Schoenhut "baby" face. It is all original and circa 1913. Esther Schwartz Collection.*

ABOVE LEFT: Illustration 11. A 14in (36cm) wigged version of the Schoenhut "baby" face. This model was used as a boy or girl. H&J Foulke, Inc. *ABOVE RIGHT: Illustration 12.* 16in (40cm) baby with a composition type head, unmarked but possibly by Lenci. The body is pressed cloth with a coat of heavy paint; the outfit is the type and quality worn by Lenci dolls. This baby is very similar to one that has a tagged outfit sold by the Toy Museum of Atlanta at their March 1987 auction, lot number 739. The resemblance to the Fiammingo head is evident. It is circa 1930. Yvonne Baird Collection.

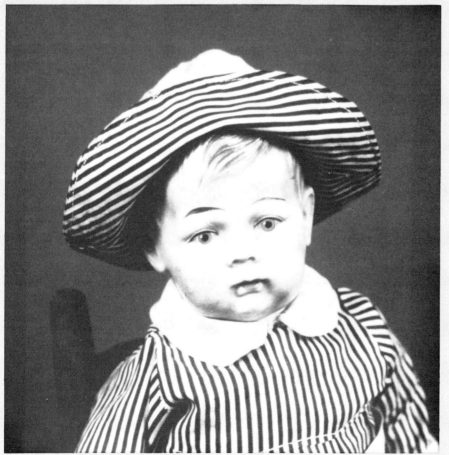

Illustration 13. 18in (46cm) character boy with a composition head appears to be Effanbee's Katie Kroose which came either as a boy or girl, some with wigs, some dressed in European peasant-type costumes. Obviously, inferred from the name given by Effanbee, it was based on the Käthe Kruse Doll I. It is circa 1918. Betty Harms Collection.

the bust? Or are some based on the bust itself, and others on the Kruse *Doll I*? At this point we do not know.

However, it is interesting to speculate and to wonder just what qualities the Fiammingo head possesses to give it such wide appeal. Why was this head chosen so widely, and not some other head among thousands which must have been produced in the past 500 or more years? It has to be the feeling which the head generates in the observer, an emotional reaction, a response to the inherent goodness and sweetness of a child with this face, his look of innocence and the natural innate adult response of needing to protect and nurture what appears to be an innocent sweet child. □

Pincushion Half-Dolls

by Catherine Cook

Who designed the first half-doll and realized the potential that led to the tremendous industry with hundreds of people involved in designing and manufacturing them? Few records were kept in this early period and time has obscured their names.

By 1880 an extremely large number of porcelain factories in Germany, England and France were manufacturing half-dolls.

The half-dolls of glazed china and porcelain were made in several sizes, 1in (2.5cm) to 9in (22.9cm), and 2000 different figures are known.

Two major types were made: one with molded clothes and the other as nude figures. They show endless ingenuity in design and construction, and are a social commentary and mirror chronically the life-styles of their period.

Fewer half-dolls were made with molded clothes and are, therefore, more rare.

Half-dolls were first used for tea cozies and met a need in the continual serving of tea, and also provided an attractive addition to the tea table. This led to the designing and manufacturing of some of the most beautiful and rarest of the half-figures.

Different series were made: one of medieval figures, the other of historical figures.

With the introduction of the half-dolls to America in considerable quantity, they were first used as decorations for pincushions. At this period pincushions held a more prominent place and elaborate beaded ones were already in use.

Of great interest were the half-dolls dressed in contemporary styles. One of the most popular was the "Flapper" half-doll with cloche hat on a chunky pincushion resembling the short Charleston skirt.

It is too bad when the pincushions have been removed for they comple-ment the designs of the half-figures.

Other half-figures were used as decoration for powder boxes and other items related to the toilet table, and complete dresser sets were made.

Half-figures of children were also manufactured including little Dutch girls, but in more limited number.

Heads also were made and used for decorating the pincushions and as handles for small articles and stoppers for cologne bottles.

Two others seen, and also professionally made, had bisque shoulder heads with set-in eyes and mohair wigs and wore be-ribboned red satin bonnets, and the puffed pincushions were of red satin.

Some of the more important porce-lain companies marked their half-dolls, but other manufacturers did not, especially the smaller items, as they did not consider them worth marking.

Although very popular when first made and continuing for many years, half-dolls were overlooked by doll collectors; but because of their close relationship to dolls, a few found their way into doll collections.

With today's great interest in dolls making their collecting difficult and their escalating prices prohibitive for some, the half-dolls are appearing again for sale.

Also with today's interest in decorative covers for kitchen utensils, the tea cozy has again made an appearance as a cover for the teapot.

Illustration 1. 3in (7.6cm) porcelain half-doll, 7in (17.8cm) assembled; arms bent at elbows and jointed at shoulders with elastic and wooden peg; blonde mohair wig, painted brown eyes; white satin wedding gown trimmed with silk lace of the 1920 period, long bridal veil of net with cap, carries shower bouquet of velvet flowers with ribbons streamers, silk lace-trimmed petticoat over cone-shaped pincushion; professionally made, excellent workmanship, and one of the loveliest costume half-dolls seen; costume authentic for the 1920 period in the United States; any trademarks covered by clothes; probably made as a gift for a bridal shower.

Illustration 2. 4in (10.2cm) glazed china nude half-figure, 7in (17.8cm) assembled and sitting on a box for powder; light brown hair arranged down on each side to cover the ears and brought to the back of the head into a pug, gold band across forehead with pearl in center, and a cluster of delicate molded flowers over each ear — petals and leaves are individually molded and applied; very nicely molded face and hands, arms away from body; dress of green silk taffeta with full gathered skirt tied with gold cord at the waist, same material is used to cover the cardboard box for powder and is trimmed with gold lace and braid. The half-doll sits on one side of the cover and the back of the skirt lifts up to reveal an arrangement of silk flowers and leaves in blues and greens and makes a lovely dresser top ornament. There is a mirror inside the cover of the box. It is not possible to check for markings.

Illustration 3. 3in (7.6cm) glazed china half-doll with molded clothes, simple low-necked white bodice; blonde hair with pug at back of neck; yellow cap bonnet with molded pink roses over each ear and deep pink ties; blue eyes and very nicely decorated face, arms away from body, with right arm in back at waist. This was a popular design and many were made. It is marked "5160" at the bottom of the waist in back.

Illustration 4. 1⅜in (3.4cm) glazed china head wearing a poke bonnet of white, with brim lined in green and tied with lavender ribbon; blonde hair and brown eyes; mark inside of neck " $\frac{?}{6}$." Although purchased in a shop in Venice, Italy, she looks as if she might be a character from a Dickens' book.

TOP LEFT: Illustration 5. 4½in (11.5cm) pincushion doll of glazed china with molded clothes, blue blouse with yellow bertha collar with blue pompon at neck at top of right shoulder, white hat with brim lined in dull orange; café au lait hair, brown eyes and slightly parted lip, left arm away from body and bent at elbow with hand at waist; marked on outside bottom of blouse: "M.A. Germany." Pincushion, 4½in (11.5cm) in diameter and 2in (5.1cm) deep, is of blue sateen trimmed with ecru lace and braid.

TOP RIGHT: Illustration 6. 2¾in (7.1cm) pincushion half-doll of glazed china with molded clothes, white strapless bodice with pink bow at neck front; molded blonde hair with pink ribbon band and curls at back of neck, right arm bent and away from body with hand at waist; flat pincushion, 7in (17.8cm) in diameter, of pale pink cotton with shirred rows of ecru lace; no mark.

BOTTOM LEFT: Illustration 7. 2½in (6.4cm) glazed china pincushion doll with molded clothes, arms bent at elbows and away from the body, left arm at side of neck; yellow strapless bodice edged at neck in orange; black painted hair combed to top of head with blue and gold Spanish type comb, blue eyes; very poorly incised "Germany" and "M15" at bottom of waist. Spanish designed half-dolls were quite popular.

ABOVE: Illustration 8. 2in (5.1cm) glazed china doll head used for commercially-made pincushion of pale pink material with tiny applied paper flowers; arms believed to be those made for a china doll. *Barbara J. Rand Pegurri Collection.*

TABLE OF CONTENTS

Page 151

Page 90

Page 150

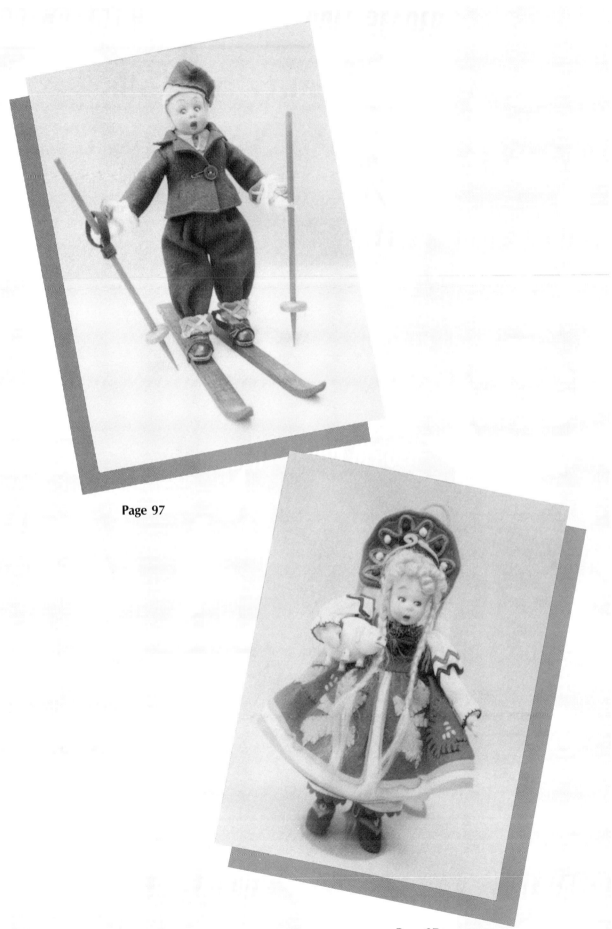

Page 97

Page 97

Artistic Beauty of Dolls

by **Dorothy S., & Evelyn Jane Coleman**

Throughout the centuries the artistic beauty has been probably the most important attribute of popular dolls. All of us realize the irresistible appeal of a beautiful artistic doll. No one can dispute the artistic beauty of a Jumeau bébe and it is not surprising that about five million Bébés Jumeau were produced every year at the beginning of this century, before World War I. The appreciation of the artistic beauty of a doll is usually a subjective response. This is indeed true for doll collectors and for purchasers of dolls in general. Most people purchase a doll because it appeals to them and they are influenced by their apprcciation of its artistic beauty. The exceptions to this are some of the very widely advertised dolls that may be similar to earlier dolls that had had little commercial success, possibly because of their lack of real artistic beauty. Dolls that are seen everywhere have a special popularity appeal regardless of the absence of artistic charm.

Since our appreciation of the artistic beauty of dolls is so very important, it is interesting that at the United Federation of Doll Clubs, Inc. (UFDC) conventions and regional exhibitions the judging does not include the artistic beauty of the dolls. (This is probably due to the fact that determining the artistic merit is based on a subjective reaction to it rather than an intellectual reaction to the doll.) Judging is supposed to be based entirely on four factors: authenticity, originality, rarity and condition. The artistic beauty is not included because its evaluation would be a personal point of view. However, for the collector who enjoys having the doll and for the producer who enjoys selling the doll, the artistic beauty is usually the most important factor.

Several organizations have been formed to further the production of artistic dolls and thus help both the

Illustration 1. *19in (48cm) Jumeau doll wearing original Jumeau clothes. A blue cloth label with gold lettering was attached to the dust rufflel. It reads: "Bébé Jumeau//Médaille d'Or// Paris." The outer garments are blue including the blue kid single strap shoes which are labeled: "Jumeau//Médaille d'Or//Paris//Déposé."* Sylvia Brockmon Collection.

doll purchasers and the doll producers. One of the first of these organizations was the Art Alliance of America which was formed in 1914 and had its name changed to National Art Alliance in 1932 when it was incorporated. This society was in existence for over 50 years and covered a period when

American dolls were probably among the most artistic in the world, a fact that was no doubt partially due to the work of the Art Alliance of America.

---

*One wonders if Helen Sargent was distantly related to John Singer Sargent.

"Cinderella and the Glass Slipper." Group of dolls designed by Dorothy W. Heizer. In the Artists' Toy Exhibition.

Illustration 2. Dorothy Heizer cloth dolls were exhibited by the Art Alliance in the Art Center, New York, in December 1925. The theme of this group of five dolls is "Cinderella and the Glass Slipper."

Throughout its history, Helen Sargent* Hitchcock (Mrs. Ripley Hitchcock) of New York City, who designed dolls, was an officer, sometimes president, of this organization. In 1914 Mrs. Hitchcock and others founded the Art Alliance at a time when World War I had just started in Europe and the supply of foreign-made dolls was beginning to be curtailed. Up to that time, most dolls have been made in Europe, especially Germany. When hostilities began it became necessary for the Allies to produce their own dolls. To further the production of American dolls and to keep high artistic standards was one of the aims of the Art Alliance of America.

The purpose of this organization, as stated in the *American Art Annual* published by the American Federation of Arts, Volume II, 1914, was: "To promote co-operation between artists, art students, artisans, publishers, manufacturers, advertisers and all others who are engaged in artistic activities; to give expert advice to art

Illustration 3. Helen Sargent Hitchcock's wooden Flexy dolls were exhibited by the Art Alliance in the Art Center, New York, in December 1925. These six dolls in a beach and pool scene show that "She folds, she floats, she's flexible and funny." The original faces were painted by Lucille Patterson Marsh and made by Converse of Winchendon, Massachusetts.

students and employers and a department of general information; to hold exhibitions." There were several exhibitions in 1914.

By 1916 the Art Alliance had 600 members and it put on an exhibit titled "Art Associated with the Child." About 3500 people came to see this exhibit during the two weeks that it was shown. The following year, 1917, there was an exhibit of dolls from France. Many of these dolls had bisque heads and hands sculptured by the French artist, Louis-

Aime Lejeune, a member of the French Legion of Honneur. The Callot Sisters, famous couturières, designed the clothes for some of the dolls that were in this exhibition. (See color plate 40 in *The Collector's Encyclopedia of Dolls, Volume Two*.)

In February 1918 the Art Alliance of America had an exhibition of Toys in New York. About this time the *American Art Annual* was listing the following women doll designers as well as the Art Alliance: Grace Drayton, Maud Tousey Fangel, Helen Trowbridge and Rose O'Neill Wilson. Generally there was about an equal number of men and women doll designers.

Soon after the war ended the membership in the Art Alliance of America exceeded 1000 and Mrs. Ripley Hitchcock remained as first vice president.

The Art Alliance moved from 10 East 47th Street in New York City to larger quarters in 1920. The new location was at 65-67 East 56th Street. This same building was dedicated in 1921 and became the location of the Art Center where numerous exhibitions were held. The Art Center was a holding company which included, besides the

The Flexy Doll. "She folds, she floats, she's flexible and funny." Pronounced a new standard doll. Designed and patented by Helen Sargent Hitchcock. The original face was painted by Lucille Patterson Marsh.

Art Alliance, the Art Directors Club, the Society of Craftsmen, the Society of Illustrators and others. Mrs. Ripley Hitchcock was the president of the Art Center and later she became honorary president. Charles Dana Gibson was the first vice president of the Art Center.

The *Art Center Bulletin* was published monthly except in July and August beginning in September 1922. The January 1926 issue of the *Art Center Bulletin* lists Mrs. Ripley Hitchcock as president, Charles Dana Gibson as first vice president and among the members of their advisory committee were Daniel Chester French, Charles Scribner, Jr., Louis Comfort Tiffany, Viscount Exmouth (Edward Addington Hargreaves Pellew), a British flying hero in World War I and other famous people.

This January 1926 issue of the *Art Center Bulletin* contains an article titled "The Art Alliance Exhibition of Artists' Toys," written by Helen Appleton Read. This exhibition included an exhibit of Dorothy Heizer dolls titled "Cinderella and the Glass Slipper" and an exhibit of the Flexy dolls designed and patented by Helen Sargent Hitchcock. The faces of these dolls were painted by Lucille Patterson Marsh and the exhibit was in the form of a beach and swimming pool. One of the dolls was floating in the water and another doll had feet in the water. The article on artists' toys in the *Bulletin* begins with a quotation from Stewart Culin, a curator at the Brooklyn Museum who was especially interested in dolls. (See the Stewart Culin entry in *The Collector's Encyclopedia of Dolls, Volume Two*.) Stewart Culin is quoted as saying: " 'Had I my way I would give more thought to children's toys even at the expense of some other details of their education.... The subject is one which our toy makers, with the best of intention do not understand fully....' These sentiments might be taken as the guiding and inspirational thought back of the collection of toys which the Art Alliance of America at 65 East Fifty-sixth Street, assembled in its galleries during December [1925]. Believing that in the designing of toys and dolls there is a fertile field for the artist designer, the Art Alliance arranged the exhibition with an educational intent as well as one of mere display, hoping that it

might inspire the American designer to express himself in this medium....

"No, it is merely one of those branches of industry into which a larger amount of art and imagination may enter, but which the American artist designer, with a very few exceptions, has passed by....

"...the supposition often voiced by those versed in the laws of child psychology, which is that artistic content plays no part in a child's preference for a toy, is contradicted by the tremendous sale of [certain] articles.

As an evidence of the field that this branch of design offers to the American artist and further proof of the rarity with which it is made use of, I must cite the cases of 'Kewpie' and 'The Bye-Lo Baby' dolls both designed by American sculptresses, Rose O'Neil [sic] and Grace Putnam. These dolls have appealed to thousands of American children. 'The Bye-Lo Baby' I am informed is the best seller in every doll department....

"Among the artist designers included in the Art Alliance Exhibition [is] Helen Dryden, who has designed a set of paper dolls which are lifelike enough to appeal to the child mind and are yet wholly charming as regards color and design....Mrs. Ripley Hitchcock, president of the Art Center, is showing a unique wooden doll which she has designed and which has just been put upon the market. It differs from other wooden dolls in that it has various characteristics not generally conceded to wooden dolls — it folds, floats and is flexible.

"The committee chosen by the Art Alliance to assemble and to give advice on the subject of collecting artistic toys had among its members Tony Sarg, Rose O'Neil [sic], John Martin [publisher of an artistic children's magazine], Mrs. Stewart Culin [painter] and Julia Daniels. The last named is the gifted young designer of nursery friezes and illustrations for children's books....

"To make the exhibition more than a mere display of toys Stewart Culin, who is the recognized authority in this country on the subject of toys...loaned examples from his collection of antique and modern toys. He also allowed the Art Alliance to show extremely rare hand-colored plates which set forth the story of toys from their earliest beginnings....

"Tony Sarg, the master toymaker of this country, loaned a group of his wooden dolls and some ancient wax dolls which have served as models for some of his world famous marionettes...."

Also in December at the Art Center there was a members' competition of pictorial photographs and the first choice photograph showed two naked dolls, one sitting and one standing, both looking toward a toy duck. This photograph by J. Vanderpant of New Westminster, British Columbia, was named "A Ducky Story."

Mrs. Ripley Hitchcock became honorary president of the Art Alliance of America in 1930 but there was no mention of the Art Center in the *American Art Annual* after 1932 when the Art Alliance of America merged with the National Alliance of Art and Industry which was located in the R.C.A. Building in New York City. The combined society was incorporated in 1932 under its new name and Mrs. Ripley Hitchcock remained the honorary president. The National Alliance of Art and Industry existed "To serve manufacturers seeking greater beauty for their products: artists who adapt their taste, skill and vision to the needs of industry; and the public interested in the union of beauty and utility in industry."

At the beginning of World War II the National Alliance of Art and Industry was located at 119 East 19th Street in New York City and its purpose was "To be of service to manufacturers, artists and the public, interested in promoting good artistic standards in industrial products." Mrs. Ripley Hitchcock had returned to her earlier position of being vice president.

The National Alliance of Art and Industry was listed in the *American Art Annual* as late as 1964 but it is not mentioned in the 1967 *American Art Annual*. Thus the Art Alliance and its successor, The National Alliance of Art and Industry, was in existence in New York City for over half a century and no doubt was an important factor in the artistry developed in American dolls during that period. It is interesting that Mrs. Ripley Hitchcock, who designed dolls, was an important officer of this society for many years.

During the first half of this century many famous artists designed dolls, and the clothes for dolls were sometimes designed by outstanding French couturiers and couturières such as the Callot Sisters, Doucet, Lanvin, Paul Poiret and others. Surely today there must be many designers with artistic talent who can create dolls of outstanding beauty. Organizations such as the National Institute of American Doll Artists, Inc. (NIADA), the Original Doll Artist Council of America (ODACA) and others, have been formed recently to encourage artists in the designing of artistic dolls.

Dolls today are designed and produced all over the world so that an organization limited to America is anachronistic. About thrcc years ago the International Doll Academy (IDA) was formed to promote the appreciation and production of modern dolls. This international organization has many of the same goals and purposes as the earlier Art Alliance of America, namely to encourage the artistic appreciation and manufacture of aesthetic dolls. The dolls produced each year compete first to be nominated for their artistic beauty by the IDA members. These nominees are exhibited at various places in America and their pictures are shown in major department stores and other retail shops that sell dolls. The public is asked to vote for one of the five dolls that they like best in each of ten categories. The dolls that receive the most votes are then given the coveted DOTY® (Doll Of The Year®) award. It can readily be seen that the public is usually going to vote for the dolls with the greatest artistic appeal, beauty and charm. Thus the public can express its preferences and the producers learn what the public likes best. In this way the dolls can actually be judged on that elusive and subjective, but all important, attribute — their artistic beauty. □

Illustration 4. *One of the DOTY® award nominees in the "Collectible Doll — All Other Mediums" class 8, No. 021. The doll is named* Alice *and has a porcelain head, human hair wig, paperweight glass eyes, porcelain and wooden ball-jointed body and is 15in (38cm) tall. The muslin print dress has hand-smocking and the shoes are leather. Lynne and Michael Roche were the designers and creators of this doll.*

Effanbee's *Little Lady — Anne Shirley*

by **Barbara Lutz Comienski**

Photographs by **James Comienski**

During the composition era of doll making, many companies created extremely lovely dolls which we continue to enjoy today. One of the most charming and most versatile of these dolls was Effanbee's *Anne Shirley*, later known as *Little Lady*. From her debut in 1936, until her final appearance in 1949, in the advent of hard plastic, this doll played many different roles: child star, doll artist's creation, historic fashion mannequin, skating star, innocent little girl or mature young lady. Because of her many striking variations, this doll has endeared herself to collectors for five decades.

The first dolls Effanbee referred to as *Anne Shirley* actually bear *Patsy* family markings. Capitalizing on RKO's 1934 hit film, *Anne of Green Gables*, Effanbee gave several existing *Patsy* family dolls long reddish-blonde braids and little girl dresses reminiscent of the movie. However, by 1935, a new doll design appeared. As competition for Ideal's sensationally popular *Shirley*

Temple doll, Effanbee sculpted a portrait doll of the child star of *Anne of Green Gables, Anne Shirley*. (More details about this star's career can be found in John Axe's *The Encyclopedia of Celebrity Dolls*, published by Hobby House Press, 1983.) A newly propor-

BELOW LEFT: Illustration 1. 17½in (44cm) *Little Lady* as *Anne Shirley*; all composition, fully jointed, with reddish-blonde mohair wig and blue sleep eyes with eyelashes. Although Anne in the film was not a highland dancer, the Scottish costume on this doll would recall the Canadian setting of the story. The costume consists of black wool tam and jacket, a red, green and yellow plaid cotton fabric "plaid" and kilt, red knee socks and black dancing sandals of the style Effanbee often used at that time. Both the head and back are marked "EFFANBEE//U.S.A.," showing that this

is a slightly later doll of the early 1940s. **MIDDLE: Illustration 2.** *Life* magazine for April 3, 1939, features on the cover a real child holding one of the Dewees Cochran designed *American Children* manufactured by Effanbee. This doll is the type termed as the "shy, sensitive 'French' type...." **BELOW RIGHT: Illustration 3.** 21in (53cm) *American Child*/Portrait doll designed by Dewees Cochran for Effanbee, 1937 to 1940; all composition, fully jointed, with ash blonde human hair wig styled in a Dutch bob and blue sleep eyes with eyelashes. She appears to be the mold meant to typify the "good-natured type." She wears her original red leather oxfords with fringed flaps and pink striped white stockings. Her blue cotton dress (under her coat) is similar in style to the one shown on the *Life* cover. Her black and white checked wool coat is trimmed with maroon velvet, the same shade as her maroon felt boater hat. A charm is attached to the coat collar. Note the leather gloves completing her ensemble, made possible by her beautifully sculpted individual fingers. Her head is marked: "EFFANBEE// AMERICAN//CHILDREN:" her back is marked: "EFFANBEE//ANNE-SHIRLEY."

tioned body featured large hands with separated fingers. Human hair wigs and sleep eyes were other appealing features of these dolls. During her reign as the mainstay of Effanbee's line for 14 years, her size ranged from an initial 14½in (37cm) to 27in (69cm) in the late 1940s. These first *Anne Shirley* dolls retained the reddish-blonde hair and continued to wear outfits reminiscent of the film, but as the doll's role changed, so did her costumes. The head is unmarked in these late 1930s dolls; the back is marked: "EFFANBEE//ANNE-SHIRLEY."

Anne Shirley soon assumed several different faces as part of the *American Children* series. Effanbee commissioned the renown doll artist Dewees Cochran to sculpt a series of realistic children's faces and these were used in conjunction with the *Anne Shirley* body. These dolls were so lifelike that they were featured on the cover of the April 3, 1939, issue of *Life* magazine, quite an honor given the turbulence of world events at that time. The *Life* article discussed four "types" of faces, all with closed mouths, but doll researchers have shown open mouth styles as well numerous times. The child and doll shown on the cover of *Life* were described as the "shy, sensitive 'French' type,...with oval face, delicately pointed features." The other styles were described as " 'Germanic' type, with classic features, softly molded mouth, the roundest eyes; good-natured type, with pug nose, eyes farthest apart, full lower face;...self-confident type with well-defined features, prominent chin." Ranging from 15in (38cm) to 21in (53cm), these *American Children* also varied in having either painted or sleep eyes. All had human hair wigs in various styles besides the four featured in *Life*, and those purchased clothed, had lovely designed wardrobes. The head is marked: "EFFANBEE//AMERI-CAN//CHILDREN;" the back is marked: "EFFANBEE//ANNE-SHIRLEY."

The open mouth *American Child* face was used not only for these portraits, but for a 1939 *Snow White*, and some models of the early 1940s *Ice Queen*, undoubtedly a competitor to Alexander's *Sonja Henie*. (Other models of the *Ice Queen* used the standard *Anne Shirley* face.) This open-mouthed portrait face sometimes was only marked "EFFANBEE" on the head.

Illustration 4. 14in (36cm) replica historical dolls. These were available for purchase, in contrast to the 21in (53cm) display dolls. These were all composition, fully jointed, with human hair wigs and painted eyes. All have unmarked heads of the *Anne Shirley* mold. Their bodies are marked: "EFFANBEE//ANNE-SHIRLEY." They date from 1939. The doll on the left represents "1658 — Carolina Settlement." A brunette with waved hair drawn back in a bun and painted brown eyes, she wears a 17th century forest green dress with gold lacing and trim in an elaborate pattern. Her long train is lined in gold. The middle doll, a blue-eyed blonde with a pompadour, represents "1720 — The Pioneering American Spirit" in her turquoise calico gown with red and white flowers and red-lined overskirt. Note her metal gold heart bracelet which is marked on both sides: "EFFANBEE//DURABLE//DOLLS." The doll on the right represents "1682 — Quaker Colony." Her dress is much plainer, gold with a black laced weskit, white collar and cuffs and a green apron. She has brown eyes and her gray hair is styled in a simple bun.

Illustration 5. Several more examples of 14in (36cm) replica historical dolls. The doll on the left, referred to as "1816 — Monroe Doctrine," has blue eyes and black hair in an elaborate hairdo of side curls and a braid wound around the head in back. Her equally elaborate dress features a narrow red and white striped underskirt and a white overdress with a pleated side inset, pleated insets in the sleeves and fine red braid trim. Her metal heart bracelet reads "EFFANBEE" on both sides. The second doll from the left represents "1840 — Covered Wagon Days" in her pointed bodice, sky blue dress trimmed in white lace and pink rosebuds. In her light brown hair, which is dressed in ringlets, she wears matching rosebuds. She has blue eyes. Her metal heart is marked on both sides: "EFFANBEE//DURABLE//DOLLS." The third doll, a brown-eyed redhead, bears the name "1896 — Unity of Nations Established." Her hair is swept up in the Gibson Girl style. The large sleeves, peplum waistline, white jabot and white braid ornamentation of her peach-colored dress also define the period. The doll on the right represents the last doll of the series, "1939 — Today." A brown-eyed blonde with a pageboy hair style, she is dressed in a gown by Coco Chanel consisting of a purple skirt, attached white bodice of multiple lace ruffles and wide green sash.

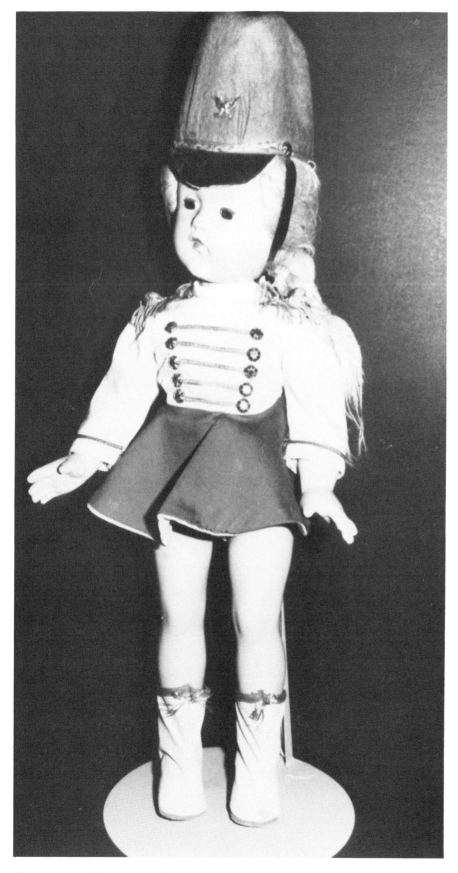

In 1939, Effanbee launched a nation-wide traveling exhibit "The Romance of American Fashion." Three sets of 30 21in (53cm) *American Children* dolls with painted eyes, on the *Anne Shirley* bodies, were costumed lavishly in a documentary presentation of the history of American fashion. So comprehensive was this display that it started with an Indian of 1492 and concluded with a model in a 1939 Chanel evening gown. Their human hair wigs were also styled authentically. Stores exhibiting these dolls offered 14in (36cm) replicas for sale. The replicas had the standard *Anne Shirley* face and body. However, unlike the usual *Anne Shirley*, these dolls had painted eyes. Their human hair wigs were also elegantly styled. Variations in eye and hair color sometimes emerge with these dolls. These dolls have no markings on the head, but bear the "EFFANBEE//ANNE-SHIRLEY" logo on the back. Their underwear is historically accurate, with hoop petticoats or wire cages supporting panniers. The replica gowns, although made of cotton, show infinite detail in pleating, ruching or ruffles.

After the early 1940s, the "Anne-Shirley" logo and tie to the celebrity was dropped. The doll assumed a new identity: *Little Lady*. The mold remained the same for both head and body; only the markings changed. Now the head and back both bore "EFFAN-BEE//U.S.A." Previously, all of these dolls had worn the famous Effanbee gold heart bracelets; war shortages put an end to that. War shortages also forced innovation. Note that both **Illustrations 6** and **7** show *Little Lady* dolls with yarn hair. Other innovations to capture the wartime market included insertion of magnets in the hands to allow the dolls to hold metal objects such as mirrors or majorette batons. In addition, from approximately 1939 to 1942, some models of the doll had a torso music box that could be wound to play "Happy Birthday" or a lullaby.

Little Lady's figure seemed adapt-

Illustration 6. 17in (43cm) *Little Lady* as a majorette; all composition, fully jointed, with brown sleep eyes with eyelashes. During the war years, Effanbee converted to using cotton yarn hair, as shown by this doll's pale blonde braids. She is dressed in a one-piece outfit of corded cotton with a white bodice and shorts and red skirt lined in white. Gold epaulets and gold metal buttons give the costume flair, as does her tall red felt hat and white leather boots. Many of the *Little Lady* majorettes had magnets inserted in their hands in order to hold flags or batons, but this doll seems not to have this added feature. Both her head and back are marked: "EFFANBEE//U.S.A." she is from the mid 1940s.

able to a wide range of ages. The mid 1940s saw the doll used to represent a sophisticated lady in her black negligee, bra and panties. In the late 1940s she resumed her role as a mannequin for historic fashion (such as *Little Lady Gibson Girl*) or evening gowns. Nonetheless, most collectors think of her child roles, when they think of *Little Lady*. From party dresses to school dresses to even raincoats, the everyday fashions of a child of the 1940s were authentically captured by this charming child.

In 1954, Effanbee reissued *Little Lady* in vinyl. Her tenure of only a few years, as compared to her previous 14 year reign could be attributed to the medium, or even to changes in society. However, whether she represents history, a sophisticated lady, a real or an idealized child, collectors will continue to cherish Effanbee's composition *Anne Shirley*, the epitome of a "little lady." □

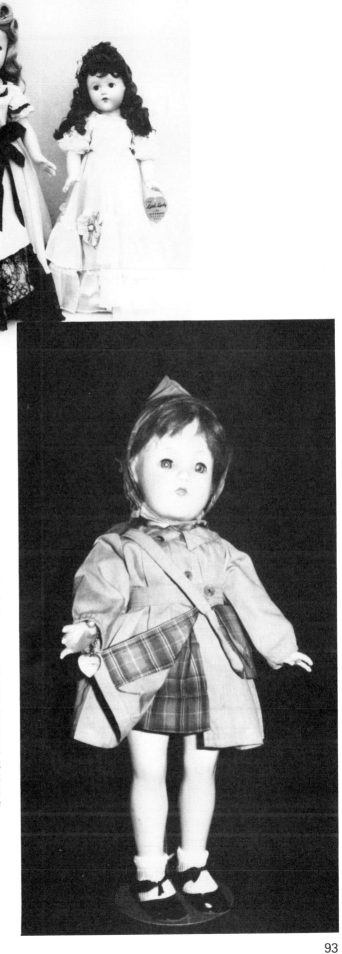

Illustration 7. 21in (53cm) *Anne Shirley* and 18in (46cm) *Little Lady* in evening gowns. *Anne Shirley*, on the left, is all composition, fully jointed, with an ash blonde human hair wig in long loose curls and blue sleep eyes with eyelashes. Her white satin slip and gold shoes are under a white organdy gown with tiny gold dots, trimmed in black lace and a large black velvet sash that matches her purse. The head is unmarked; the back is marked: "EFFANBEE//ANNE-SHIRLEY." She is from the early 1940s. On the right is a tagged *Little Lady* doll from the war years; all composition, fully jointed, with brown sleep eyes with eyelashes. Her auburn hair with marcelled waves is of cotton yarn. She also wears gold sandals. Her gown of pink organza has a ruffled square neckline, two ruffled tiers to the skirt and two ruffles on the sleeve. The dress is trimmed with a large blue fabric flower which matches an identical one in her hair. Her heart-shaped paper tag states on one side "I am//Little Lady [in script]//An//EFFANBEE//DURABLE//DOLL" and on the other side "A new EFFANBEE Playmate." Both her head and back are marked: "EFFANBEE//U.S.A." She is from the mid 1940s. *Pam and Polly Judd Collection. Photograph by Polly Judd.*

Illustration 8. 17½in (44cm) *Little Lady* dressed as a child; all composition, fully jointed, with a long human hair ash blonde wig with bangs, green-blue sleep eyes with eyelashes and painted shell pink fingernails. She wears replacement shoes and under her coat a one-piece dress of a navy taffeta bodice and navy and red plaid taffeta skirt and collar with separate navy taffeta panties. Her khaki trench coat with separate hood is lined in this same plaid taffeta fabric. The ensemble is completed by her matching khaki book bag trimmed in plaid taffeta. Her metal heart bracelet reads on both sides: "EFFANBEE//DURABLE//DOLLS." Both her head and back are marked: "EFFANBEE//U.S.A." She is from the late 1940s.

Novelty Dolls From the House of Lenci

by **Polly & Pam Judd**

Illustration 1. A traditional old Lenci box holds this 18in (46cm) "rag-type" boy with a hand-knit sweater and fur hat.

Many doll collectors have enjoyed the wonderful felt art deco dolls created by Madame Lenci in the 1920s and 1930s. However, this same company also made other lovely, less expensive dolls for select stores in Italy, the United States, aboard ships and around the world. These are not as well-known, but they have the same style and detail as the more expensive models.

Lenci also made wonderful miniature toys and accessories to accompany the wonderful bright costumes of their dolls. Today the company is reproducing their earlier models, and they are also remaking the more inexpensive dolls as well as accessories and toys.

A boy cloth doll with a large fur hat was found still tied into his original 1930s box in never-played-with condition and is shown in **Illustration 1.** He is 18in (46cm) tall and made of felt. His soft-sculptured face has vivid color and his eyes are painted yellow and black. His lips are red appliqued felt and he has the Lenci flair and attention to detail.

Today this modern version of the cloth doll shown in **Illustration 2,** can be found in selected stores and mail-order companies. This 18in (46cm) girl was purchased in 1980 in the Lenci shop in the Galleria in Milan, Italy, but it is sold today in the United States. She, too, has a wonderful painted soft-sculptured face with felt appliqued lips.

Lenci made many accessories in wood including the unusual wooden peg doll shown in **Illustration 3.** The tiny 6in (15cm) doll has the same costume as a long-necked lady doll advertised in *Playthings* magazine in May 1923. Her dress has the same quality, color and detail as the large 13in (33cm) doll. She is well labeled.

Two uniformed miniature dolls from the 1930s, shown in **Illustration 4,** represent two elite corps of Italy. The doll on the right is a *Bersagliere*

Illustration 3. Lenci dressed this 6in (15cm) wooden peg doll in the same costume as a larger 1923 cloth doll. Her blue felt dress and yellow felt hat is bright today. She carries a felt-trimmed purse, one of the many accessories made by the company. *Ingeborg Tomoletz Collection.*

(soldier). The man with the plumed hat is a *Carabiniere* (special policeman). Both have unusual carved wooden swords hanging from their belts. These delightful characters are still being made today in a type of hard plastic and are available for the children of Italy.

After World War II hard plastic was used for dolls because it was more durable than the celluloid and composition of the 1930s. The 6in (15cm) provincial doll from Valsarentino, shown in **Illustration 5** on the right, has a lovely plastic color. Her face is well painted and has the same two-tone lip detail as the earlier felt art dolls. Her well-made necklace is engraved with the word "Torino" (Turin). The Lenci tag is sewn into her skirt.

Another hard plastic 6in (15cm) provincial doll from Sardinia, shown in **Illustration 5** on the left, also has quality clothing. The waistband of her felt clothing is hand-embroidered and her trim is sewn with metallic thread. She also has a well-painted face with the two-tone lips.

Very popular today are the tourist hard plastic dolls in the Lenci box with the cellophane cover. One favorite is

Illustration 4. The uniforms of the Italian soldier and policeman are well-tailored and ornate. Each has a wooden sword.

Illustration 5. Both 6in (15cm) provincial dolls are made of hard plastic and have the same beautiful details as the cloth dolls.

Illustration 6. Popular with tourists, the 7in (18cm) *Vatican Guard* is handsome in his bright red and yellow uniform.

the *Vatican Guard*, seen in **Illustration 6**. *Vatican Guard* is 7in (18cm). He is still available in Italy.

Wood was used for miniature toys and accessories which complemented the costume and the doll. The miniature 9in (23cm) provincial doll, shown in **Illustration 7**, carries a pig with a wonderful painted expression on his face. Other animals produced included bunnies, giraffes, Oriental dogs and birds in cages. The tiny toys are art treasures in themselves.

Lenci used felt flowers with many of the costumes. This tiny 8½in (22cm) Mascotte flower seller boy, shown in **Illustration 8**, carries a felt basket with flowers and waves a multicolored bouquet. He has a handkerchief with felt trim in his pocket. This is another Lenci touch used for many dolls.

A miniature 9in (23cm) skier from the 1930s, shown in **Illustration 9**, still glides dangerously down the slopes with a very surprised look on his face. His ski equipment is well-balanced and beautifully crafted. Other sports accessories found on dolls are croquet mallets, soccer balls, golf clubs, tennis rackets and baseball bats.

By the end of the 1950s hard plastic dolls were replaced by soft vinyl dolls which the children loved to hold. Their features were much simpler than the earlier dolls and the children could use their imagination when playing with these dolls. This was a trend in both Iatly and France during this period. The rooted-hair sleep-eyed doll, shown in **Illustration 10**, is 14in (36cm) tall.

Other novelty dolls include tea cosies, ladies' purses, bellhops, candy boxes, lamps, puppets and marottes. Other accessories reported in Lenci catalogs are hoops, parasols, pots of flowers, diabolo games, drums and drumsticks, stickhorses, Oriental lanterns, pails and many many more.

Today's collectors can still find the unusual older Lenci dolls at flea and antique markets, doll shows and garage sales. They have the same appeal as their more expensive counterparts. Elena Scavini (Madame Lenci) was devoted to "quality" dolls and accessories of all types as her advertisements proclaimed. With that philosophy she turned a hobby into an doll business which is still attracting new customers today. □

Illustration 7. The 9in (23cm) little girl with the pink pig has an orange felt dress with other colored felt hand-appliqued on it. Her pink headdress is very ornate.

Illustration 8. The 8½in (22cm) flower peddler waves multicolored felt flowers. His green jacket has elaborate black felt trim.

Illustration 9. This 9in (23cm) miniature Lenci skier has well-made wooden skis and poles, but he still seems to be having problems controlling them.

Illustration 10. Lenci made provincial dolls in soft vinyl with sleep eyes. This 14in (36cm) doll has a red felt skirt with a yellow felt band and a blue cotton apron. It represents the province of Rome.

97

Nancy Ann Storybook Dolls

by **Marjorie Miller**

Illustration 1. 4½in (11cm) *Little Sister Goes To A Party* (number 53) and 5½in (14cm) *Big Sister Goes To A Party* (number 63) from the Little and Big Sister Series. Both dolls have brown mohair wigs, black sleep eyes and pink ribbons around the hair. The short white satin dresses with flower print are both the same and have lace trim. The dolls are wearing white panties and the shoes are painted white. *Randi Kulik Collection.*

Illustration 2. 6½in (16cm) *Debut* (number 75) from the Commencement Series. This doll has blonde hair, black sleep eyes and a white satin ribbon with flowers around her hair. Her long white sheer dress has lace trim, gold and white braid trim, white flowers at the waist and white lace at the neck and arms. She wears a white satin underskirt, long pantaloons and black painted slippers. *Randi Kulik Collection.*

The original Nancy Ann Storybook dolls which were made of plastic with sleep eyes, mohair wigs, jointed arms and legs and had movable heads on the 5½in (14cm) and 6½in (16cm) sizes, were manufactured by Nancy Ann Abbott and her partner, Mr. Leslie Rowland, from 1950 to 1964. The plastic dolls with sleep eyes, jointed arms and legs, 3½in (9cm) and 4½in (11cm) tall do not have movable heads. These dolls, undressed, are shown in the book, *Nancy Ann Storybook Dolls*, page 169, Illustration 406, and page 170, Illustration 408.

The quality of the design of the dolls and the material used to dress them is comparable to that of the early Nancy Ann Storybook dolls. However, in the early 1960s, one can note the difference in the material used as well as the designs for the costumes. This was due, in part, to the illness which prevented Nancy Ann Abbott from designing the costumes and influencing the purchase of the material to be used. Mr. Rowland's supervision as to the quality of good workmanship for the costumes of that period is well noted.

The Nancy Ann Storybook Doll Company went into bankruptcy in 1964. In 1967, Mr. Albert Bourla reintroduced the Nancy Ann Storybook dolls at the Toy Fair in New York. These plastic sleep-eyed dolls, as well as their costumes, were made in Hong Kong, and were sold in the United States until 1973.

Presently on the market is another reintroduction of the Nancy Ann Storybook doll, this time by the Jesco Company. The marking on the back of these dolls is: "NANCY//ANN// DOLLS//JESCO//INC//1985// CHINA." They are plastic with painted eyes, jointed arms and legs and heads that swivel.

The dolls shown in this article are the original Nancy Ann Storybook dolls and are marked on the back: "STORYBOOK//DOLLS//U.S.A.// TRADEMARK//REG." □

TOP: Illustration 3. 6½in (16cm) *Nun* (number 81) from the Religious Series. There are three types of habits represented in this series: white, brown and black. The doll in this illustration has a long white habit with a black headdress, a firm cotton material covering her forehead while the collar around her neck is of the same material. A gold cross is attached to a black cord at her waistline and she wears long white cotton pantaloons and painted high boot type black shoes. *Randi Kulik Collection.*

MIDDLE: Illustration 4. 4½in (11cm) *Flower Girl* (number 85) and 4½in (11cm) *Ring Bearer* (number 84) from the Bridal Series. The *Flower Girl* has long blonde hair, black sleep eyes and a light blue ribbon with circular solid design satin thread as trim on top of the ribbon around her hair. She wears a long light blue organdy dress with a white flower design. The trim above the hem of the doll's dress is the same as that on the top of the ribbon in her hair. She wears a white cotton undershirt with white lace trim, short cotton panties with white lace trim and painted white high boot type shoes.

The *Ring Bearer* has short brown hair, black sleep eyes and wears light blue taffeta pants and a sheer light blue shirt with white lace trim across the front of the shirt. He has a small blue flower at the right side of his waist and wears white painted high type shoes. *Randi Kulik Collection.*

BOTTOM: Illustration 5. 5½in (14cm) *Winter* (number 93) from the Seasons Series. She has auburn hair, blue sleep eyes and wears a black felt hat with a large red feather, a long dark green taffeta dress with a red ribbon around her waist and red rickrack trim around the skirt, long pantaloons and black painted slippers. *Anne Lien Collection.*

TOP: Illustration 6. 5½in (14cm) *Here Am I Little Joan* (number 111) from the Mother Goose Series. She has auburn hair and black sleep eyes. She wears a small yellow felt hat with a blue ribbon with a bow on top on her head and a calf-length yellow taffeta dress with two rows of light blue rickrack as trim around the skirt, long yellow taffeta pantaloons with one row of light blue rickrack trim and black painted slippers. *Randi Kulik Collection.*

MIDDLE: Illustration 7. 5½in (14cm) *Topsy* (number 126) from the Fairytale Series. This is an unusual boxed doll, the only one I have seen like it. There are small tufts of cotton accompanying the doll. She is a plastic sleep-eyed doll with black short hair and a large red bow on top of her hair. She wears a long white cotton dress with a red dot pattern, long white pantaloons and painted high boot type shoes. *Anne Lien Collection.*

BOTTOM: Illustration 8. 5½in (14cm) *Mary Had A Little Lamb* (number 152) from the Fairytale Series. She has auburn hair, black sleep eyes and wears a yellow felt bonnet type hat with yellow ribbon ties on her head and a long yellow organdy dress with small white lines which form a square pattern. Blue rickrack trims the waist, the lower edge of the skirt and the hat. She also wears white pantaloons and black painted slippers. *Becky Mays Collection.*

TOP: Illustration 9. 5½in (14cm) *Sunday's Child* (number 186) from the Dolls of the Week Series. She has brown hair and black sleep eyes. She wears a large white felt hat with a cluster of flowers on the right side with white ribbon ties, a dress with a white taffeta bodice and underskirt with white organdy overskirt and two rows of white lace trim on the overskirt, short panties and black painted slippers. This doll is shown in one of the special insert type boxes for Easter. The outside of the box has the white and pink dots. *Judy Berry Collection.*

MIDDLE: Illustration 10. 6½in (16cm) *July* (number 193) from the Dolls of the Month Series. She has blonde hair and black eyes. She wears a large red felt hat with blue ribbon ties, a long red and white taffeta dress with white lace trim at the bodice and around the skirt, white pantaloons and black painted slippers. *Ann Lien Collection.*

BOTTOM: Illustration 11. 6½in (16cm) *Sally* (number 310) from the Operetta Series. She has blonde hair and black sleep eyes. She wears a hat of white lace with white flowers and white ribbon bow, an ankle-length dress of black taffeta with white lace trim and a small organdy apron with white lace trim, a white underskirt with lace trim, short panties and black painted slippers. *Randi Kulik Collection.*

TOP: Illustration 12. 6½in (16cm) *Only A Rose* (number 406) from the All Time Hit Parade Series. She has blonde hair and blue sleep eyes and wears a large pink straw hat with lace and pink flower trim, a long pink flower print organdy overskirt over her dress with a ribbon at the waist and a large pink flower above the wide white lace trim of the skirt, a pink taffeta underskirt, pantaloons and black painted slippers. *Ann Lien Collection.*

MIDDLE: Illustration 13. 5½in (14cm) *Violet* (number 123) from the Garden Series. She has brown hair, blue sleep eyes and a light lavender ribbon around her hair with a cluster of violet flowers on the right side. The bodice and underskirt of her dress are light lavender taffeta, the overskirt is organdy with lavender ribbon at the right side of the waist and she wears pantaloons and black painted slippers. *Kathy Bookstin Collection.*

BOTTOM: Illustration 14. 6½in (16cm) *Topaz* (number 308) from the Jewel Series. She has brown hair, blue sleep eyes and wears a large yellow felt hat with gold trim and yellow ribbon ties. She wears a long golden taffeta embossed dress with two rows of gold cord trim around the skirt, bodice and waist ending in a bow at the right side, a yellow gold glass jewel on the left side of the bodice, pantaloons and black painted slippers. *Becky Mays Collection.*

Illustration 1. This 14in (36cm) *Skookum* brave is typical of the *Skookum* Indian dolls manufactured, hand-assembled and distributed by the H. H. Tammen and Arrow Novelty Companies from 1914 to about 1950. The label on the bottom of the foot reads: "Trade mark registered *Skookum* (Bully good) Indian U.S.A. patented."

Illustration 2. This 12in (30cm) couple (brave and squaw) is fashioned in the same way as all Skookum dolls. Their bodies are built of sticks and straw, and the legs are made of sticks. A blanket is folded around the body in such a way as to indicate arms beneath.

Illustration 3. The squaw, seen in **Illustration 2**, is shown from the front. Note that she wears wooden beads while most of the brave's are of glass. Like all *Skookum* dolls, they wear real Indian blankets that have been cut for this purpose. Early *Skookum* dolls wear soft leather boots, later ones wear felt boots. Some were decorated. Those dolls manufactured in the last years have plastic boots.

Oregon was green with new spring life, and the sun shimmered on the Columbia River.

On its bank lay an Indian child sick with fever, his mother hovering nearby. They listened intently to the old medicine man chanting incantations, his aged feet shuffling in rhythm to the singing of spirits only he could hear.

He held a stick figure, a manikin doll, in the child's right hand, shaking it, and beseeching the child's higher spirit to return to the body so healing could occur.

From this prototype manikin emerged the "Skookum" Indian doll. "Skookum" means strong spirit in Chinook Indian jargon, a language believed to have originated in far earlier times. Chinook Indians were part of a nation known as "Flatheads," not to be confused with the so-called Flathead Tribe of western Montana. Their inner

lives sought an upward connection with the spirit world the medicine man was evoking.

Strangely enough, the healing spirit of skookum seemed to travel full circle when H. H. Tammen, Denver *Skookum* doll manufacturer, died in 1924 and left half of his great fortune to the Children's Hospital of Denver, one of the finest children's hospitals in the country. The dolls were produced in Denver from 1914 until about 1950.

Tammen, often described as "quite a character," began doing business in Denver in 1881, the year Denver became the capital of Colorado. His firm manufactured and sold minerals, novelties, animal specimens and various types of collections. It also provided Indian curios, furs, game heads and souvenirs — including *Skookum* Indian dolls — for tourists attracted to the Rockies by the lure of Indians, cowboys and game hunters. This developed into a nationwide wholesale business. In 1895, Tammen and Frederick

Gilmer Bonfils joined forces in cofounding the *Denver Post*.

A story is told of how Tammen would give away small figurines he called Navaho spirit idols to anyone who would take them. These figurines had a meaning similar to that of *Skookum* dolls. They also served as the trademark of the Tammen Company.

The first *Skookum* doll patent was held by Mary McAboy and appears in the February 1914 Official Gazette of the United States Patent Office of the Denver Register. It was described as an ornamental doll figure or toy design. The squaw was shown alone and also holding a baby. The brave wore a felt hat that became popular with Chinooks after they were introduced into the area by American fur traders. The first doll heads were made from dried apples.

An outstanding feature of the dolls that Tammen manufactured were the side-glancing eyes on their composition heads. Most of them looked to their right. According to the "Doctrine of Souls and Disease Among the Chinook Indians," published in 1892, when a sick person's soul chose the path leading to the right, the patient would recover. When the soul took the path to the left, death occurred. Thus, the manikin doll represented a guardian spirit which, with the help of the medicine man, could turn the sick person's soul from a left- to a right-leading path.

Skookum Indian dolls were advertised in the Tammen Company catalogs as "the original and greatest Indian Character Doll," and represented the "true Indian type." Tammen's dolls were almost all of the same physical type, however, although garbed like such other tribes as the Navaho, Apache, Sioux, Chippewa and Blackfoot.

Designed in the likenesses of the Chinooks, the dolls have very expressive faces. Their elongated heads were fashioned to reflect the most unusual trait of Chinook physiognomy which, according to explorers Lewis and Clark, was "the flatness and width of forehead which they artificially obtained by compressing the head between two boards while in the state of infancy and from which it never afterwards perfectly recovers." Tammen's dolls do not represent the true very flathead configuration, however. If they had, the dolls might not have appealed to the tourist trade for whom they were intended.

Lewis and Clark also commented in their journal that the Chinooks were monogamous and lived in a state of comparative happiness. Tammen, possibly knowing this fact, had the *Skookum* Indian dolls packaged as families.

Mrs. Loreen Anderson, a 70-year-old North Denver resident, recalls working for the Tammen Company during the 1940s assembling *Skookum* dolls for 25 cents per doll. She applied for the job because she could do it in her home while her young son was at school. Each Saturday Mrs. Anderson and her son would return completed dolls to the Tammen factory on Larimer Street and pick up parts for more dolls. Among the materials she received was half of a full-size Indian blanket which she would cut into doll clothing pieces. Mrs. Anderson was able to put together between 20 and 25 dolls every week for over a year.

She reminisces about the difficulty of folding the doll arms "just right,"

ABOVE: Illustration 4. The skirted squaw shown here is 10in (25cm) tall and has the side-glancing eyes typical of all such dolls. Looking right is believed to signify taking a right-leading path that indicates good health and life. A few rare dolls have left-glancing eyes.

LEFT: Illustration 5. The squaw shown here is carrying a baby that is made of padding wrapped in the form of an infant, with a mask added for its face. The brave is 14in (36cm) tall, and the squaw is 12in (30cm) tall.

American International 1986 Toy Fair

DOLLS
DOLLS
DOLLS
DOLLS

by the **Editorial Staff**

1. *Cynthia*, a 15½in (39.4cm) porcelain doll by The Littlest Ballet Co.

2. The *Tennis Lady, Teddy Clown* and the *Gentleman* by Margarete Steiff.

Manufacturers and their artists alike offered collectors choice new models at the 1986 American International Toy Fair held in New York in February. The 1985 Dolls Of The Year™ (DOTY) Award nominees and "Public's Choice" Award dolls have exerted a profound influence on dolls. The results of the DOTY balloting have made the industry aware of the public's desires. **Doll Reader** is pleased to give collectors a glimpse of the 1986 dolls *before* they appear in your favorite store as Toy Fair is only open to business entities.

Doll Reader views its coverage which represents the diversity of tastes and styles of Toy Fair as our responsibility to give you indepth information so that **you the collector can collect whatsoever appeals to you!**

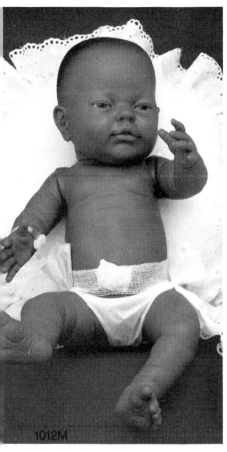

3. *La Newborn* with open eyes by Barval.

4. *Ginger Rogers* and *Fred Astaire* 19in (48.3cm) dancing movie stars by World Doll.

Barval Toys, Inc.

For 1986, Barval has introduced to its *La Newborn* line of realistic dolls a new 16in (40.6cm) size and has added a black doll. Both are available with open or closed eyes and either anatomically correct or non-sexed (the black doll only available in a non-sexed model).

Also of interest is *La Baby,* a 10in (25.4cm) doll which is mechanical. The baby has a pacifier and when it is removed, the baby cries — when replaced, the baby stops crying. The black *La Baby* is non-mechanical.

The 21in (53.3cm) size *La Baby*, "Heart to Heart" series is another mechanical Barval doll. When pressure is put on the baby's chest, a "heartbeat" can be felt.

(*Note:* For photograph of *La Newborn* see #3, above left.)

5. The *White Swan* by Avigail Brahms. This 22in (55.9cm) porcelain doll is part of "The American Ballet Series." Costume is made of imported silk tulle; bodice is imported Chinese silk satin trimmed with white feathers and brocaded beadings. Hand blown glass eyes and mohair wig.

6.

7.

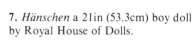

6. *Somebody* by Dolls by Jerri.

7. *Hänschen* a 21in (53.3cm) boy doll by Royal House of Dolls.

8. *Rosamunda*, the recreated pouty face at 19in (48.3cm) tall by Lenci.

8.

Thomas Boland & Co., Inc.

Thomas Boland & Co., Inc., had an exciting line of artistic originals at Toy Fair. Many are one-of-a-kind dolls or are made in limited quantities. Dolls from his magnificent display are always the talk of buyers at Toy Fair. This year proved no exception. Included is but a sampling of the creative and artistic dolls featured in the exhibit.

9.

9. *Mickey* with two of three *Bakers* by William Wiley.

Yolanda Bello (11)

Second in Yolanda Bello's "Cognac and Lace" Series is *Sondra*. Costumed in a black silk dress, fringed shawl, black silk patterned hose and a garter. *Sondra* is very fashionable with her 14K gold jewelry. Holding the customary brandy snifter, she sits in an elegant hand-carved mahogany chair upholstered in velvet. (See February/March 1986 **Doll Reader**, page 128, #4, for *Gretchen* and *Babette* by Bello.)

Brigette Deval (12)

Offered were her unique sculptures that are converted to wax over porcelain with beautiful hand-blown glass eyes and costumed where possible with antique fabrics and lace. See *Illustration 12* of this article for one of the many different styles offered by Brigette from Italy.

Hal Payne

Carved dolls and animals from alder wood from 12 to 24in (30.5 to 61cm) are this artist's specialty. These

10.

11.

10. *Marilyn Monroe* one-of-a-kind sculpture by Carl Hanforth. Carl's work is currently being shown in the first floor windows of the Gift Building (5th Avenue at 26th Streets, New York City).

11. *Sondra* by Yolanda Bello.

12. *Tasha* a one-of-a-kind wax-over-porcelain doll by Brigette Deval.

unique designs are ball-jointed with stainless steel springs to increase posability. Design standouts included *Country Girl* in a calico costume and a group of dolls fashioned after turn-of-the-century children, *Mama's Little Urchins*.

Susan Wakeen

Cynthia (*Illustration 1* of this article) is the 1986 Littlest Ballet's release. The 15½in (39.4cm) all-porcelain doll is jointed at the hips and shoulders, and the head moves. The 375-piece limited edition has paperweight eyes and human hair wigs. Each doll is signed, numbered and dated.

12.

13. Faith Wick's all-porcelain limited edition *Blue Fairy, Pinocchio* and *Gepetto* from the well-known story.

William Wiley

The book *In the Night Kitchen* by the famous illustrator Maurice Sendak served as the inspiration of three dolls from Manhattan Sandcastle. *Mickey* and two of the three *Bakers* are shown in *Illustration 9*. These dolls have porcelain heads on cloth bodies with wire armature. Limited to 25 of each doll.

Peter Wolf

Louis XIV, the Sun King of France, received a one-of-a-kind costume treatment, dressed in the costume Louis wore in a ballet as Apollo, the Sun King. The doll is between 12 and 15in (30.5 and 38.1cm) tall.

14. *Scarlett* (2255) by Alexander.

15. *Scarlett's Jubilee®* (1500) by Alexander.

14.

15.

Madame Alexander

Doll Reader bestowed its first *Lifetime Achievement* DOTY crystal award to Madame Alexander on February 14 in New York City. Madame was recognized for her enhancement of hundreds of different doll models for collectors and for being instrumental in building the doll industry since 1923. An exclusive interview with photographs featuring Madame Alexander will appear in the May 1986 **Doll Reader**.

This reporter in covering Toy Fair for the last ten years has never seen as many doll and costume changes as were in evidence in the Alexander Doll showroom. A reporter must choose, and Scarlett as a theme comes to the head of the class. The 21in (53.3cm) *Scarlett Portrait* (2255) doll is costumed in a white dress with a rose floral print accented by green velvet ribbons, a green parasol, and topped by a straw hat with flowers. Readers will recognize this as the dress from the barbecue at the opening of both the book and movie. *Sacrlett's Jubilee* (1500) is a redressed 14in (35.6cm) doll resplendent in the famous velvet bustle full-length gown with jacket and velvet bonnet.

Anili

Anili dolls, which are among "the finest Italian felt dolls," were shown for the first time at Toy Fair by their exclusive U.S. distributor, Pittsburgh Doll Company. Each doll and costume are individually made by hand and have many unique features, such as

hand-painted eyes. No two are exactly alike. These pressed felt dolls are from 16in (40.6cm) to 25in (63.5cm) tall and are dressed in felt of lush colors combined with the finest Swiss organdy and taffeta. They are trimmed with the felt applique and flowers that Elena Scavini, their originator, was so famous for. The large lady dolls, like *Rosemarye*, are complemented by a family of smaller toddlers and children as well as a line of small dolls and animals called the "Anili Toys." For 1986 there are five new models of dolls that include a lanky clown called *Wolfango*.

16. *Rosemarye* by Anili.

16.

17. *Amy* from the "Cherished Memories Series" by Phyllis Parkins.

19. Dakin's *Bag Lady* designed by Faith Wick.

The Collectables, Inc.

Amy and *Andrew*, 14in (35.6cm), of the "Cherished Memories Series" are nostalgic children sculpted and manufactured by Phyllis Parkins. These adorable children are outfitted in Victorian-style costumes. *Amy* wears a matte taffeta ecru dress decorated with French trim and silk ribbon. She holds her lovely Teddy Bear. *Andrew* in his burgundy velveteen and ecru costume has a handmade stickhorse.

Corolle

Madame Catherine Refabert introduced *Ophelie*, a 22in (55.9cm) doll wearing a "Pollyanna" dress with ballet slippers and pantalets. *Ariane*, a toddler doll 24in (61cm) tall, is dressed in a white snowsuit accented with a striped scarf. Her long blonde rooted hair and blue sleep eyes compliment the new soft vinyl skin of this "pudgy" doll.

Dakin

Dakin's Elegante line includes *Rumpelstiltskin* and the *Miller's Daughter* of vinyl and designed by Faith Wick. *Rumpelstiltskin*, 12in (30.5cm) tall, wears a box-pleated tunic and wool cape. He is accessorized with a felt elfin hat and gold leather pouch. The *Miller's Daughter*, 22in (55.9cm), wears a pink sheer fabric-draped hat and a crepe de chine dress and comes with her famous wooden spindle and gold thread.

Another addition to the line, also designed by Faith Wick, is the 12in (30.5cm) vinyl *Bag Lady*. Dressed in a camel-colored patch coat and "stylish" hat, she carries a small print handbag and woven bag holding her "treasures."

Dolls by Jerri

The porcelain dolls by Jerri McCloud are more innovative than ever and are going to continue to be collector favorites. Some of the 1986 dolls will have mohair wigs that are handmade in Germany and are a perfect scale for doll hair.

The gowns on the girl dolls are even more intricate and elaborate than in the past as evidenced by *Somebody* (*Illustration 6* on page 112 of this article). *Somebody* is the doll that completes the set of *Nobody*.

20. *Rainy Day* from the Saturday Evening Post Cover Collection by Signature Collection.

21. *Muhammed Ali* by Effanbee.

22. *Jackie Gleason as Ralph Kramden* and *Art Carney as Ed Norton* by Effanbee.

23. *Melissa* by From the Heart Originals.

Signature Collection

Four new dolls have been added to the series by the Signature Collection based on covers of the *Saturday Evening Post* by Norman Rockwell. These all porcelain dolls are *Rosie the Riveter; Going Out*, a young girl seated at a dressing table getting ready to go out; *Hollywood*, which shows an actor ready to have his makeup applied; and *A New Hat*, a young girl trying on a new hat. A new addition to the Saturday Evening Post Cover Collection is *Rainy Day* based on a cover by Linedecker. This blonde-haired porcelain headed doll is in a red dress and carries a large black umbrella, and has a porcelain dog.

Effanbee

Effanbee's most stunning 1986 offerings are five new celebrity dolls in vinyl. *Jackie Gleason as Ralph Kramden* and *Art Carney as Ed Norton* are from "The Honeymooners," an early television favorite. Both are 16½in (41.9cm) tall. *Muhammed Ali* is the second entry in the "Great Moments in Sports" series and is 18in (45.7cm) tall. *John F. Kennedy* is 16in (40.6cm) tall and is a good rendition of the 35th President. A flashy 18in (45.7cm) *Liberace* is the eighth "Legend Series" doll, a group that began in 1980 with the *W.C. Fields* doll.

Each of these dolls has unusually careful and accurate sculpting and is a good portrait of the celebrity represented. Each will have a limited production that will be restricted to 1986 only.

From the Heart Originals

Artist Lynne Laber's 1986 fabric and felt limited edition dolls are the second and third releases of the "Our Little Cousins" series. *Melissa*, the birthday cousin, is a darker skin-toned doll dressed in sky blue underdress and white eyelet yoked pinafore. To complete her outfit she has a full lace slip, bloomers, and Mary Jane shoes.

Meghan has blue-green eyes and freckles. She has red hair fashioned in ponytails and sausage curls. *Meghan* is attired in a teal textured dress with white collar and cuffs and a floppy hat.

Both dolls are limited editions of 300, signed, dated and numbered.

GTC

Eva-Marie Reick of German Toys & Crafts, Inc., introduced 25⅝in (65.1cm) *Sabine*, a doll she specially designed to sit by herself. Blonde-haired *Sabine* comes dressed in a sailor suit. 23in (58.4cm) *Marina*, who also sits unaided, wears a white pinafore over a pink dress. *Barbara*, 25⅝in (65.1cm) and blonde-haired, is a new doll dressed in a pink pinafore over an off-white blouse. All of Eva-Marie Reick's dolls have new outfits this year.

24.

25.

26.

27.

24. 1986 Silver Anniversary Limited Edition *La Patineuse* by Suzanne Gibson.

25. *Samantha* by Götz.

26. *Veronica* by Gorham from the "Southern Belle Series."

27. A Lollipop Series doll by Gillian Heal.

Suzanne Gibson

To commemorate Suzanne Gibson's 25 years in doll designing, Reeves International, Inc., is featuring *La Patineuse*, a silver anniversary limited edition doll (2000 dolls) in a classic skating outfit of green velvet trimmed in rabbit fur with a pair of silver skates and fur muff. Suzanne also designed a 12in (30.5cm) *Alice*, a limited edition based on the character from the Lewis Carroll classic together with her friends the 10in (25.4cm) *Rabbit*, 6in (15.2cm) *Dormouse*, and 11in (27.9cm) long *Cheshire Cat*. All animals of this set are by Steiff. *Alice* is a limited edition of 3000 sets.

The storybook series, which has been re-introduced in an 8in (20.3cm) size, features *Mary Had A Little Lamb* with a Steiff lamb as a 1986 limited edition (2000 sets). Others in the storybook collection are *Little Miss Muffet with Spider, Polly Put Her Kettle On with Tea Kettle* and *Little Girl With Curl and Parasol*.

Four dolls have been added to the Smithsonian Institution First Ladies series: *Angelica Singleton Van Buren, Harriet Lane Johnston, Lucretia Rudolph Garfield* and *Mamie Doud Eisenhower*.

Götz

Samantha is the first limited production doll for Götz. Limited to 5000 pieces worldwide, she is 21in (53.3cm) tall and has red hair and green eyes. Her lovely costume includes green velvet dress trimmed in white, a matching velvet hairbow and a parasol. *Samantha* comes with a certificate of authenticity and is signed and numbered.

Gorham

Gorham's new musical bride, *Elizabeth*, is 16in (40.6cm) tall and has a porcelain head, hands and feet. She wears an elegant bridal gown of satin and lace and a tiara and veil. She plays "I Love You Truly."

A new doll in their "Southern Belles Series" is 19in (48.3cm) *Veronica*. She has a porcelain face and paperweight eyes. Wearing a cornflower blue taffeta gown accented with pink nosegays and a coordinating hat, she plays "Beautiful Dreamer." *Veronica* is numbered, hallmarked and dated — open edition. (The February/ March 1986 **Doll Reader**, page 128, #7, featured *Colette* by Gorham.)

Halfpenny Houses

Gillian Heal's *Lollipop Dolls — Emily, Mary, Victoria* and *Daisy* (see February/ March 1986 **Doll Reader**, page 128, #8), are wearing dresses of floral fabric designed by Gillian Heal. The other two, *Tom* and *Charlotte*, wear knitted clothes.

28.

30.

29.

31.

28. Horsman's *Tynie Twins*, replicas of their 1924 baby.

29. The *Princes in the Tower* set with *King Richard III*, *Boy King Edward V* and *Boy Richard, Duke of York*.

30. *Kewpie Kards* are featured by Jesco, Inc., for 1986.

31. "Children's Party" by Lissi Dolls.

Horsman

The second in Horsman's five-year program of reproducing a nostalgic doll from the past is a replica of a baby first manufactured in 1924. This lovely doll is being produced as boy and girl. *Tynie Twins*, these 14in (35.6cm) boxed set replicas have soft bodies and faux composition arms and legs and are attractively priced. The babies' expressions are slightly frowning, like babies about to cry. The clothing is a copy of 1924 infant styling.

Also featured in the 1986 Horsman line is *The Horsman Family*, five girls and one boy. Exquisitely dressed, these include 21in (53.3cm) *Lynette*, 17in (43.2cm) *Antoinette*, 16in (40.6cm) *Leslie*, 19in (48.3cm) *Yvette*, 16in (40.6cm) *Yvonne* and 16in (40.6cm) *Terri-Anne*, the latter in a beautiful christening dress with matching hat and pillow.

House of Nisbet

The famous Portrait Gallery photograph of Queen Victoria in widow's dress has been made into a doll and added to the Wax Doll Collection by House of Nisbet.

Two new 16in (40.6cm) vinyl portrait models of *Princess Diana*, one in formal state dress and one to commemorate her visit to the United States, have been added to the line. An 18in (45.7cm) *Prince William* in sailor suit and *Prince Harry* in sunsuit join their mother.

The new limited editions include *Peter Bull*; the *Statue of Liberty*; *Elizabeth I*, which is a replica of an early Nisbet doll; and *The Princes in the Tower* set (illustrated) which includes *King Richard III* and his nephews Boy King Edward V and *Boy Richard, Duke of York*.

A new Alison Nisbet doll is a 15in (38.1cm) *Gibson Girl* in a striking black gown accented with jewels and a fuschia feather boa. (See the February/March 1986 **Doll Reader**, page 130, #20 for Alison Nisbet Morning Doll.)

Jesco, Inc.

1986 is the tenth anniversary of Jesco, Inc. For this occasion President Nancy Villaseñor has designed new costumes for the various vinyl *Kewpies*, including some winsome *Christmas Kewpies* in plaids and winter attire. A really exciting 1986 *Kewpie* is a 6in (15.2cm) hard plastic doll with jointed arms that is packaged in a box, a *Kewpie Kard* (see illustration) which has Rose O'Neill artwork on the front. These cards are appropriate for various holiday and anniversary occasions.

The 6in (15.3cm) *Nancy Ann Dolls* line is expanded and a highlight is the "American Ladies Series," four deluxe styles with brass ornaments carried by each doll that is wearing "liberty fabrics."

Lissi Dolls

Lissi Dolls are made in the Sonneberg-Neustadt area of West Germany, which has been a doll producing region of Germany since 1600.

Some Lissi Dolls that will have great appeal to collectors are made with cloth bodies that are jointed on discs, a method perfected in Germany in the late 19th century. These are the 18in (45.7cm) "Children's Party" boy and girl and the "Cycling Tour" boy and girl in the same size. The Bavarian "October Festival" (see illustration) boy and girl are appropriately costumed for fall and are 19¾in (50.3cm). The "Outing to the Moor" couple are 21¾in (55.3cm) and wear charming country-style costumes. These dolls all have vinyl heads with rooted hair and sleep eyes.

Some cute babies, the "Half-Hour Baby," now come wih rooted hair and hand-painted closed eyes, as well as with glass eyes. They are 11in (27.9cm), 17in (43.2cm), and 21in (53.3cm). All of the pastel clothing features smocking or eyelet trim.

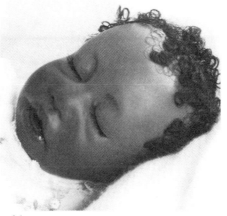

32.   34.

32. *Bird of Paradise* and *Madame Butterfly*, two 14in (35.6cm) "Flying Foxxies" by Marin with hand-painted porcelain heads.

33. *Barbie*® and *The Rockers*™ dolls by Mattel, Inc. Left to right: *Derek*™ doll, *Barbie*,® *Dana*,™ *Diva*™ and *Dee Dee*.™

34. *Dear One* by Middleton Doll Company.

35. *Audrey* a 20in (50.8cm) hand painted face with blonde hair. Double-layered, delicately patterned cotton dress designed by Pierre Cardin.

35.

33.

Lenci

New from Lenci is the reintroduction of the pouty face for several of their models: 19in (48.3cm) *Rosamunda (Illustration #6)*, wearing a white ruffled layered dress with black trim and green jacket holding flowers and her yellow hat; 19in (48.3cm) *Marta* in her blue dress with white and pink organdy apron and carrying a feather duster; 19in (48.3cm) *Glenda* costumed in a brown pinafore with orange and yellow flowers on it, over a white blouse, and wearing her wide brimmed orange hat; 22in (55.9cm) *Adriana* in a white dress with blue trim and a blue bow in her hair; and 22in (55.9cm) *Carola* wearing a green coat and hat with fur trim and carrying her white muff.

In the 13in (33cm) size the new dolls: *Alice* wearing an unusual scalloped dress in shades of yellow and orange with a wreath on her hair; *Aldo* in brown short pants and white shirt with a brown tie; and *Diana* costumed similarly to *Chiara* (see November 1985 **Doll Reader**, page 164).

Lloyderson Dolls

The leading collector dolls from Lloyderson Dolls are the Marin dolls from Spain. There are more than 50 new models for 1986, including three new concepts. One *avant garde* group

is the four models of the 14in (35.6cm) "Flying Foxxies" (porcelain heads/cloth bodies), creating fantastic creatures covered with feathers, sequins and rich materials. There are 10 models of the 16in (40.6cm) "Teen Classics" (porcelain heads/cloth bodies). These girls have such titles as *Spring Dame*, *Farmer's Daughter* and *Gypsy Girl*. The "City Characters" are of a pale colored vinyl depicting modernistic clowns and harlequins of 22in (55.9cm) (*Dallas Extravaganza, Miami Creation* and *Chicago Fantasy*). The Marin "Selection Line" of traditional Spanish costumes is offered in a 14in (35.6cm) size as well as 18in (45.7cm) versions.

Mattel Toy Company

Mattel's *Barbie*® is presented in several new 1986 models. *Magic Moves Barbie* has a switch that allows her arms to move up and back to push her hair in place or to perform other gestures. *Dream Glow Barbie* and *Ken* have sparkling costumes with stars on them that glow in the dark. A line of fashions for both dolls also has the glow in the dark ability; there are also a bed and a vanity for *Barbie* with the same aspect.

Astronaut Barbie is a space explorer dressed in a glittery space suit that can change into a sparkly skirt and tights. *Barbie and the Rockers* are

Barbie and her new friends *Derek*, *Diva*, *Dana* and *Dee Dee*, all wearing trendy fashions in neon colors. This group has a stage for swimsuits that match. The girls have the longest hair ever on *Barbie* dolls. For 1986 there will be a special collector's edition porcelain *Barbie* that is similar in design to the early *Barbie* dolls. Also in the Department Store Special line will be a *Greek Barbie*.

The Middleton Doll Company

Lee Middleton's fabulous *First Moments* sleeping baby of 1985 now has a 21in (53.3cm) baby brother called *Bubba Chuckles*. He has rooted blonde hair and blue eyes and is dressed in green. *Dear One* is a cute 18in (45.7cm) sleeping black preemie with real lashes. *First Moments*, Lee's first big success, and a 1985 Dolls Of The Year nominee, now also comes with open eyes as well as sleeping eyes.

Mundia

Mundia has an extensive new line of dolls, both in all-cloth and porcelain. The 14 Mundia dolls are costumed by Pierre Cardin and additional models dressed by Cardin will arrive in the United States in mid-summer. All of the cloth dolls have hand-painted faces and synthetic hair.

37.

36. *Minet-Cherie* by The China Doll comes in a smocked dress, party dress and coat and hat with pram - a doll and dog as accessories.

37. 1986 *Sari* by *Sasha* Dolls.

38. Pat Campano's "Footlight Fantasy" from Schmid.

36.

38.

Heidi Ott
It was reported that this Swiss doll maker is cutting back on her doll production by about 50 percent. There are costume changes on many models.

Lynne & Michael Roche
Original Daisy, 14 to 17in (36 to 43cm) and *Minet-Cherie*, 5in (13cm) are new for 1986. All the dolls are hand-crafted by Lynne and Michael Roche at their studio in Bath, England, using real hair wigs, glass paperweight eyes and, whenever possible, pure cotton, wool and silk for costuming. *Florence*, a 1985 DOTY nominee is still in their line.

Rothschild
In addition to the new *Betsy McCall*, *Edith — The Lonely Doll*™ is offered in both a 12in (30.5cm) vinyl size in a pink cotton dress and an 8in (20.3cm) hard plastic size with bending knees. The 12in (30.5cm) *Molly* has four new outfits.

Royal House of Dolls
Miss Elsa of Royal House of Dolls offers the collector a number of new

selections for 1986. Her *Royal Court Collection* consists of four (12in [30.5cm]) dolls with new faces, elaborate hairdos and fancy ballgowns (*Candice, Constance, Carolyn* and *Cynthia*). To join *Gretchen*, a 1985 DOTY nominee, is the 21in (53.3cm) *Hänschen (Illustration #7)* who is dressed in a Tyrolean outfit. An 18in (45.7cm) *Grandmother*, a new addition and a remake of a 1959 Royal doll is offered this year. She is wearing a dress, cape and purse in shades of purple and pink. Another new series is the *Daughter* and *Mother Collection* featuring 12in (30.5cm) daughter and 15in (38.1cm) mother in coordinating outfits. The *Royal Calendar Collection* features 12in (30.5cm) dolls representing the month of the year. *May, August,* and *December* are offered this year.

The second limited edition doll in the *Night at the Opera Series* is 15in (38.1cm) *LaScala* in a heavy red, blue and gold brocaded gown. She has a feather jewel in her elegantly styled hair. In the *Mary Jane Growing Up* in the USA Series, *Maine* and *Colorado* are new with *Missouri* and *Michigan*

scheduled to follow. The five dolls in the 1986 *Limited Edition Christmas* collection are in outfits of a different fabric wearing old-fashioned styled gold outfits with touches of Christmas colors of green and red.

Sasha Dolls
Sasha Dolls announced the introduction of four new models for 1986. It was also announced that after these dolls were sold and after whatever little inventory remained of previous models was sold, *Sasha* dolls would cease to be made. John and Sara Doggart, guardians of *Sasha*, have decided to retire and, as of press time, have found no one who could continue the tradition and style of workmanship under which *Sasha* is made. Very limited quantities of the 1986 *Princess Sasha, Sasha Sari* (see illustration), *Sasha Hiker* and *Sasha Skier* have already been made and no further production is contemplated.

Schmid
The "Footlight Fantasy" trio by Pat Campano is a delightful group artfully dressed to coordinate with

39. Faith Wick's *Wicked Witch.*

40. *Concha* and *Carrie* by Judith Turner.

41. *Ginny* from the *Encore Collection* made of porcelain.

their respective musical themes. *Buffo,* in his colorful tails and gold bow, plays "Music, Music, Music," while *Fritz,* the hobo, in an appropriate costume including patches, plays "If I Were A Rich Man." The third clown, *Happy Hooper* wears a lavender wig and hooper costume of orange, yellow and lavender stripes. He plays, "That's Entertainment."

Silvestri

Silvestri's 1986 Faith Wick artist doll is the 29in (73.7cm) porcelain *Wicked Witch,* signed by the artist and in a worldwide edition of 1313. In addition, all of Faith Wick's *Alice* series has been produced in mini-size as Christmas ornaments.

Also new in the Silvestri line is *Pickles,* a 33in (83.8cm) clown designed by Mary Lake-Thompson, and 13½in (36.9cm) *Catherine* of the "Fancipants" series by the same artist.

Steiff Dolls

In the decades since Margarete Steiff last produced her distinctive felt dolls, collectors have sought after examples. Because of the low number available versus the demand by collectors, prices on the collectors' market have escalated. Margarete Steiff has decided to once again recreate very special examples from their archives and museum. The *Tennis Lady* and the *Gentleman* (see *Illustration 2*) are being made in 1986 and in a limited edition.

Turner Dolls

Among the 1986 line of dolls by Judith Turner are 18in (45.7cm) *Concha* and *Carrie.* Each limited to 250 pieces, they have a porcelain head, arms and legs. *Concha* has black hair and wears a christening outfit, while *Carrie* has blonde hair and wears an appropriate baby costume.

Chelsea is another in the 1986 line. Also limited to 250 pieces, she is 26in (66cm) tall, has a porcelain head, arms and legs, blue eyes, blonde hair and wears a lovely original white fur costume.

Vogue — Ginny

Ginny, the 8in (20.3cm) Vogue classic manufactured by Meritus Industries, will radiate even more collector appeal in 1986 as Vogue introduces an all new collection of vinyl and porcelain dolls and new "traditional" hard plastic bodied dolls.

Designed especially as collectibles, the hard plastic body *Ginny* dolls feature the same "little girl" look, and the hair is stylable because it is rooted. Rooted hair on 8in (20.3cm) dolls is unusual.

Ginny will be adorned in a whole new wardrobe of fashions this year including costumes from the Lollipop Collection, the Holiday Collection, the Fantasy Collection and the Ovation Collection. In addition, *Ginny* now has her own furniture including a shiny brass bed with a ruffled spread and canopy, a travel trunk and a wooden bed, vanity and wardrobe.

Mr. and *Mrs. Santa Claus* have been added to the Famous Pairs Series and are dressed appropriately.

The *Coronation Ginny* is making an encore appearance as are *Little One, Communion, Angel* and *Ballerina.*

121

42. 14in (35.6cm) *Little Women Series* by Robin Woods. Clockwise starting at the left: *Meg, Jo, Amy* and *Beth*.

43. New octagonal display case offered by World Doll is an accessory to the *Princess Collection*.

44. Left to right: *Colin, Patrick* and *Jean* by R. John Wright.

Robin Woods

Robin Woods, Inc. has acquired the rights to Associated Dollmakers, whose leading sculptors were Yolando Bello and Avigail Brahms and now are offering vinyl editions. Ms. Woods' philosophy of doll making is to produce dolls that are meant to be playthings, not just collectibles that must be kept in the original boxes. The "Childhood Classics" collection is a feature of the line with such storybook characters as *Little Women, Anne of Green Gables Pollyanna* and *Larissa* from *Dr. Zhivago*. The costumes are very special with detailed miniature prints in pleasing color combinations, and they are also washable and durable. The faces on the vinyl dolls are hand painted, giving them more individualism.

The Robin Woods line still includes her traditional mask face, soft body dolls like *Stevie as Yankee Doodle*, a little boy on a wooden rocking horse.

World Doll

Celebrity dolls continue to be an integral part of the offerings of World. New for 1986 are *Fred Astaire* and *Ginger Rogers*, 19in (48.3cm) vinyl (see *Illustration #4*); *Judy Garland* from *Easter Parade*, 18in (45.7cm) vinyl; the *Can Can* Doll (Toulouse Latrec move over!); and a group of 8in (20.3cm) vinyl dolls known as the *Princess Collection* (see illustration). The *Princess Collection* included five different dolls noted for their intricate costumes. An accessory, the plastic octagonal display case (see illustration) received much favorable comment. It is produced for ease of hanging vertically (8in [20.3cm] dolls of many manufacturers will fit nicely) or horizontally (great for miniature scenes). The consumer retail price of $10 was judged very reasonable.

R. John Wright

John continued in the tradition of his 1985 Dolls Of The Year Limited Edition Doll (All Other Mediums) with *Christopher Robin - Series 2*. The 19in (48.3cm) *Christopher Robin* is dressed in pants, shirt, suspenders and Wellington boots. Both boy and bear are protected from the rain by an umbrella. The *Childhood Classics* series continues with a 20in (50.8cm) *Little Red Riding Hood*.

Here the similarity stops as John has initiated a new design look to the faces of his beguiling felt children dolls.

The new series called *Little Brother, Little Sister* features faces sculpted directly from the two eldest children of the Wrights. Collectors will be amazed with the posability offered by the new ball and socket neck joint and by the realistic look of rooted mohair wigs. *Arthur*, is 18in (45.7cm) and *Lillian* is 20in (50.8cm), and they are limited to 250 of each. Other dolls in this series (see illustration) are *Patrick* a red haired "urchin" in bib overalls; *Colin*, a 20in (50.8cm) little brother with red hair and vest; and *Jean*, an 18in (45.7cm) little sister.

45. 1986 *Christmas Doll* by Zapf.

46. *Molly Mayfly* by Johannes Zook Originals.

This *sampling* of new dolls introduced and shown at the 1986 American International Toy Fair provides you with a starting point for your quests. Visit your favorite local or mail-order, full-service doll store, toy or department store to see these dolls and many other worthy examples to consider adding to your collection. You may wait to see actual models where they can be closely examined, but the collector vies to "be first" and some of the job is in the "hunting"!

Thank you for voting for the "Public's Choice" for *1985 Dolls Of The Year*. Doll manufacturers have already started to speak to your tastes in the changes and new models offered in 1986. The **1986 Dolls Of The Year** program has been kicked off and ballots will be available at your local retailer, doll, toy or department store in late May. The International Doll Academy is now carefully examining the 1986 doll submissions from world-wide doll manufacturers. Everyone is carefully awaiting IDA's nominations! □

Zapf Dolls

The *1986 Christmas Doll* is 20in (50.8cm) with red dress, white apron, and real leather shoes. The body is signed by Brigitte Zapf, the designer. The 1985 *Easter Doll* at 21½in (54.6cm) with rabbit suit (yes, floppy rabbit ears) and is accompanied by a basket for gathering Easter eggs.

Johannes Zook Originals

Many new porcelain dolls were introduced at Toy Fair. Another new model is *Molly Mayfly*, a 20in (50.8cm) porcelain fairy with silver-speckled leotards with a translucent overlay and wings. The intricate blonde wig completes this piece.

47. Margarete Steiff of Germany will re-issue two of their felt dolls in 1986. *Tennis Lady*, which was first made in 1913, is dressed in white sport costume and hat and *Gentleman*, which was first made in 1914, is dressed in frock coat and top hat. These dolls will be limited to 3000 each (1500 of which will be distributed in the United States). Accompanying these two dolls is the *Teddy Clown* (replica of 1926 bear) that comes fully jointed, squeeze voice and dressed in a clown hat. *Tennis Lady, Gentleman* and *Teddy Clown* are exclusively available and distributed in the United States by Reeves International.

48. England's Sasha Dolls, Ltd. introduces *Princess Sasha* as their 1986 Limited Edition. The sixth in a series, *Princess Sasha's* outfit consists of a pink frilled dress which is accented at the hip with a wide blue velvet sash. A blue velvet cape, lined in pink to match her dress and shoes completes the outfit. Only 3500 *Princess Sasha* will be made (each numbered and accompanied by a signed certificate of authenticity). Distributed exclusively in the United States by International Playthings.

Cloth Dolls, A Collector's Delight

by **Barbara Guyette**

Illustration 1. 6½in (16cm) *Benjamin Franklin* from the Bicentennial Commemorative Doll set by Hallmark Cards, Inc.; all cotton cloth; full color printed details front and back; seam joints at hips, elbows and knees; removable coat over printed clothing with lace trim cravat and cuffs; printed label sewn into seam of doll; sold packaged in "house" shaped box that opens like a greeting card to reveal inner display window doll compartment. Doll may be removed from box through a flap at the top of the box. 1976.

Who among us does not have a special place in their heart for a rag doll? Since man first produced fabric, there have been rags with which to create dolls. But alas — rag dolls are fragile dolls, and many times showed considerably less artistic skills than their carved counterparts. For this reason, cloth dolls were often discarded, with all but the elaborate ones from wealthy families preserved, due in part to the quality and the fine workmanship of the more expensive cloth doll.

Authenticated examples of cloth dolls before the year 1800 are rarely seen, even in museums. Cloth dolls are usually included in textile collections rather than in doll collections. It is also true that collectors have tended to neglect rag-type dolls in favor of more beautiful ones. Cloth doll appeal seems to be favored by collectors of folk art.

It has not been until recent years that doll collectors have realized the true worth of the cloth doll. If one seeks out the good examples of early cloth dolls, it will be seen that many are extremely fine, with their construction and artistry holding its own among the wax and wooden dolls of the same period.

It was the American toy maker that first realized the need to create a sturdy doll that would stand up to the rugged pioneer life. Their most successful products were the ones that could stand up to rough conditions and did not need the careful handling, as did the dolls of their European counterparts.

The greatest advance in the history of the cloth doll developed from the introduction of cheaper textile printing methods. In the late 19th century, rag dolls were printed and sold in sheet form, a process which revolutionized

traditional methods. Doll designers and manufacturers flocked to the textile mills to explore the possibilities of the new techniques. It was the cloth distributors and printers rather than the doll makers that produced some of the earliest printed dolls. These doll sheets were sold by the panel or yard, from drapers' shops, and in dry goods stores, making them widely available as they had never been before. The sheet on which the doll was produced bore instructions such as "Sew together, and stuff with cotton batting, and sawdust."

This technique of printing dolls was particularly suited to creating dolls of a novelty nature, such as dolls for advertising, and dolls with a different character printed on each side. The printed cloth doll craze even saw the production of life-size cutouts that could be costumed in life-size clothes!

One of the most successful and well-known cloth doll sets was the celebrated Palmer Cox Brownies, patented in 1892. They were 12 in number and all came on 1yd (.91m) of printed cloth. The Brownie Camera is said to derive its name from the figures, whose popularity was overwhelming. The yard of Brownies cost a mere 20¢!

The Hallmark greeting card company continued in the cloth doll traditions of the past when, in 1976, they produced a set of our exquisitely detailed Bicentennial Commemorative portrait dolls. The set, which included, *George* and *Martha Washington, Benjamin Franklin* and *Betsy Ross*, was based on historical research and sold as exact replicas of their prototypes. Each came packed in a uniquely designed "house" that represented either the character's home or surroundings in which he or she functioned. Open the "door" and you will find a brief biographical sketch of the occupant. The back of the package identifies the building the package represents.

Due to the excellent quality of the dolls and their inexpensive price tag,

Illustration 2. *George* and *Martha Washington* dolls from the Bicentennial Commemorative collection. A set of four dolls included *George* and *Martha Washington, Benjamin Franklin* and *Betsy Ross* (not shown). The dolls make up the first group of collectible cloth dolls produced in 1976 by Hallmark Cards, Inc., Kansas City, Missouri. All dolls were considered miniature portraits of their prototypes.

Illustration 3. Hallmark Cards, Inc., produced a second group of collectible 6½in (16cm) printed cloth dolls, the Holiday Dolls. Shown, left to right: *Winifred the Witch, Santa Claus, Indian Maiden* and the *Little Drummer Boy*, with their box "houses."

the dolls were extremely sought-after, particularly by doll collectors. Each member of the set, in package, sold for $2.50.

Within the following two years, the Hallmark company introduced a second group of similar cloth dolls, known as Holiday Dolls. The holiday set included *Winifred the Witch* for Halloween, an *Indian Maiden* for Thanksgiving, *Santa Claus* and the *Little Drummer Boy* for Christmas. All were packaged as the set before them, in appropriately decorated,

"house" boxes, each with a printed holiday message on the inside.

Now the doll collecting boom had really hit the Hallmark company! The year 1979 saw the release of a series of six dolls called Collectible Doll "Famous Americans" Series I. The members of the set were such notables as *Annie Oakley, Babe Ruth, Chief Joseph, George Washington Carver, Amelia Earhart* and *Susan B. Anthony*. Each packaged doll sold for $4.00.

In 1980, a Series II of "Famous Americans" was produced, but never

marketed to the public. Instead, the labeled Hallmark dolls were sold through special offers, unboxed, but with a certificate of authenticity. This set included *Molly Pitcher, Davey Crockett, Mark Twain, Clara Barton* and *P. T. Barnum*.

The illustrations featured here show all of the Hallmark cloth dolls, with the exception of *Betsy Ross*. Do you have one in your collection? They help us to celebrate our recent achievements in the art of the cloth doll! □

125

CLOCKWISE: Illustration 4. *Winifred the Witch* is shown here, snugly packaged in her holiday house box. A Halloween poem about her is printed on the inside of the box door. Each doll of the Holiday Set sold for $3.00, perfectly packaged in its own display case!

Illustration 5. A close-up of *Babe Ruth*, Collectible Doll "Famous Americans" Series I. Shown with *Babe* is his personal history printed on the inside of the door of the display box.

Illustration 6. *Annie Oakley, Babe Ruth* and *Chief Joseph*, three dolls from the Collectible Doll "Famous Americans" Series I set by Hallmark Cards, Inc., shown with their original boxes.

Illustration 7. Collectible Doll "Famous Americans" Series I, left to right: *George Washington Carver, Amelia Earhart* and *Susan B. Anthony*, shown seated in front of their open display boxes.

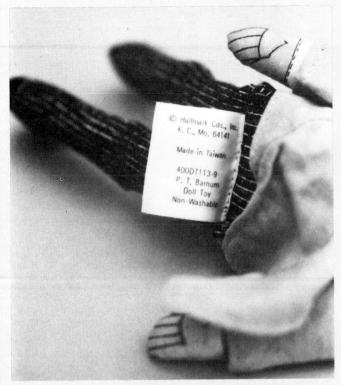

Illustration 8. Each Hallmark cloth doll has a label sewn into a seam. In addition to the information shown on the tag, the reverse side gives information on material contents and state license numbers.

Illustration 9. A stack of Hallmark doll boxes. End flaps show the various labeling of each different doll series.

Illustration 10. The final series of Hallmark cloth dolls, Collectible Doll "Famous Americans" Series II, produced but never boxed or marketed. From left to right: *Mark Twain, Clara Barton, Davey Crockett, Molly Pitcher* and *P. T. Barnum.*

Illustration 11. The *Martha Washington* doll was packaged in a box which represents her Mt. Vernon home. Each of the unique Hallmark boxes includes a brief history on the back.

The Latest Doll Faces at Toy Fair 1988 Part One

Every year sees new and stimulating doll designs being born. Some years see the birthing of an extraordinary group of dolls and concepts. 1988 is such a year! There is a bevy of porcelain, cloth, hard plastic, vinyl, and wooden dolls for collectors to choose from. For those that said that dolls will not be made any longer in America — do we have news for you. Young and growing American doll companies are releasing stimulating and exciting models guaranteed to please, and sure to start additional collections. The best from the old world continues to fascinate collectors, even though the drop in the dollar's value will mean that we must dig deeper into our pockets. There are so many models worthy of special picturing and describing that it will take several issues of **DOLL READER** magazine to do them justice. So get out your pencil and paper and start rating the dolls from one to ten — and we guarantee you.will create a long wish list!

1. Annette Himstedt

Annette Himstedt is the creator of those adorable "Barefoot Children," and now she has turned her talents to making another series of life-like children called "Blessed Are The Children." The 30in (76cm) dolls include *Kasimir*, a *Japanese girl*, *Malin*, *Makimura* and *Fredericka*.

2. The Collectables

Tabatha is 3rd in a series of porcelain Fairy Dolls in a limited edition of 1,500. She is dressed in aqua chiffon, has lavender eyes, and is in a setting of trees and a pond. 12½in (32cm) high, she is signed, dated and numbered by the artist. Phyllis Parkins, the designer won two DOTY® Awards for 1987 and her doll models were snapped up during Toy Fair.

Tabatha is the 3rd in a Series of Fairy dolls. Limited edition of 1,500. Dressed in aqua chiffon, lavender eyes, pond and tree is all cold cast porcelain. 12½in (32cm). Signed, dated and numbered by artist, Phyllis Parkins.

3. Alexander Doll Company, Inc.

Madame Alexander was the first recipient of the DOTY® Lifetime Award in 1986. This year's Alexander dolls are a reflection of the quality of the costumes expected from this concern. Four of the new 14in (36cm) dolls from the "Classic Series" are: *Bo Peep*, *Mary Mary*, *Bessy Bell* and *Mary Gray*. There were a multitude of costume changes and new doll models — more so than in recent memory.

Dolls by Pauline are introducing two new Oriental dolls, *Lan Tau* (a boy) and *Ping Chow* (a girl). The dolls have porcelain heads, hands and feet on cloth bodies and are appropriately dressed — *Lan Tau* wears a costume with dragon decoration embroidered on the front (for the Year of the Dragon) and Ping Chow's costume is decorated with chickens (designating purity). The dolls stand 18in (46cm) tall and are a limited edition of 1,500 each.

Madame Alexander — shown are four of the all new 14in (36cm) dolls for 1988 from the Classics Series. Upper right — *Bo Peep*; lower right — *Mary Mary*; upper left — *Bessy Bell*; lower left — *Mary Gray*.

4. Corolle

Reflecting the style of the French Impressionists are *Gigi* and *Rosanne*. *Gigi* is a blonde doll wearing a floral print dress trimmed in eyelet and a pink straw hat decorated with pink roses. *Rosanne* has brown rooted hair and wears a white print dress with large pink and aqua flowers and a full-sleeved striped blouse all trimmed with white eyelet. The 21in (53cm) vinyl dolls were designed by Catherine Refabert.

Gigi (left) and **Rosanne (right) by Corolle.**

5. Dakin

This year's *Ginny* Line includes many specials, among them in the "Fantasy Collection" is *Ginny* as a *Court Jester, Pollyanne* and a *Miss Ginny 1988*, all hard plastic dolls. Collectors are pleased that *Ginny's* new owners are meeting their needs so cleverly.

Ginny as Court Jester, by Dakin.

4.

5.

6. Gorham

"Bonnets and Bows" is Gorham's first limited collection of all-porcelain, fully-jointed dolls. *Jesse* has brown hair and blue paperweight eyes. He wears burgundy velvet knickers, white satin shirt and an argyle sweater. He comes with his very own wooden rocking horse. *Jesse* stands 17in (43cm) and is limited to an edition of 1,000 dolls.

Jesse, by Gorham.

7. Hildegard Günzel

This year Hildegard Günzel introduced a new line of 30in (76cm) vinyl dolls, all of them with her special touch of realism and beautifully costumed. Shown here are *Edith* and her companion doll *Matthias* dressed in plum velvet with white lace trim, and the charming *Doris* wearing an outfit described by the artist as "white eyelet rompers."

New vinyl dolls by Hildegard Gunzel. Left: *Edith*. **Right:** *Matthias*. **Foreground:** *Doris*.

6.

7.

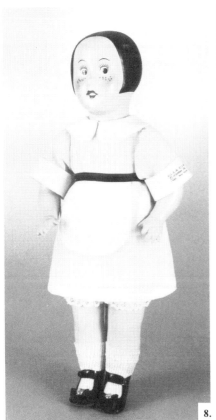

8. Horsman

This year, Horsman presents the replica of their 1925 *Ella Cinders* doll based on the rags to riches comic strip character created by Bill Conselman and Charlie Plumb. *Ella Cinders* stands 18in (46cm) tall, has black painted hair, round painted eyes, freckles and a cloth body. The doll's vinyl components look just like the original composition material from which the dolls were first made. She is limited to a 3,000 piece numbered edition.

9. Wendy Lawton Dolls

For her 70th anniversary the Gruelle family licensed Lawtons to produce *Marcella and Raggedy Ann*. *Marcella*, who was Johnny Gruelle's daughter in real life, is a 14in (36cm) tall porcelain doll and carries a miniature *Raggedy Ann* cloth doll. This is a limited edition of 2,500 dolls.

8.
9.

11.

10.

10. The Littlest Ballet Co., Inc.

Julie and *Jason*, baby dolls, are 22in (56cm) tall. *Julie* wears a pastel colored dress, and *Jason* is outfitted in a blue jumpsuit. Both vinyl dolls are a limited edition of 2,500 pieces or one year's production.

11. Great American Doll Company

Martina, by artist Rotraut Schrott, radiates simple charm and a Mona Lisa smile that has mystified generations. Her shoulder head, arms and legs are made of "Cernit," a synthetic resin sculpting clay. The arms and legs are wired and bendable, and she has a cloth body, human hair wig and painted eyes. *Martina* is 24in (61cm) tall.

Martina, by GADCO.

12. Mattel

Showing one of their strongest lines ever, Mattel has discovered the doll collector! *Barbie®, Whitney* and *Ken* are all "Perfume Giving" as well as doctors. Shown here in our report is *Perfume Pretty™ Barbie®*.

Perfume Pretty™ Barbie® with signature *Barbie®* fragance.

13. The Middleton Doll Company, Inc.

The Middleton Doll Company presented *Simplicity*, a 20in (51cm) vinyl doll dressed in a three-piece burgundy corduroy suit with white blouse and knee-high black patent leather boots. She has a dark synthetic wig and acrylic paperweight eyes.

Simplicity, by the Middleton Doll Company, Inc.

12.

13.

14. Louis Nichole

Raffina, by Louis Nichole, is an all-porcelain 16in (41cm) doll wearing a costume of inverted pleated chiffon with silk style edging on capelet and hemline. She has a long brown human hair wig tied on back with a matching bow.

Raffina, by artist Louis Nichole.

15. Margarete Steiff Dolls

1988 is the first year the new line of hard plastic Steiff dolls are available in the United States. *Babette*, a 20in (51cm) doll with hand-painted face and arms, fabric body with jointed legs, and human hair wig, is dressed in the best fabrics. In all, there are six models at 16½in (42cm) and six models at 20in (51cm). Each doll comes with the "button in ear" and a 24-karat gold-plated Steiff brooch and certificate of authenticity.

Babette, by Margarete Steiff GmbH.

14.

15.

16. Vlasta Dolls

The Vlasta line of porcelain dolls are elaborately costumed with rows of English batiste, lace and ribbons. *Marney*, Pat Thompson's most successful doll this year, is 16in (41cm) tall with blue eyes and blonde hair. She comes with her little dog *Quentin*.

Marney, designed by Pat Thompson for Vlasta Dolls.

17. Helga Weich Dolls

Helga Weich dolls are handcrafted with wooden heads with hand-painted faces, soft bodies, human hair wigs and handmade clothes. Helga's studio is located in the hilltops surrounded by the beautiful forests of Franconia, West Germany.

Helga Weich dolls. Left: *Elizabeth* 18in (46cm). Right: *Caitlin*, 18in (46cm). Foreground: *Ingrid*, 13in (33cm).

Tiffany, a Vlasta doll from Thompson Associates, stands 19in (48cm) tall to the top of her elaborately decorated hat. The doll's head, hands and feet are of poured synthetic material and hand-painted; her wig is of English mohair. She is costumed in mauve cotton batiste with cotton netting on the sleeves, French lace trim, and hand-embroidered plisse trim from France.

18. 19. 20. Robin Woods

The "Camelot Castle Collection" of 14in (36cm) vinyl dolls by Robin Woods includes *Little Arthur, Young Lancelot, Little Queen Guinevere, Lady Elaine, Lady Linet*, the evil *Morgan Le Fey* and *Amuse*. Beautiful wigs and gorgeous detailing makes these a "must" for serious collectors.

Little Queen Guinevere.   Young Lancelot.

Little Arthur.

16.

17.

18.

19.

20.

The Latest Doll Faces at Toy Fair 1988
Part Two

Anna Marie, by Karin Heller.

1b. *Chuck* and *Megan* are two new all wood dolls created in a limited edition by Ha Payne. The dolls are 19in (48cm) tall, ball and spring-jointed at the neck, shoulders elbows, wrists, hips and knees which makes them fully posable. The handmade mohair wigs and costumes complete the picture of two young country children. Two black dolls named *Cody* and *Tish* will also appear at Toy Fair this year.

1a.

1.   **Karin Heller Dolls**

For 1988 Karin Heller of West Germany has created eight new designs in cloth dolls 19in (48cm) tall. These are brother and sister pairs, among which are *Anna Marie* (illustrated) and her brother/companion doll *Johann*. Karin Heller scale model wooden dolls' houses and furniture to fit her 18 to 20in (46 to 51cm) dolls are now available in the United States.

1a. Celebrating *Dolly Dingle's* 75th anniversary. House of Global Art and award-winning designer Bette Ball will present this limited edition Diamond Jubilee doll at Toy Fair 1988. The doll comes with a "diamond" heart pendant and a music box that plays "Diamonds Are A Girl's Best Friend." Articulated for posing, the doll has porcelain head, hands and legs on a cloth body, plastic eyes and a synthetic wig that is "curlable." *Dolly Dingle* stands 16in (41cm) tall.

2. R. John Wright Dolls, Inc.

Walt Disney's *Snow White & the 7 Dwarfs* are all felt dolls by R. John Wright and limited to an edition of 2,500 each. The first 1,000 will be as matched numbered sets. *Snow White* is 17in (43cm) tall; the *Dwarfs* are 9in (23cm) tall. *Snow White-Rags*, 17in (43cm) tall, wears the tattered costume worn early in the film and carries a wooden bucket. This edition is limited to 1,000 dolls.

Walt Disney's *Snow White & the 7 Dwarfs*, by R. John Wright. *Left to right: Sleepy, Happy, Sneezy, Doc, Bashful, Dopey* and *Grumpy. Snow White* is in the back.

3. Victoria Impex Corporation

Nosegay is a set of all porcelain dolls consisting of mother, 14in (36cm), child, 6in (15cm) and small fairy, 4½in (12cm), all set on a wooden base with grass. This is the second piece from the "Enchanted Moment Collection" designed by Cindy M. McClure and limited to 1,500 pieces.

Nosegay from the "Enchanted Moment Collection" by Victoria Impex Corporation.

4. Bello Creations

Yolanda Bello's newest original porcelain doll is *Zephyr*, a seductive 17in (43cm) black lady cast in one piece to the waist, and reclining on a white polar bear rug.

***Zephyr*, by Yolanda Bello.**

5. American Beauty Dolls

A series of twelve 18in (46cm) hand crafted felt dolls were designed and produced by Shirley Peck of California. All of the dolls are in extremely limited editions and each is signed and numbered by the artist and has a "Certificate of Authenticity."

***Miss American Beauty Rose*, by American Beauty Dolls.**

6. Madame Alexander

Dressed in the most fashionable styles of the 19th and 20th centuries, the *Portrettes* bring back the romance of the past. These 10in (25cm) hard plastic dolls have delicately beautiful faces and costumes of rich materials, laces, charming hats and elaborate hairdos.

***Portrettes*, by Alexander Doll Company, Inc. *Flower Girl* and *Babette*.**

7. Avigail Braham

Avigail Braham's ballerina dolls received great acclaim when they first appeared a few years ago, but her current line of dolls shows this artist's great versatility. Attention to details, especially in her 20in (51cm) one-of-a-kind dolls (shown here), was even more apparent this year at Toy Fair. Oddly, none of these dolls have names.

8. Dolfi/Artex of Europe

Dolfi presents *Verena*, a 13in (33cm) fully jointed hand carved wooden doll with hand painted features. She wears a peach print dress with puffed sleeves trimmed with lace and accented with peach ribbons, and a peach pinafore with snaps on the back and a large bow.

***Verena*, a fully jointed wooden doll by Dolfi/Artex of Europe. *Photo by John Axe*.**

9. Effanbee

The all-new porcelain *Patsy* (girl and boy editions are available) is fully jointed and stand 13½in (34cm) tall. *Patsy* is dressed in a black silk velvet dress with matching lace-trimmed bonnet. The boy version wears silk velvet shorts, suspenders and matching cap. It has been announced that 1988 will be the last year for *Patsy*.

Porcelain *Patsy*, by Effanbee.

4.

5.

6.

7.

8.

10. From The Heart Originals

Emily and *Margaret* are fully jointed, 20in (51cm) felt dolls with synthetic wigs and painted eyes. Designed by Lynne Laber, *Emily* wears a green and rose calico print dress with pinafore, clay colored prairie bonnet and brown shoes. *Margaret* wears a green and pink print dress with rose calico pinafore, teal colored prairie bonnet and brown tie shoes. Both dolls are 20in (51cm) tall and limited to 250 pieces each.

Emily (left) and *Margaret* (right), by From The Heart Originals.

11. Suzanne Gibson

Astride his masterful stick pony, *Yankee Doodle Dandy* is dressed as a turn-of-the-century boy, 8in (20cm) tall, with a feather in his tricorne hat. This is a treasured limited edition set for 1988.

Yankee Doodle Dandy, by Suzanne Gibson.

12. Goetz (Götz) Dolls

Antje, Jan, Monica and *Max* are from the Marianne Designer Collection by Goetz Dolls. They are dressed in classic German outfits with human hair wigs and leather shoes. The dolls are vinyl, 18in (46cm) tall, and limited to an edition of 300 pieces each.

Left to right: Antje, Jan, Max and *Monica* by Goetz Dolls.

13. Good-Krüger Dolls

Everything Nice is the second vinyl design by Good-Krüger Dolls and a natural companion to the first vinyl doll called *Sugar and Spice*. She has a beautiful red wig which is French braided and looped with ribbon. Her arms, legs and torso are jointed.

Everything Nice, by Good-Krüger Dolls.

14. Heidi Ott

The *African Girl* and *African Boy* dolls are 19in (48cm) tall; *African Baby* is 13in (33cm) tall. The boy wears a muted green plaid peasant shirt with striped black cropped pants. The girl wears a red and green paisley shirt, light peach cotton cropped pants, white sox and black shoes; she carries the baby in a cradle on her back.

African Boy, African Girl and *African Baby*, by Heidi Ott.

15. House of Nisbet

The *Garter of Arms*, 8in (20cm) tall, is among the newest of the House of Nisbet dolls and is featured on the color dust jacket of *The Peggy Nisbet Story*, recently published by Hobby House Press, Inc. He wears a colorful gold and red costume and a plumed hat. In his hand is the official proclamation of the Crowning of Queen Elizabeth II.

Garter of Arms, from House of Nisbet.

16. Horsman

Billiken, "the god of things as they ought to be," has been re-introduced this year by Horsman in its 1909 Teddy Bear version standing 11½in (29cm) tall, with jointed arms and legs.

Billiken, by Horsman.

17. Dolls by Jerri

Meredith, designed by Jerri McCloud, is a 16in (41cm) all-porcelain doll with red human hair, glass eyes, beautifully costumed in a slate blue drop waist dress and maribou feather decorated chiffon hat.

Meredith, a limited edition from Dolls by Jerri. **Photo by John Axe.**

18. Jesco

Kuddle Kewpie is a deluxe 20in (51cm) soft-bodied doll with vinyl head, molded hair and painted eyes. She wears a Peter Pan collared puffy sleeved blouse with a pink pinafore and soft turned down sox.

Kuddle Kewpie, by Jesco.

19. Pacific International Corporation

Lyndi, by doll artist Linda Dwinell, is a 20in (51cm) all porcelain doll with blonde ponytail wig and blue glass paperweight eyes. She is a limited edition of 1,000 and is signed and dated by the artist.

Lyndi, by Pacific International Corporation.

20. Lissi Bätz

Samantha, Sally and *Bob* by Lissi Bätz are soft bodied with vinyl heads and hands, painted eyes, and stand 19¾in (50cm) tall. Attached to their plaid costumes are Lissi Bätz gold name pins.

Left to right: Sally, Bob and *Samantha*, by Lissi Bätz.

21. Louis Nichole

Tatiana (left) and *Raffina* (right) are two of Louis Nichole's latest creations with porcelain shoulder heads, arms and legs on a stuffed cloth body. Both 16in (41cm) dolls are beautifully costumed in the Louis Nichole tradition.

Tatiana (left) and *Raffina* (right), by Louis Nichole.

21.

22.

23.

23. Johannes Zook Originals

Megan is a 20in (51cm) vinyl doll with a cloth body. She has green eyes and auburn "crimped" hair. She wears a mint green country print dress with a cream colored pinafore, cream tights and sand colored shoes.

Megan, by Johannes Zook Originals.

24. 25.

26. Gillian Heal Limited Edition Dolls will introduce *Tansy* for 1988 at Toy Fair. This English fabric doll has hand painted features by the artist herself and wears a classic English style party dress with front panels painted and embroidered by Gillian with tiny beads and ribbons. No size given.

22. World Doll, Inc.

New to the 12in (30cm) "Gone With The Wind Collection" are *Ashley* in Confederate uniform and *Melanie* in a blue dress and bonnet.

Ashley and Melanie, from World Doll, Inc.

24. Zapf Dolls

Among the many 1988 high-standard German vinyl dolls from Zapf some are of special note: The "Children of Easter" are *Christian* and *Candice*, both 19-2/3in (50cm) tall, dressed as children of wealthy European families at the turn-of-the-century in matching velvet costumes with real leather shoes.

Christian and Candice, Children of Easter, by Zapf.

25. Royal House of Dolls

There are five new dolls in the Christmas Series — *Tess*, 17in (43cm); *Tammy*, 13in (33cm); *Timmy*, 13in (33cm); *Tara*, 15in (38cm); and *Tiffany*, 17in (43cm). The vinyl dolls are all dressed in colorful red and green costumes, some with added accessories.

Christmas Series, by Royal House of Dolls.

26.

Fabulous Maud Tousey Fangel

by **Mary Lou Ratcliff**

Maud Tousey Fangel was born in 1881 in Tousey House on Professors Row at Tufts Campus, Medford, Massachusetts. Her father was Head of Divinity at Tufts College.

From her earliest days she loved to draw and paint. She was the pride of her mother and father and was encouraged to pursue a career in art. She was among the privileged to study art in those days. Her art education included the Boston School of Fine Arts, Cooper Union where she was awarded a scholarship, and Art Students League in New York.

A talented young woman, Maud Tousey's illustrations appeared in *Harper's Bazar* as early as 1907. In 1908 *The Boston Sunday Post Magazine* cover featured a beautiful lady in color, along with a story illustrated in black and white by Miss Tousey. Interestingly, the story was about art students in a big city. Shortly thereafter, she approached *Good Housekeeping* magazine with a portfolio of her drawings. The Art Director, Guy Fangel, was so impressed with the appealing and fresh touch of her pastels that he bought some of the paintings and even took her to lunch. Their meeting had a happy ending; later they were married and would work together for many years.

A son, Lloyd, was born in 1910. He was his mother's first unpaid model. By the time he was three years old he had posed for nearly 1500 drawings.

Maud and Guy Fangel moved to Westport, Connecticut, in 1916. Well-known sculptors Laura and James Earle Fraser, artist Hugo Ballin, illustrator Henry Raleigh and Rose O'Neill, artist, writer and creator of the Kewpies, were among the many creative people who lived in

Westport, which was gaining the reputation as a colony for artists of all arts. Most of the artists had studios in New York where they wintered.

It is evident that Maud loved children. She had a special talent of portraying the innocence and charming expression of her subject. Her son paid a tribute to his mother many years later.

He said: "The previous and wonderful baby and mother and child paintings had been done by Mary Cassatt, but MTF brought in a freshness, a new approach, using pastels which she felt brought the more sensitive feeling through to express the delicate touch of the child, and the tenderness of the yearning between child and mother."

Maud Tousey Fangel sketched covers and illustrations as well as advertisements for all sorts of products linked with children. Her art appeared in leading publications such as *The Delineator, Designer, Good Housekeeping, Woman's Home Companion, Ladies' Home Journal* and many American periodicals. Her work also appeared in *Die Dame* and other German and European publications and as far away as Australia.

Mrs. Fangel was the first artist to draw the Dionne Quintuplets, born in Canada May 28, 1934. She was commissioned by a number of leading companies of the United States to portray them. She moved into the Canadian Clinic with the babies and sketched them from life daily through their first year.

She also was the first artist to draw a set of paper dolls of the Quints as babies, complete with a large bassinet, wardrobe and accessories which consisted of 211 pieces. These were published by the Merrill Publishing

Company in 1935.

She designed and painted a cover for a book of paper dolls titled *Baby Bunting* published by Samuel Lowe and Company, Kenosha, Wisconsin. No publication date is shown.

Suddenly there is great interest among art collectors in Maud Tousey Fangel's original artwork. However, among doll collectors her most sought-after work is art in cloth dolls produced by Georgene Novelties, Inc. — Averill Mfg. Co. of New York. The original drawings and dolls have comparable price tags, even though in the late 1930s the dolls could be purchased for 59¢ in leading department stores.

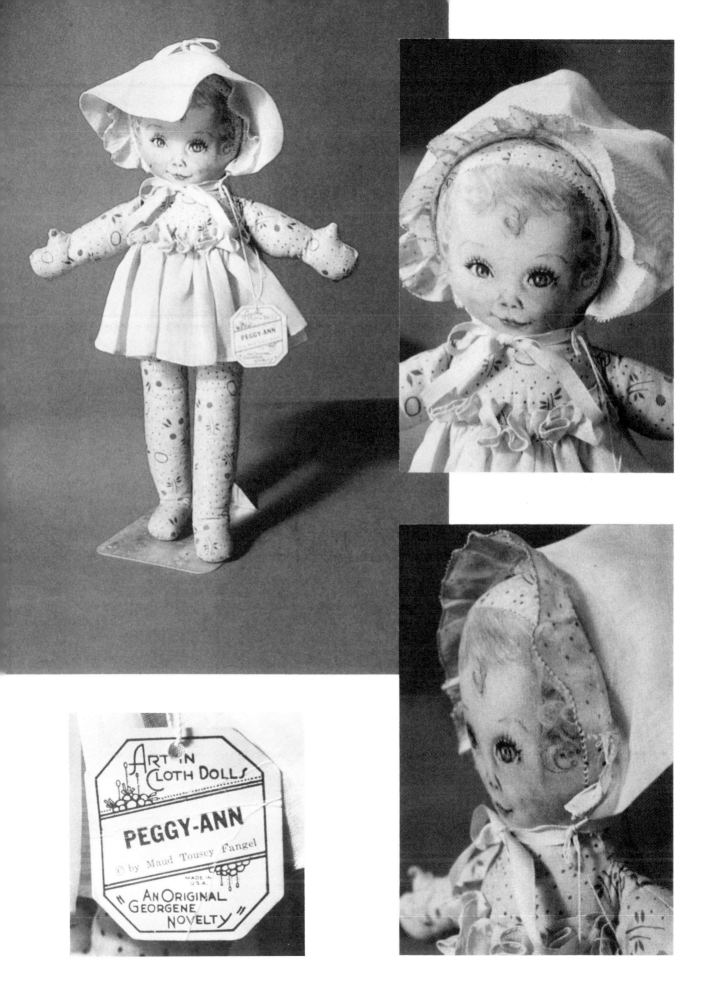

ART IN CLOTH DOLLS

PEGGY-ANN

© by Maud Tousey Fangel

MADE IN U.S.A.

AN ORIGINAL GEORGENE NOVELTY

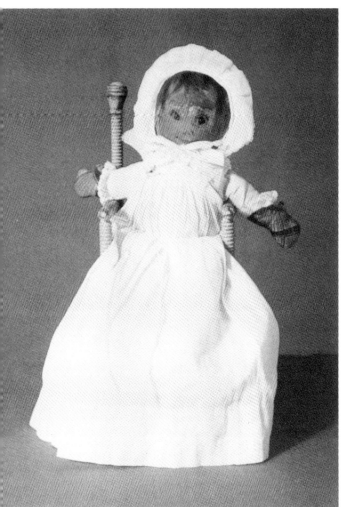

TOP LEFT: Illustration 5. *11in (28cm) baby, constructed differently; unlike the others shown, the body is made of pink sateen rather than printed material. The short and stocky legs are straight with a knee seam. She has brown eyes and blonde hair. One initial of the signature is barely visible. The clothing is not original.* Millie Clark Collection. **TOP RIGHT: Illustration 6.** *13in (33cm) bent-leg baby, extremely well constructed with darts and seams in the legs so the knees are flexible and bend. The fabric for the body is a tiny flowered print of yellow roses and blue forget-me-nots on a white background with original bonnet and skirt of the same material. The bonnet is trimmed with a 2in (5cm) organdy ruffle. Mrs. Fangel's work is evident in the painting of the natural blonde curls, the brown expressive eyes with detailed eyelashes and the sweet expression on the baby's face, along with her initials on her left ear.*
LEFT: Illustration 7. *16in (41cm) baby with long straight legs measuring 8in (20cm), one-half of her height. The body is made of red, green, blue and white plaid fabric. These bold colors are not typical of the artist's use of pastels. Painted almond-shaped brown eyes, watermelon mouth and wisps of brown hair are different than others shown. The face has the appearance of Mrs. Fangel's early advertising art. Unfortunately a former owner repaired the face with glue. It is doubtful that her long white dress is original. The bonnet has been attached permanently obscuring the signature.*

LEFT: Illustration 8. *Uncut Dionne Quintuplets paper dolls with Maud Tousey Fangel's signature in the lower right-hand corner. Titled* QUINTUPLETS, *it was published by Merrill Publishing Company in 1935. Carolyn Hall Collection.*

RIGHT: Illustration 9. *The* QUINTUPLET *paper doll cut-out book, seen in Illustration 8, consisted of 211 pieces, a page for each Quint with toys, clothing and accessories. The uncut page shown is Emelie's. Note the way her name is spelled. Carolyn Hall Collection.*

LEFT: Illustration 10. *Cut paper dolls from the front cover of the* QUINTUPLET *paper doll book, seen in Illustrations 8 and 9, resting in a bassinet, which was the back cover of the book. The bassinet measures 16in (41cm) in length. Carolyn Hall Collection.*

143

LEFT: Illustration 11. *Front cover of* Baby Bunting *cut-out paper doll book designed by Maud Tousey Fangel and published by Samuel Lowe & Co., Kenosha, Wisconsin.* Carolyn Hall Collection.

BELOW: Illustration 12. *Back cover of the* Baby Bunting *cut-out paper doll book, shown in* Illustration 11, *with the baby doll.* Carolyn Hall Collection.

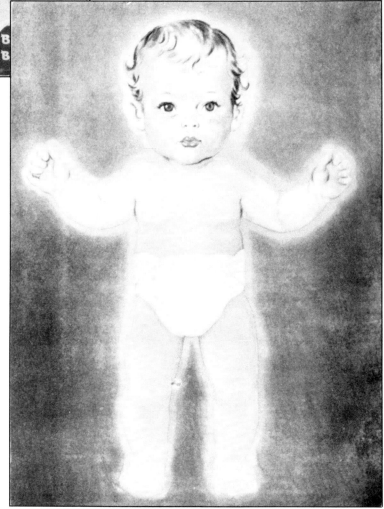

The lithographed faces were designed and painted by Mrs. Fangel. Brown eyes seem to be predominant as three of the four examples shown have brown eyes. Hair styles ranged from finely detailed blonde curls to brown wispy strands of painted hair.

Names of *Sweets* and *Peggy-Ann* have been noted on original paper wrist tags. *Sweets* is portrayed as a baby and it is of interest to note that she has appeared with two different faces and hair styles.

A variety of cotton material was used for the bodies ranging from pink sateen and small printed flowers to a gaudy plaid design. Most often the clothing was fashioned from the same printed fabric with a removable skirt and bonnet trimmed with organdy. However, some of the babies wore organdy dresses and bonnets or pink rompers and hats. *Sweets* has been seen in both costumes.

Illustration 13. The cover of the book, Babies, *illustrated by Maud Tousey Fangel and published by Whitman Publishing Co., Racine, Wisconsin, in 1933. The book contains 16 beautiful colored drawings and is a wonderful example of her love for children.*

The bodies are well constructed consisting of numerous pieces sewn together. The lower part of the body is contoured to allow the doll to sit securely without the aid of any support.

The design and body construction of the bent-leg baby is very interesting. Darts and gathers form a wrinkle to simulate a knee and give the appearance of a bent leg. The foot is designed in a similar manner to form the heel and instep, and is used on the dolls with short and long legs. All the dolls have mitt-type hands.

The dolls are usually signed on the left ear with initials "MTF" and a "©" underneath blending into the ear pattern. Unfortunately many times part of signature is lost in seam stitching the flat face to the rounded head.

Maud Tousey Fangel is listed in *Who's Who in American Art, Mallet's Index of Art* and as a member of the *Society of Illustrators, NY.*

Even into her 80s she sketched from dawn to dusk. Her philosophy was "Each new day is a glorious gift."

She passed away on September 30, 1968, shortly before her 88th birthday. Red chalks, lithographs, crayons and pastels of cherubic babies she had painted lined the foyer of the beautiful church in Westport, Connecticut, at her memorial service in November 1968. No mention was made that any of her dolls attended. □

Charming Charmin' Chatty

by **Barbara Guyette**

How would you like to own a doll that could speak eloquently on a variety of subjects, teach you a foreign language, and even play games with you — and win! Many children of the early 1960s found that they had just such a friend in *Charmin' Chatty* by Mattel Toy Company.

Few people today realize what a fascinating and unique doll she was, and still is, to doll collectors.

Talking dolls were invented long before *Charmin' Chatty's* day. The first American-made talking doll was manufactured and patented in 1878. The talking mechanism, similar to a phonograph, was housed in the metal torso of the doll. The doll itself was German-made with a bisque head. Other firms began to produce talking dolls in the years that followed. The Edison doll was by far the most successful, being manufactured in large numbers.

The mechanism of the Edison doll was given a "voice" by the use of cylindrical records inserted into the doll. *Charmin' Chatty* talked by means of small plastic records inserted into the doll's body. Both operated with similar concepts.

It seems people were just not content with inactive make-believe friends! They wanted their dolls to be participating companions, not earnest listeners! In 1882, William Webber of Massachusetts invented singing dolls! He was an organ maker by trade who turned to doll making. A miniature organ-type music box within a cloth stuffed doll body played a variety of tunes, allowing the doll to "sing."

However, *Charmin' Chatty* could hold the record for diversity! She was one of the most active dolls you would ever want to meet.

OPPOSITE PAGE: Illustration 1. 24in (61cm) *Charmin' Chatty* by Mattel Toy Company; plastic and vinyl body, rooted saran hair in choice of auburn or platinum color, side-glancing sleep eyes with molded eyelashes, closed mouth; records fit in slot in side of doll; pull ring for voice; came with two records. Doll wore a red, white and blue two-piece sailor dress with red tights and blue and white plastic shoes. She came with a pair of black plastic eyeglasses. Marking on back of body: "Charmin' Chatty//Mattel Inc.//1961//Hawthorne, California, U.S.A.//U.S. Pat. 3,017,187//-Pat'd in Canada, 1962//other U.S. and foreign patents pending." Jointed at shoulder, neck and hips; legs widespread when sitting.

The 24in (61cm) tall doll came with a set of two-sided records containing several phrases each. Each outfit or set included a similar record on a specific subject associated with the costume. For example, the record included with a hospital gown and medical accessories was titled "Let's Play Nurse." The most expensive costume set, which sold at the time for approximately $8.00, was a traveling coat and hat with a doll-size foreign language dictionary and record. The doll could converse in phrases in several different languages, and then explain the English translation!

Her records were inserted into a slot in the side of the plastic body. They were held in place by a small black lever. She would talk when a string, located at the back of her neck, was pulled. The record could be changed entirely, or just turned to the opposite side when desired. The speaker was contained in the chest. The advantage of changing the records allowed the doll to have almost limitless random conversation. A complete list of records, not including two game records and the foreign language record, is as follows: Restaurant/Shopping; Animal Noises/Scarey; Pajama Party, side 1 and 2; Ridiculous/Mother; Let's Play

Illustration 2. A selection of records which, when placed singly into *Charmin' Chatty's* talking mechanism, allowed her to speak. Each 3in (7.6cm) diameter white plastic record contained several phrases on each side. A record came with every costume or accessory set, in addition to the two records that came with the doll.

Illustration 3. Each piece of clothing for *Charmin' Chatty* had her label sewn into it.

Illustration 4. *Charmin' Chatty* always wore this outfit when eating out or on a shopping spree. Outfit included a red with white dots short-sleeved front buttoning cotton shirt with a denim look and cotton skirt and vest trimmed with bands of shirt fabric and red rickrack.

Nurse, side 1 and 2; Cinderella, side 1 and 2; Outdoors/Indoors; Proverbs/Poems, Hear a line - make a rhyme; Birthday Party, side 1 and 2; Good/Famous; Get Acquainted, side 1 and 2.

Shown in the accompanying illustrations is the wide variety of costumes and accessories that were available for *Charmin' Chatty*. Additionally, as was often the case with popular dolls of her period, sewing patterns were available to add to her stylish wardrobe. McCall's pattern number 7269 gave instructions to create a robe and nightgown; a cape, hat and boots; a dress and panties; a turtleneck shirt; tights and jumper; and a hand-knit sweater and socks.

Charmin' Chatty could easily have been labeled the most versatile and accomplished doll a little girl could own! □

Illustration 5. Outdoors or indoors, she is always ready for work or play! This set features a smock-type tie-on red cotton play dress with red and white print pockets and a triangle head scarf, all trimmed with blue binding. Red tights footed with blue vinyl slippers with brown soles complete the outfit.

Illustration 6. Come over for a pajama party! Outfit includes a pink and white rosebud print cotton nightgown, with pink cotton scuffs, a hair net and plastic curlers.

Illustration 7. Have you ever played a game with a doll? *Charmin' Chatty* could participate in four specially designed ones, and even win at them! Two games came in each box, and each included a voice record for the doll. The games were: Stock Number 499, Chatty Skate 'N Slide and Chatty at the Fair; Stock Number 498, Chatty Animal Round Up and Chatty Animal Friends.

Illustration 8. Shown here are the following: a white cotton hospital gown from the "Let's Play Nurse" playset and the dress of tatters from the "Cinderella" playset.

Illustration 9. *Charmin' Chatty's* sweet child-like features mimic those of a typical real-life eight-year-old girl of the 1960s. Here she holds a plastic birthday cake with eight candles from the birthday party accessory set. Her party dress is handmade using McCall's pattern number 7962 for the *Charmin' Chatty* wardrobe.

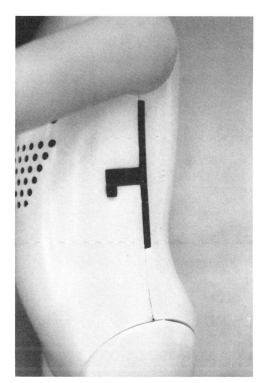

Illustration 10. The records that allowed Charmin' Chatty to talk were inserted into a slot in the side of the plastic body. They were held in place by a small black lever.

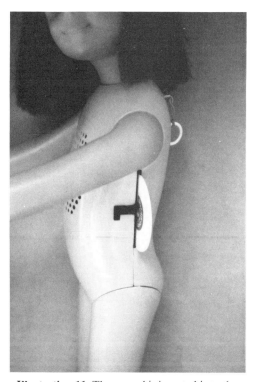

Illustration 11. The record is inserted into the slot in *Charmin' Chatty's* body, the lever is moved through the slot from position A to position B. The doll would randomly choose phrases from the record when a string at the base of her neck was pulled.

Dolls That Walk, Talk and Steal Your Heart

Toy Fair 1987

Part I

The Winds of Winter were cold in New York City in February 1987, but the hot new designs of the manufacturers will warm the hearts of children and collectors alike. This article is one of three parts in **Doll Reader** magazine to show and describe a choice selection of some of these new models.

Visit your favorite doll store, department store, gift store or write your favorite mail order source of dolls to find out when the dolls that walk and talk and steal *YOUR* heart away will be available.

Gina, an original creation by Jerri McCloud, is limited to only 1,000 pieces and stands approximately 16in (41cm) tall. Dressed in a blue smocked dress and bonnet, she carries her own teddy bear and security blanket.

2. *Tasha,* by The Collectables.

The Collectables, Inc.

Tasha, by The Collectables, is a 14in (36cm) tall confection consisting of porcelain head, hands and feet, and a wire armature body for poseability. Her long blonde wig and elaborate costume are in contrast to the fluffy white duck who is her steed — a whimsical touch that lends an air of fantasy to this doll (**Illustration 2**.)

Also new this year from The Collectables are *Snow Fairy Tree Top Angel, Mother's Little Treasure II,* and *Bear Head* and *Fairy Baby* ornaments.

Madame Alexander

Madame Alexander's dolls have long been regarded as "something special" and "a joy forever." 1987 has a bevy of new beauties. The 10in (25cm) "Portrettes" with the *Cissette* face are being reintroduced in Summer 1987 and will include: *Rosette* (#1115), *Daisy* (#1110), and *Jasmin* (#1113). (See **Illustration 1.**) Also reintroduced, but not pictured here, will be *Lily* (#1114). *Iris* (#1112) and *Violetta* (#1116). Among the many other new dolls are the new 21in (53cm) "Portrait Dolls" *Scarlett* (#2247 with layered white gown), *Sarah Bernhardt* (#2249, with reddish-brown outfit), and the piece de resistance *Marie Antoinette* (#2248, with flowered print court dress). Newly costumed dolls in the "Storyland" and "International" series will have a different face, the so-called "Maggie Mix-Up" face.

1. Alexander's 10in (25cm) "Portrettes" *Daisy* (left) and *Jasmin* (right).

which is patterned after their well-known, sweet-faced logo doll head found on all of their packaging and advertisements in **Doll Reader**.

A limited edition of 1,000 *Brer Bear* and *Brer Rabbit* has also been created to complement Jerri's *Uncle Remus* doll. *Brer Bear* stands 18in (46cm) tall, made of dark brown plush with plastic eyes and is wearing a shirt, vest and pants. *Brer Rabbit* is 16in (41cm) tall, made of light brown plush with plastic eyes, and wears a vest, shirt and pants. The first 500 of each of these creations by Jerri will be saved to match up with the *Uncle Remus* doll. The doll 500 will be sold individually.

From The Heart Originals

Kevin, standing 20in (51cm) tall, is dressed in navy blue knee pants, with plum knitted vest and matching knitted hat. He has blonde hair, brown eyes, and carries his own brass horn. He's available alone or as a matched set with his sister *Caitlin*. (See **Illustration 5**.) *Caitlin* is also 20in (51cm) tall, and is dressed for play in plum corduroy rompers with calico to match her ruffled blouse and matching bonnet. She comes with her very own muslin horse. Both dolls are limited to an edition of 300 each.

Suzanne Gibson

Red Riding Hood, by Suzanne Gibson, and the *Wolf*, by Steiff, made their debut at Toy Fair 1987. *Red Riding Hood* is an all-vinyl doll, 8in (20cm) tall, dressed in the traditional red hooded cloak, and carrying a wicker basket of flowers. The *Wolf* is light grey mohair with brown facial markings. It has been some years since Steiff has made a wolf. (**Illustration 6**.)

Le Petite Patineuse, also by Suzanne Gibson, is a charming boy and girl couple dressed in Victorian skating outfits. The dolls are all vinyl and stands 8in (20cm) tall. All of the above dolls are 1987 limited editions.

Karin Heller

DOTY award winner Karin Heller introduced *Annie*, her latest doll, at Toy Fair in New York City. Standing 18in (46cm) tall, *Annie* is made of stockinette material, with jointed head and legs, light brown braided hair, and wears glasses. Her costume is a blue and white dress with red cape, navy blue picture hat, and traditional Black Forest hand woven straw shoes. (**Illustration 7**.)

Paul Crees

Among the new wax portrait dolls introduced this year by British doll artist Paul Crees was his 30in (76cm) version of *Jean Harlow* dressed in a long white gown worn by this famous Hollywood star in the film "Dinner at Eight." (**Illustration 3**.)

Crees' portrait doll of *Elizabeth Taylor* dressed in a gold lame costume as "Cleopatra" was another of his stunning creations that attracted much attention at Toy Fair this year.

Dolls by Jerri

Uncle Remus is a departure from Jerri's usual designs. He has porcelain head, arms and legs and a cloth body. Standing 16in (38cm) tall he is completely poseable, including his head. (See **Illustration 4**.)

Dolls by Jerri are planning to release their *Logo Doll*, the design of

3. *Jean Harlow* by Paul Crees. **4.** *Uncle Remus*, by Dolls by Jerri. **5.** *Kevin*, by From The Heart Originals. **6.** *Red Riding Hood*, by Suzanne Gibson, and *The Wolf*, by Steiff. **7.** *Annie*, by Karin Heller.

8. *Ginny Let's Go Places,* by R. Dakin & Co.
9. *Bastian* and *Fatou,* by Annette Himstedt.
10. House of Nisbet's *Nativity Collection.*

Ginny

Mothers and collectors have waited breathlessly since the acquisition of the names *Vogue* and *Ginny* by R. Dakin & Company from Meritus Industries last year. Neither will be disappointed! The line is refreshing and stunning. Some old favorites are back, such as the hard plastic *Ginny* introduced last year. The same molds are used again this year in exciting new ways.

The "Ginny Going Places Collection" (See **Illustration 8**) includes 18 designs featuring the vinyl *Ginny* created in 1985. Included are old favorites such as *Little One,* along with new outfits like *Mardi Gras* and *Broadway.*

In the "Ginny Fantasy Collection" hard plastic designs, such as *Miss Ginny,* top the line, with old favorites like *Mommy's Attic* and *Fairy Tale Princess* returning.

New ideas, such as the "Ginny Portraits" and "Famous Pairs Collection," focus on historical and nursery rhyme characters.

The "Holiday Collection" features special occasion outfits, such as *Easter Bunny, Witch, Pilgrim* and *Christmas Girl.*

The "Ovation Collection" for the mass market stores shows *Ginny* in contemporary American looks.

Yes, *Ginny* is back to charm the collector and delight the child. However, the porcelain *Ginnys* are being discontinued, and will not be carried in the Dakin *Ginny* line.

Annette Himstedt

The first of a collection of six dolls by Annette Himstedt of Paderborn, West Germany, produced for Mattel Toys is "The Barefoot Children" series. The first three, *Paula, Ellen* and *Käthe,* were introduced late last year. This year *Lisa, Bastian* and *Fatou* came on the scene. Each of the 26in (64cm) dolls has vinyl facial features with handsketched eyebrows and glistening eyes that are filled with emotion. The dolls have carefully sculpted toes, fingers and nails, and all are dressed in multi-layered ensembles made of natural fabrics that bear the designer's label. (**Illustration 9.**)

House of Nisbet

The Nativity Collection by House of Nisbet consists of nine Christmas dolls wearing brilliant costumes, with hand-carved and painted wooden head, hands and feet made in the Tyrolean mountains of Northern Italy, and area long famous for its beautiful wood carvings. The dolls, ranging from 8 to 9in (20 to 23cm), include *Mary, Joseph, Baby Jesus,* the *Three Kings,* a *Shepherd,* a *Shepherd Boy* and an *Angel.* All have poseable bodies. (**Illustration 10.**)

Two new 16in (41cm) versions of Sarah Ferguson in her wedding dress were also introduced this year by House of Nisbet in porcelain and vinyl.

House of Nisbet and their representative Tide-Rider, Inc., are introducing the "Nisbet Collectors Club" through a network of specialist dealers as headquarters in their locality.

11. *Queen of the Nile*, designed by Lloyderson and made by Marin of Spain. 12. *Corky* dressed as "Adventure Scout," "Star Ship" and "Big Game," by Playmates. 13. *Night at the Opera*, by Royal House of Dolls. 14. *Josie*, by Thompson Associates.

Marin

Queen of the Nile and her companion *Pharoah of Egypt*, made by Marin of Chiclana, Spain, were featured art dolls in the Lloyderson "Flying Foxxies" collection this year. Exotically costumed in lavish fabrics with much gold trim, *Queen of the Nile* has a porcelain head and hands, black wig, painted blue eyes, and measures 14 by 23in (36 by 48cm). The dolls are limited to an edition of 2,500 each worldwide. (**Illustration 11**.)

At the popularly priced end of the Lloyderson line are their *Blossom Kids*, soft sculptured dolls 20in (51cm) tall.

Playmates

Cricket's brother *Corky* is new this year from Playmates. *Corky* can hold a conversation and his eyes and lips are synchronized for realism. *Corky* is available dressed in four different outfits with corresponding tapes. (**Illustration 12**.)

Several new versions of Playmates' popular doll *Jill* were also introduced this year by Playmates.

Royal House of Dolls

Night At The Opera debuted in Royal House of Dolls' showroom this year. Dressed in a stunning gown of pale blue, and with her white hair piled high upon her head, she stands 15in (38cm) tall and her vinyl body is jointed at the arms and legs (**Illustration 13**.)

Reintroduced this year was a new version of *Lonely Lisa*, the 17in (43cm) tall sad-faced doll which first appeared in the 1950s and carried through to the mid 1970s. She has a vinyl head and poseable cloth body.

Doll Reader wishes to say "Happy 10th Anniversary" to Miss Elsa, President of Royal House of Dolls in her 10th year with her own doll manufacturing firm.

Thompson Associates

New to Pat Thompson's "Vlasta" line of exquisitely dressed dolls is *Josie*, a 26in (66cm) doll with porcelain head, hands and legs, and a cloth wired body for poseability. She wears an extravagant silk dress trimmed with French laces and over 100 handmade silk flowers. (See **Illustration 14**.)

Colene, another 26in (66cm) doll in the Vlasta line, also has porcelain head, hands and legs with a cloth wired and poseable body. She is dressed in silk organza with silk underskirt, silk ribbons, and 282 pure silk handmade flowers.

15.

16.

15. *Gum Drop,* by Boots Tyner Originals. 16. *Rhett* and *Scarlett,* by World Doll Company. 17. *Patrick,* by Johannes Zook Originals.

Boots Tyner Originals

Gum Drop was Boots Tyner's special new doll this year. Both the girl and boy versions have porcelain-like vinyl heads and hands on a cloth body. Head, hands and legs are jointed for poseability. The girl has blonde hair and blue-green eyes. The boy version has brown hair and eyes. Both dolls are 20in (51cm) in length and wear coordinating blue and pink outfits with "bum hats." (See **Illustration 15**.) (Ed. note: World Doll is introducing Boots Tyner's 13in [33cm] vinyl dolls *Lizette* [dressed in play clothes and "Cheer Leader"] and *Mathew* [costumed in a *Football* and *Cowboy* outfits].)

World Doll

World Doll has produced a smaller version of their "Gone With The Wind" dolls — *Scarlett* (11in [28cm]) in green velvet, *Rhett Butler* (12in [31cm]) in black tuxedo and smoking jacket, and *Melanie* (11in [28cm]) wearing green printed white ruffled dress. Added to the collection this year is *Mammy* (10in [25cm]). (**Illustration 16**.)

On display also, and new for this year, was a series of porcelain dolls by Louis Nichole. The *Victoria Bride Doll* dressed in exquisite laces, which is Nichole's trademark, was the most elaborate.

Johannes Zook Originals

Patrick, a 24in (61cm) tall doll, has porcelain head, arms and legs, and an articulated cloth body with special hip joints that allow him to sit without the support of a stand. He has blonde human hair, and can be had with brown, blue or hazel blown glass eyes with real hair lashes. *Patrick* is available in two outfits — a blue and white pajama set or a red velour footed and hooded outfit. *Patrick* is limited to an edition of 100 pieces and will be signed, numbered and have a certificate as well. (See **Illustration 17**.) A vinyl version of *Patrick* will be available in late Summer 1987.

17.

18.

18. *Pamela,* designed by 198 DOTY® Award Winner Susa Wakeen, is a beautiful inte pretation of "Clara" from th Nutcracker Ballet. She is 16 (41cm) tall, dressed in a lace ar satin tutu and a limited editic of 250 and manufactured by Tl 'Littlest' Ballet Company, In (For 1987, Cherish Intern tional, Inc. will be introduci "The Susan Wakeen Collectio in vinyl.)

Close-up on Chuckles

by Patricia N. Schoonmaker

Seldom do we know how a doll such as *Chuckles* received its name. *Playthings* magazine in July 1927 explains that this cheerful toddler "Chuckles with joy and happiness at being able to *stand alone*." Evidently this was an effort to create a doll just a little different from the many, many models which were made to compete with Effanbee's *Bubbles*. (*Bubbles* existed as a toddler doll as well as a bent-legged baby, but the former were far more scarce.)

Playthings also stated that "Baby's First Step is typified by 'Chuckles.' Sweetest of all dimpled smiling faces with the advanced human appeal of standing and sitting kiddie legs!" *Chuckles* was made in five sizes with composition breastplate head, arms and legs. Some models had metal sleep eyes, and others glassene, sometimes green in color. There were a few painted eye models.

The doll is a satisfaction to collectors with her name and company clearly marked on the shoulder back. *Chuckles* came with a good-sized circular label pinned to the dress front which read, "The new standing CHUCKLES Baby Doll, Century Dolls."

The Century Doll Company, of 62-68 West 14 Street, New York, New York, offered a sample assortment to buyers for $50.00 which included the following:

½ dozen 14in (35.6cm)
1/3 dozen 16in (40.6cm)
¼ dozen 18in (45.7cm)
¼ dozen 21in (53.3cm)
1/6 dozen 23in (58.4cm)

This seems an incredible bargain in light of the prices of today!

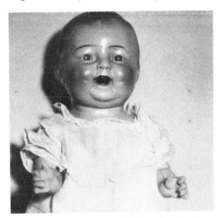

Illustration 4. 14in (35.6cm) *Chuckles;* composition shoulder head, arms and legs; painted hair; sleep eyes of metal; original dress and petticoat; marked on back of shoulder "CHUCKLES//A CENTURY DOLL." *Georgia Cannon Collection. Photograph by Georgia Cannon.*

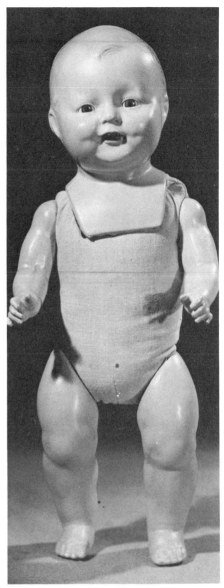

Illustration 2. Doll undressed to show body construction. *Betty Lopez Collection.*

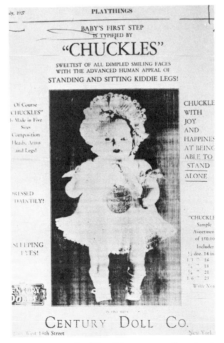

Illustration 1. 16in (40.6cm) *Chuckles* with all-original rose-pink clothing. It is trimmed with white lace and pink ribbons. *Betty Lopez Collection.*

Illustration 5. *Playthings* magazine trade advertisement for July 1927.

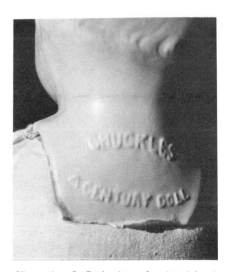

Illustration 3. Back view of painted head showing the name and company mark. *Betty Lopaz Collection.*

Dolls That Walk, Talk and Steal Your Heart

Toy Fair 1987

Part II

2a. *Kathy* is a 1987 limited edition of 2500 pieces created by Marianne Goetz of Goetz Dolls. Each doll will be hand signed by Mr. Franz Goetz. Kathy has flowing auburn hair, brown magical eyes and is dressed in a white eyelet dress with a bouquet of flowers. A 22K gold bracelet, with her name engraved on it, completes her outfit.

1. *Hermine*, by Corolle.

2. *Annie*, by Karin Heller. **Doll Reader** received so many inquiries, we decided to show this cloth German schoolgirl in color.

Corolle

1.

Hermine, by Corolle, is a 16¾in (43cm) soft bodied doll with vinyl head and hands, blonde wig and sleeping eyes. She wears a white lace dress and pink hat (**Illustration 1**). *Hermine* and her companion doll, *Hortense*, come in a round box with pastel painted cover. The dolls are limited to an edition of 1,000 world-wide, signed and numbered.

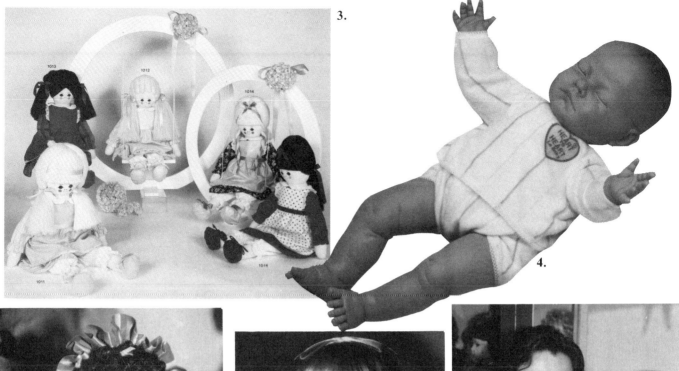

3.

4.

5.

6.

7.

Amanda Jane Dolls

Handmade in England, Amanda Jane Dolls have embroidered faces, pure wool hair and removable outfits made of quality materials. Each doll is individually numbered and recorded. New this year are *Sophia* (1011), *Daisy* (1012), *Dorothy-May* (1013), *Dulcie* (1014) and *Martha* (1015). (**Illustration 3.**)

Barval

Softly press on its chest, and Barval's *Heart-to-Heart* baby responds with a realistic heart beat. Part of the La Baby™ dolls series for 1987, *Heart-to-Heart* has vinyl head, arms and legs and a soft body. Barval's *Shaking Baby* reacts realistically to a touch by a child, as do some other dolls in their current line.

Yolanda Bello

Dulcie, a 16in (41cm) doll with her dog, appeared at Toy Fair this year. She has a porcelain head on a wire armature cloth body. *Dulcie* is limited to 250 pieces. Also by Ms. Bello was another of her brandy snifter doll creations called *Cognac and Lace*, consisting of a female and male doll toasting each other.

Cherish International

Under a license from The Littlest Ballet Company, Cherish International, Inc. is now producing *Jeanne*, a 1985 DOTY® Award winner, in vinyl in limited edition. Other Susan Wakeen designed dolls to be made by Cherish in vinyl, are *Lisa, April* and *Melanie*. Each doll is 17in (43cm) tall and poseable.

3. Front left and right: *Sophia* (1011) and *Martha* (1015). **Back row:** *Dorothy-May* (1013), *Daisy* (1012) and *Dulcie* (1014). **4.** *Heart-to-Heart* baby, by Barval. **5.** *Dulcie and her dog*, by Yolanda Bello. *John Axe photo.* **6.** *Jeanne*, made in vinyl by Cherish International, Inc. **7.** Brigette Deval holding her *Virginia* (left) and *Chinese Boy* (right) dolls.

Brigette Deval

Virginia, by Brigette Deval, is a 25in (64cm) doll, wax-over porcelain, and limited to an edition of 100 pieces. Her *Chinese Boy* doll is wax-over industrial clay (terra cotta), and stands 20in (51cm) tall. He is "one of a kind."

Effanbee

Effanbee has a new vinyl Celebrity Doll in James Cagney dressed as *George M. Cohan* for the film "Yankee Doodle Dandy." Also new this year is another Effanbee vinyl Celebrity Doll, *General Dwight D. Eisenhower*, dressed in his familiar Eisenhower jacket uniform.

Goetz Dolls

Gisele, by Goetz Dolls, Inc., is a fully articulated 16in (41cm) vinyl doll with blonde hair and blue eyes. She is dressed in a white and pink ballerina costume. International Girls, *Larene*, *Leslie* and *Lee*, are all dressed in colorful knitted and corduroy outfits with handbags as an accessory. These three soft standing dolls are 21in (53cm) tall.

Gorham

Valentine Ladies, by designers Pamella and Noel Valentine, were inspired by a love for fashions of yesteryear. Each all porcelain doll is 10in (25cm) tall, hand numbered and limited to an edition of 2,500. (**Illustration 10.**)

Horsman

A Special Edition *President Ronald Reagan* doll, 17in (43cm) tall, will be produced during 1987 by Horsman. The doll will be dressed in a dark business suit with cuffed white shirt and handkerchief in the coat's breast pocket. (**Illustration 11.**)

Horsman will be donating a portion of the sales of the *President Ronald Reagan* doll to The Nancy Reagan Drug Abuse Fund through The Community Foundation of Greater Washington.

Also for this year, Horsman has created a replica of its 1926 11in (28cm) composition *HEbee/SHEbee* dolls. This is a limited edition series of 3,000 numbered pairs, and will be accompanied by a brief history about the Composition Doll Era.

8. *George M. Cohan* by Effanbee. **9.** *Gisele*, by Goetz Dolls, Inc. **10.** *Valentine Ladies*, by Gorham. **11.** *President Ronald Reagan*, by Horsman.

Pat Kolesar

Pat Kolesar's *Ugly but Snugly* creations in soft sculpture reflect her own sense of humor. These dolls were meant to bring a smile to faces, and they succeed in this endeavor. These new dolls are a diversion from Pat's earlier whimsical creations, which were also in soft sculpture. (**Illustration 12.**)

Lenci Dolls

Gertrude, by Lenci of Turino, Italy, is a 19in (48cm) felt doll dressed in orange, red and white plaid with orange tie shoes and hoop earrings. She carries a wooden broom. Her auburn hair and side glancing painted eyes accentuate her somewhat "pouty" expression.

The Littlest Ballet Company

Susan Wakeen designed *Elizabeth* for The Littlest Ballet Company. Made of porcelain and fully jointed, she stands 17in (43cm) tall and wears an apricot dress. 1987 will mark the first year that Susan Wakeen's dolls will be available in vinyl. Some of her most popular porcelain designs will now be manufactured in vinyl by Cherish International, Inc., of Austin, Texas, in accordance with an exclusive licensing agreement between Cherish and The Littlest Ballet Company.

Lawtons

Mary of the Secret Garden, designed by Wendy Lawton, is an all porcelain, fully jointed doll with inset glass eyes, standing 13in (33cm) tall. She wears a pink frock with white eyelet embroidered apron and carries a tin pail filled with Spring flowers. Her blonde wig is covered by her saucy straw hat with white ribbon tie. Mary was the unlikely heroine of Frances Hodgson Burnett's tale, *The Secret Garden*.

Mattel

12.

13.

14.

15.

12. Pat Kolesar with one of her *Ugly but Snugly* dolls.

13. *Gertrude*, by Lenci. *John Axe photo.*

14. *Elizabeth*, designed by Susan Wakeen.

15. *Mary of the Secret Garden*, by Wendy Lawton.

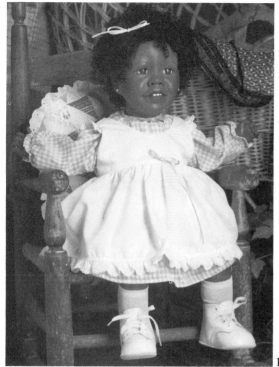

16.

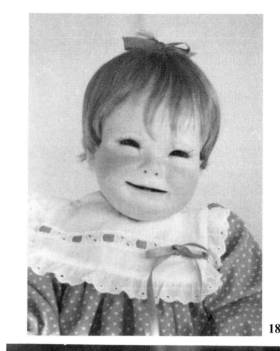

18.

17.

19.

20.

16. *Amanda*, by The Middleton Doll Company. 17. **Left to right:** *Kelly*, *Jacob*, *Zak* (seated) and *Zeak*, the rabbit, by Hal Payne. *John Axe photo.* 18. *Lollie*, by Turner Dolls. 19. *Petrushka*, by Bill Wiley. *John Axe photo.* 20. *Jenny Lind*, by Robin Woods.

21.

21. *Fiona*, designed by Louis Nichole for World Doll.

22.

Turner Dolls

Lollie is a 21in (53cm) smiling baby with porcelain head and hands, German glass eyes, soft poseable body, dressed in an original costume by her designer Judith Turner. Like the other dolls in the Turner collection, she comes signed and dated by the artist and has a Certificate of Authenticity. *Lollie* is limited to an edition of 500 pieces.

Bill Wiley

Bill Wiley's *Petrushka* has a porcelain head and chest plate on a cloth body with wire armature, and stands 24in (61cm) tall. His colorful costume is fashioned after one worn by a world famous ballet star.

Robin Woods

Among the new doll designs in the Robin Woods collection this year are *Catherine* (of Wuthering Heights), 14in (36cm) and wearing a blue velvet cloak with fur trim over a blue taffeta dress. *Jenny Lind*, the famous 19th century soprano, stands 17in (43cm) tall and is wearing a pink, lace-trimmed dress, and holding a fan. *Katie Louise*, 24in (61cm), from her American Children Collection, is wearing a calico dress and has her own Teddy Bear.

Middleton Doll Company

Amanda is a 21in (53cm) black toddler with curly hair and brown eyes. She is dressed in a checkered frock and white pinafore.

Hal Payne

Hal Payne's carved, articulated wooden animals launched his career a few years ago. Now Mr. Payne has made articulated carved wooden children with painted features and wigs. *Zak* is a 15in (38cm) 6 year old boy; *Kelly* is the name of his 15in (38cm) 6 year old girl doll; and *Jacob*, 10 years old, is 19in (48cm) tall. *Zeak*, the rabbit, is 9½in (24cm) tall.

23. The Middleton Doll Co., Inc. announces new for 1987 *First Moments* with brown open eyes. This version of the ever popular doll is made in vinyl on cloth torso and is 21in (53cm). Dressed in a three piece buttercream outfit trimmed in lace with tuft of hair in bonnet.

23.

World Doll

Fiona, designed by Louis Nichole for World Doll, has porcelain head, arms and legs and a soft body. She has an etherical wave style wig and molded and painted slippers. Her costume is antique rose cotton voile with French-style lace trim and French satin rose-buds. *Fiona* stands 16in (41cm) tall. **(Illustration 21.)**

Zapf Dolls

The *Limited Edition Easter Doll 1988* will be limited to a production of 2,000 pieces. This beautiful doll features sleeping eyes, PVC head, arms, and legs. She has washable, combable hair, leather shoes and a hand-finished dress trimmed with lace. Each doll is signed by Brigette Zapf and comes with a Certificate of Authenticity. The doll is 25½in (65cm) tall.

Drink and Wet Babies, Part I: The *Dy-Dee* Doll

by **Mary Rickert Stuecher**

Photographs by **Werner Stuecher**

All dolls from the collections of **Jean Anderson** and **Mary Rickert Stuecher**.

Illustration 2. A close-up view of the earliest *Dy-Dee Baby*. She is 15in (38.1cm) tall, has the hard rubber head on an all-rubber jointed body. Her curly molded hair and lashed glassene sleep eyes are brown. She is wearing a pink dotted swiss dress made from the 1937 McCall pattern 513 for *Dy-Dee* dolls. She is marked as shown in (A) in the text. Note the MOLDED EARS.

Fifty years ago Effanbee placed a new doll on the market. The doll could do something no doll had ever done before. After being fed a bottle of water, she would wet her diaper and need to be changed, just like a real live baby. *Dy-Dee* was the name chosen for this baby doll made of rubber, with an enameled hard rubber head, curly molded hair, glassene sleep eyes and an open rosebud mouth. A special tube inside the doll, leading from the mouth to an opening on the dolly's hip, made the "wetting" feature possible. Bernard Lipfert, who designed the doll for Effanbee, is quoted as saying it had the dumbest face he ever designed.

An advertisement in *Playthings* magazine for April 1934, announced "The New Dy-Dee Baby Arrives" and would be on display during the New York Toy Fair. The advertisement also calls *Dy-Dee* "an overwhelming overnight success."

Much of a child's play is an imitation of REAL LIFE. Playing house and pretending to be mothers and fathers, as the case may warrant, is a popular play activity for children. Dolls are a very necessary ingredient as the pretend children. The early years of this century saw the development of baby dolls that were very realistic in appearance. In the late 1920s and early 1930s the use of soft rubber for doll parts made them even more realistic to the touch. Rubber dolls were virtually unbreakable, and could be bathed, which added to the illusion of being "a real live baby" for the child mother.

A very ingenious development was a composition baby doll holding its own bottle that was attached to its hand. The Arranbee version was named *Drink'n Babe*. Directions were included to explain how the doll worked. Two small holes from the attached bottle opened into a reservoir in the hand. After filling the bottle with the fluid provided with the doll, the arm was raised to insert the nipple into dolly's mouth. *Drink'n Babe* then "drank" the liquid, as it slowly drained into the hand openings. Lowering the arm caused the liquid to flow back into the doll's bottle, ready for the next feeding. When Effanbee introduced the *Dy-Dee*, the illusion of reality was completed. The addition of a feature that enabled a baby doll to REALLY drink a bottle and then wet its diaper was the epitome of realism.

Dy-Dee was offered in five sizes. Effanbee followed the pattern of giving each size a special name as they had done for the *Patsy* Family. The sizes were 9in (22.9cm) *Dy-Dee-Wee*, 11in (27.9cm) *Dy-Dee-ette*, 13in (33cm) *Dy-Dee-Kin*, 15in (38.1cm) *Dy-Dee Baby* and 20in (50.8cm) *Dy-Dee-Lou. Dy-Dee* could be purchased singly or in a variety of cases with layettes

Illustration 1. Happy Birthday, *Dy-Dee* doll! *Dy-Dee Baby*, 1934, and today's *Dy-Dee Baby* are dressed up in their party dresses to celebrate *Dy-Dee's* 50th birthday.

Illustration 3. Arranbee's *Drink'n Babe* gave the illusion of drinking her bottle. She is all-original in her trunk. The 12in (30.5cm) doll is all-composition with a heavy celluloid hand and bottle. She is unmarked.

— some simple, others very elaborate. The layettes could also be purchased separately. A big selling point for *Dy-Dee* was the exclusive patented valve that prevented the water, after feeding the doll her bottle, from running out as fast as the doll drank.

Little girls loved *Dy-Dee*, regardless of Mr. Lipfert's opinion of the dolls. It is not surprising that they became very popular and have remained so to the present day. The *Dy-Dee* doll was soon copied by rival companies, as is the case for most successful dolls. *Dy-Dee*'s impact was so strong that any drink and wet doll of the era was commonly called a "*Dy-Dee* doll," rather than by its own company name. Some companies copied *Dy-Dee*'s construction closely, such as Ideal's *Betsy Wetsy*. Others incorporated the drink and wet feature in dolls made of composition. This soon proved disastrous to the poor babies since composition and water are not on friendly terms. Many of the competitive dolls were unmarked and were generally lower priced than the Effanbee version. An all-rubber wetting doll was offered as cheaply as 89¢. Effanbee "jobbed out" the manufacture of *Dy-Dee*'s rubber parts to the Miller Rubber Company of Akron, Ohio.

The Patsytown News, published by Effanbee and offered free to little subscribers, frequently mentioned *Dy-Dee* in its coverage. One event that was publicized was the appearance of the *Dy-Dees* at the New York World's Fair in 1939, when *Dy-Dee Lou*, the "Wonder Doll of the Day," was presented with the keys to the World's

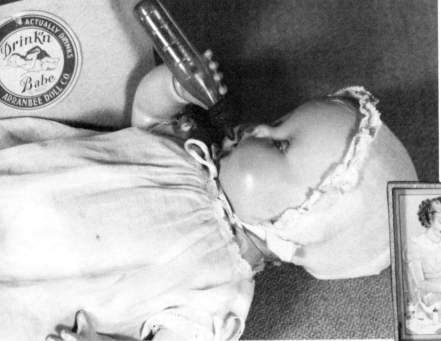

ABOVE: Illustration 4. The close-up of *Drink'n Babe* shows the two holes in her hand into which the bottle liquid drains as she "drinks." She is identified by the circular paper tag.

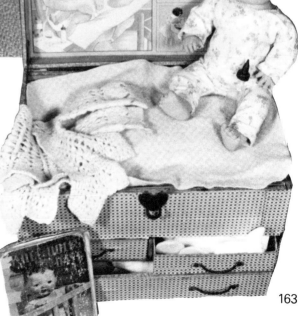

RIGHT: Illustration 5. Here is a 1930s 15in (38.1cm) *Dy-Dee Baby* dressed in her original sleeper and sitting in an early *Dy-Dee* trunk. The raggedy little book is the author's childhood *Dy-Dee Doll's Days* published in 1937.

163

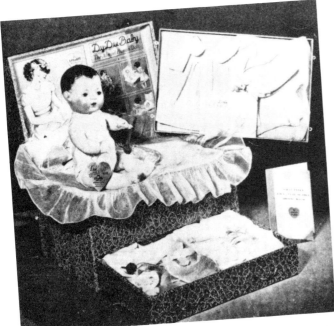

$5

DY-DEE Doll

with complete Layette

The 1936 DY-DEE doll has a layette with all the paraphernalia that the modern baby requires, from soap to a safety pin. DY-DEE is almost human, you know, and even requires a frequent change of diapers.

Aunt Patsy will be in Toytown Thursday, Friday and Saturday! Be sure to hear her talk about Dy-Dee!

Hudson's — Toytown — Twelfth Floor

HUDSON'S

A Christmas Gift Suggestion to The Mother of a Sweet Little Girl

THIS DARLING CHRISTMAS DOLL FREE

A Genuine EFFanBEE Creation

"DY-DEE IS THE DOLL I WANT!"

. . . Drinks from a nursing bottle! . . . Drinks from a spoon! Breathes like a live baby! . . . Washes with Soap and Water.

You are going to have the most delightful surprise of your life when you see the new wonder doll . . . DY-DEE Baby! Picture to yourself the charm of Dy-Dee's lovely soft cuddly body, her real baby face . . . why, Dy-Dee is almost human!

Dy-Dee is the **only** doll that can drink from a bottle sitting up or lying down!

Dy-Dee is the **only** doll that can drink from a spoon! Imagine! You can actually see her sip the water as you hold the spoon to her lips.

And then a tiny valve on her hip releases this water slowly, and you will have to **change her diaper!**

Of course, you can wash Dy-Dee Baby all over with soap and water . . . and then you can powder her, feed her and put her to sleep. And she'll sleep sitting up or lie down with her eyes wide open!

What glorious fun you can have being a real mother to such an almost human child.

There is a whole family of Dy-Dee Babies—the youngest and newest addition to the family is Dy-Dee-Wee, only 9 inches ta1—Dy-Dee-Ette is 11 inches—Dy-Dee-Kin is 13 inches—Dy-Dee herself is 15 inches and Dy-Dee-Lou is 20 inches ta1.

Manufactured by Fleischaker & Baum.

Dy-Dee Baby

Free Offer to Readers of "ACTIVITIES"

We publish a very interesting magazine called Playtime News which tells all about the doings of the famous Patsy Doll family. We will be glad to put you on the mailing list free. Just write to

Aunt Patsy, The Patsy Doll Club, 45 Greene St., New York

ABOVE: Illustration 8. *Children's Activities* magazine for December 1937 featured a half page *Dy-Dee Baby* advertisement.

This is the famous "Dy-Dee-Ette" Doll, one of the most popular we ever handled. Almost human. Opens and closes her eyes, drinks from a bottle like a real infant, and—oh yes, frequently needs changing so that she will always be dry and comfortable. The need for bathing, feeding, changing, undressing and putting to bed will keep her little mama busy and happy day after day.

"Dy-Dee-Ette" is 11 inches high, is unbreakable because her body is made of soft rubber, and she comes equipped with shirt and diaper and bottle with a real nipple.

We give this expensive doll, that you can examine and price in your local store, free, postpaid, for *securing only three yearly subscriptions to Children's Activities* at only $3.00 each. You collect and remit the full subscription price paid you for each subscription, a total of $9.00 and on receipt of these three orders with the money, this lovely dolly will be sent you postpaid. Can you imagine an easier way to earn this Christmas Gift DeLuxe?

Child Training Association, Inc., 1018 So. Wabash Ave., Chicago, Ill.

ABOVE: Illustration 9. One could obtain a free 11in (27.9cm) *Dy-Dee-Ette* for sending in three subscriptions for *Children's Activities* magazine at $3.00 each. December 1937.

Dy-Dee Baby

Attention, little Mothers! Here is the genuine EFFanBEE Dy-Dee Baby doll you have been wanting. She is 15" tall, with all of the patented Dy-Dee features—drinks from a nursing bottle, breathes and feels like a live cuddly baby. She washes with soap and water, and wets her diapers. She is dressed in shirt, birdseye diaper, and rubber panties. Her head is of hard rubber, and the body of live rubber with a satin-like finish. Entirely waterproof. Her eyes open and shut either sitting or lying down. She can drink sitting up or lying down. The layette includes Silk jacket, Batiste dress, Organdy slip, Flannel bathrobe, Flannel booties, Lawn nursing cap, Lawn slip, Diary, and Booklet. Dy-Dee bottle, nipple, Dy-Dee and her layette carrying case in an airplane luggage carrying case, and organdy dressing pad. **Price,**

164 $10.00.

LEFT: Illustration 10. A December 1937 advertisement for "Playthings for Christmas" included the *Dy-Dee Baby* and her layette in an airplane luggage carrying case.

Illustration 11. McCall pattern 513 for "Baby Clothes for *Dy-Dee* Dolls" was available in 1937.

RIGHT: Illustration 12. The Montgomery Ward catalog for Fall — Winter, 1937 to 1938 shows both *Dy-Dee* and the separate layette that could be ordered.

Illustration 13. In 1940 Effanbee added rubber ears to their *Dy-Dee* dolls. Shown are twin *Dy-Dee-Ettes*, 11in (27.9cm), one with molded hair and the other with a lamb's wool wig. The hard rubber of the head is visible where the finish has worn away. The dolls are marked as shown in (B) in the text.

Fair in a special ceremony at the Lagoon of Nations. "Aunt Patsy," Bea Orlund, traveled around the country, appearing in department store toy sections to promote the *Dy-Dee* and other Effanbee dolls.

In their effort to make *Dy-Dee* "the almost human doll," Effanbee, in 1940, added soft, flexible, rubber ears that needed cleaning with a Q-tip. The dolls also were given "the cutest turned-up noses with nostrils that are open and need cleaning, too" to quote *Patsytown News*. The 1940s *Dy-Dee* came with molded straight hair or lamb's wool wigs on their hard rubber heads. The enamel finish on these heads is so shiny and hard, it can easily be mistaken for early hard plastic. The bodies of rubber were unchanged.

In 1948 a "cryer - pacifier" was added to the accessories that came with *Dy-Dee*. By inserting the pacifier in *Dy-Dee*'s mouth and then pressing her tummy, she could now cry as well as drink and wet. She could also blow soap bubbles, using a bubble pipe, as could the earlier *Dy-Dee*. She was available in 11in (27.9cm), 15in (38.1cm) and 20in (50.8cm) sizes.

By the late 1940s a new material, hard plastic, was being used in the manufacture of dolls. Effanbee replaced the hard rubber heads with ones of hard plastic, but still used the flexible rubber ears. The bodies were still made of soft rubber as before. A 13in (33cm) size was also available, in addition to the 11in (27.9cm), 15in (38.1cm) and 20in (50.8cm) sizes.

In 1950, when American Character introduced its *Tiny Tears* dolls, the resemblance to *Dy-Dee* was very obvious. *Tiny Tears* introduced a new feature. The dolls had tiny tear holes near the eye openings and could cry "real tears," hence the name *Tiny Tears*. Effanbee continued to produce the *Dy-Dees* in quantity and held its place in the doll market. The dolls were sold separately or in trunks with layettes as before. Eventually Effanbee also added the tear holes to their dolls.

All the rubber-bodied *Dy-Dee* dolls are well marked on their bodies. The earliest markings were: (A) "EFF AN BEE//DY-DEE BABY//PAT. NO. 1 859 485//OTHER PAT. PEND." As the other patents were registered, they were added to the information on the *Dy-Dee*'s backs. They read: (B) "EFF AN BEE//DY-DEE BABY//U.S. PAT. 1 859 485//ENGLAND 380 960//FRANCE 732 980//GERMANY 585647//OTHER PAT. PENDING." Still later dolls are marked: (C) "EFF AN BEE//DY-DEE BABY//U.S. PAT. 1 859 485//ENGLAND 380 960//FRANCE 723 980//GERMANY 585 647//U.S. 2 007 784//U.S. RE 21539//OTHER PAT. PENDING."

When the doll industry replaced rubber with the newer flexible vinyl

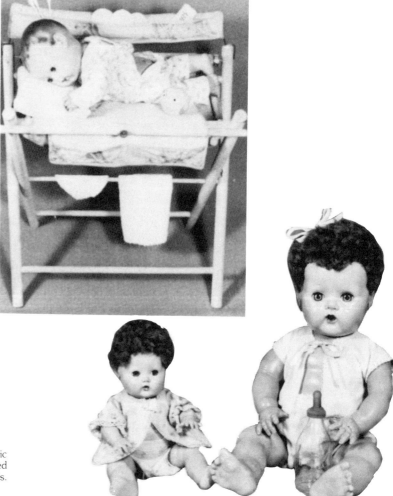

Illustration 15. The wood and cloth bathinette is from the author's Christmas, 1940. *Dy-Dee Baby's* original sleeper is unbuttoned to show the position of the opening for wetting. This 15in (38.1cm) doll has different markings. They are: "EFF-AN-BEE//DY-DEE-BABY // U.S. PATENTS // 2,007,784 // 2,037,052// 2,144,436//RE 19,849//RE 21,539//CANADA."

Illustration 14. Here is a 12in (30.5cm) *Dy-Dee* with a hard plastic head and rubber ears. The molded hair is curly. The doll is marked as shown in (C) in the text. The doll is probably from the late 1940s.

Illustration 17. These two Dy-Dee dolls are the wigged versions of the hard plastic head with rubber ears. They measure 13in (33cm) and 20in (50.8cm) and are marked as shown in (C) in the text. Their bodies are rubber.

plastics, Effanbee followed suit. The rubber bodies on the *Dy-Dee* dolls were replaced by vinyl bodies.

The all-vinyl *Dy-Dees* that made their appearance in the 1960s bear little resemblance to the earlier *Dy-Dee* dolls. Many were no longer identified on their bodies as *Dy-Dee Babies*, only on their heart-shaped paper wrist tags. For this reason these dolls are not easily identified once they have lost their tags. Several faces and body styles were used for *Dy-Dee* during this time. She came in several sizes also — 14in (35.6cm), 16in (40.6cm), 17in (43.2cm) and 18in (45.7cm), depending on the particular issue. Some dolls had the molded, painted hair; others had rooted hair. Black versions were also offered. To add to the confusion, Effanbee was also producing drink and wet babies other than *Dy-Dee*.

Montgomery Ward's 100th Anniversary, celebrated in 1973, included the *Dy-Dee* among its anniversary reissues. This doll was 17in (43.2cm) tall, all-vinyl with molded hair and dressed in a white jacket and diaper set and tied into a matching blanket.

A doll body with realistically curled chubby fingers and rather straight legs, that was first used in the 1960s, is the one used on the current *Dy-Dee Baby*. She was first introduced in the mid 1970s. She

measures 18in (45.7cm) and has a chubby, full cheeked face, small pouty mouth and very round sleep eyes. One version had molded hair and was dressed in a crocheted outfit. The most recent *Dy-Dee* comes with rooted blonde or brunette hair and wears a one-piece sleeper made from material patterned with little hearts and flowers and the words "Effanbee." A black version is also available. These dolls come with their very own teddy bears to hug. They are marked: "Effanbee//56 71" on the head and "Effanbee//1967" on the back. Only the paper wrist tag identifies the dolls as *Dy-Dee Baby*.

The *Dy-Dee* doll had another use besides that of a child's play doll. The large life-size *Dy-Dee* was promoted as "the perfect doll for pre-natal education, used by nursing classes, by Red Cross, Boards of Education, and Child Care Organizations the World Over." The 1970s all-vinyl large doll measures 21in (53.3cm) and is a heavy, sturdily built doll. The well-molded ears have openings into the head. The legs and arms are jointed so as to facilitate realistic movements.

Over the years numerous patterns were printed for *Dy-Dee* for those who chose to sew clothing for her, either for the sake of economy, for enjoyment or both. As early as 1937, McCall produced

Illustration 16. 15in (38.1cm) *Dy-Dee Baby* has a pale hard plastic head with straight molded hair and rubber ears. Her rubber body is marked as shown in (B) in the text.

a printed pattern number 513 of baby clothes for *Dy-Dee* dolls. The 1982 Simplicity pattern 5615 for 17in (43.2cm) to 18in (45.7cm) dolls shows the clothes modeled by the current *Dy-Dee Baby*.

Available at various times, to help add realism to the child's *Dy-Dee* play, were bathinettes, playpens, diaper pails and diaper bags, all fashioned like the real articles.

In the 1930s Queen Holden designed a lovely large paper doll book of *Dy-Dee* doll. A darling little child's book call *Dy-Dee Doll's Days* was published in 1937 by Rand McNally and Company of Chicago, Illinois. The book, written by Peggy Vandergriff and photographed by Lawson Fields, is the story of Peggy Ann who recieved *Dy-Dee* for her third birthday and tells of all the fun they shared.

For the collectors who love baby dolls, the *Dy-Dee* dolls, spanning a 50 year period, are certainly worthy of being included in their collections. □

Illustration 21. Today's *Dy-Dee Baby* is an 18in (45.7cm) all-vinyl doll with curled fingers and fairly straight legs. She is marked: "EFFANBEE//1967" on her back and "EFFANBEE//5671" on her head. She comes in sleepers with a bottle and teddy bear.

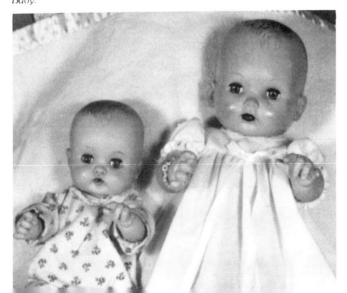

Illustration 20. A 21in (53.3cm) all-vinyl *Educational Dy-Dee* has kicked off her bootie to show her well modeled toes. The molded ears have openings into the head. The doll is marked on her back: "EFFANBEE//Dy-Dee Baby//(plus nine rows of patent numbers that are so faint they cannot be deciphered)."

Illustration 18. It is unusual to find mint-in-box *Dy-Dee* dolls. This 15in (38.1cm) doll has the hard plastic head on a rubber body and is marked as shown in (C) in the text. Her box is deep pink with a light blue label.

Illustration 19. Numerous all-vinyl *Dy-Dee* dolls were issued in the 1960s. Most of these were identified only by their tags. Shown here is a 17in (43.2cm) *Dy-Dee*, on the right, with molded hair, that is marked only: "EFFANBEE." Her body is like that of *My Fair Baby*, 14in (35.6cm), on the left. The heads are similar, but *Dy-Dee's* forehead is less protruding and her hair modeling is different than *My Fair Baby*.

Illustration 22. Simplicity pattern 5615, currently available, is for 17in (43.2cm) and 18in (45.7cm) baby dolls and shows *Dy-Dee Baby* modeling the clothes.

167

Drink and Wet Babies, Part II: *Betsy Wetsy* and *Tiny Tears*

by **Mary Rickert Stuecher**

Photographs by **Werner Stuecher**

All dolls from the collections of Jean Anderson and the author.

When a new doll innovation is successfully developed for the market, other doll companies waste no time in making their own versions available to the buying public. The most notable of the early competitors to Effanbee's *Dy-Dee* dolls was the *Betsy Wetsy* produced by Ideal. She made her nationwide debut in the autumn of 1937. The dolls were constructed similarly to *Dy-Dee*, but *Betsy Wetsy* had a prettier face. Early advertisements state that "her idonite head of hard rubber is waterproof" and her "lifelike body is of Tru-flesh rubber." The enamel coating on her head was not bonded as well as the Effanbee *Dy-Dee*'s was and repeated bottle feedings could cause the paint to flake away.

Betsy Wetsy had wavy brown molded hair and lashed sleep eyes with eye shadow to enhance their size. Some of the eyes were glassene; others were painted tin. She was marked simply "IDEAL" on her head and "IDEAL" in raised letters on her rubber back. The dolls came in one size only, approximately 11in (27.9cm), as far as is known. They were sold individually in brightly colored boxes or in suitcases with layettes.

My own childhood drink and wet doll was a *Betsy Wetsy,* received for Christmas 1937. She came dressed in a sleeveless undershirt and pink-edged diaper. Her layette consisted of a glass bottle, extra diaper, powder puffs, cotton lace-edged slip, white dotted swiss dress and bonnet, flannelette bathrobe and a pair of pink banded rayon socks. The local toy departments carried a nice selection of clothing sized to fit this doll. Subsequent Christmases brought a pink bunting of blanket flannel, flannel pajamas with feet, flannel baby jacket, and a knitted wool sweater, bonnet and bootie set. Scarce pennies were frugally hoarded to provide the amount needed to purchase cute little dime store dresses at 10¢ apiece. The rest

Illustration 1. The first *Betsy Wetsy* doll made her debut in 1937. She measures 11in (27.9cm), has a rubber body and "idonite" head. Her clothing is all original. She is marked only: "IDEAL."

of Betsy's wardrobe was hand-sewn by me from scraps provided by and supervised by my patient mother.

To attest to the popularity of drink and wet dolls in the late 1930s, I recall that ALL my playmates had them. Only a few also had the rather expensive *Shirley Temple* doll.

Both *Betsy Wetsy* and *Dy-Dee* have been offered as subscription premium dolls. One could earn a free *Dy-Dee-ette* for three yearly subscriptions to *Children's Activities* magazine in December 1937. *Betsy Wetsy* in a travel case was offered free in the December 1937 issue of *Women's World* for six subscriptions at 50¢ each or for two subscriptions to *Child Life* at $2.50 each in January 1938. The January 1938 *The Household Magazine* ran a contest to name the baby doll pictured, which was a *Betsy Wetsy*. The prize for the name chosen was $100, a fortune in Depression days!

Betsy Wetsy changed little over the next few years. In the late 1940s she was issued with a hard plastic head on a rubber body. Her eyes were oval-shaped and her mouth small. The rubber body was a dark color underneath a flesh pink rubber coating. She was marked on her head: "MADE IN USA//PAT NO 2252077" and "IDEAL DOLL" on her back.

In the 1950s she appeared with the same hard plastic head on a vinyl body. The eye openings were cut rounder and she had tear holes like the *Tiny Tears*. Some issues of the doll also had pierced nostrils to accommodate the crier which squeeked when her body was squeezed. Her head had either molded painted hair or a curly lamb's wool wig. She was available in several sizes. An advertisement in *Life* magazine in 1956 described her as follows: "She drinks, she sleeps, she wets, she weeps. And her magic flesh stays pink for life." She came boxed with a layette.

Her progression followed that of other dolls of the times. About 1959 she was given a vinyl head and vinyl body with widespread, well-defined fingers and toes. The all-vinyl *Betsy Wetsys* that followed had the same basic body and head model. Variations in eye shape and mouth painting, as well as hair styles, gave individuality to the various issues. Vinyl *Betsy Wetsys* can be found in 9in (22.9cm), 12in (30.5cm), 13in (33cm), 16in (40.6cm), 18in (45.7cm), 20in (50.8cm) and 24in (61cm) sizes. There are numerous markings in addition to "IDEAL DOLL" or "IDEAL TOY CORP."

Betsy Wetsys have been absent from toy shelves for a number of years, but were offered again in 1983 in several sizes and styles.

In direct compeition to the 1930s *Dy-Dee*, American Character Doll Company made a drink and wet baby called *Wee-Wee*. After court action for plagiarism the name was changed to *Bottletot*. The most

Illustration 2. The author and her sister, Joanne, received twin *Betsy Wetsy* dolls for Christmas 1937. The only difference was the eyes; one had brown tin eyes, the other brown glassene eyes. Shown is an original box *Betsy Wetsy* came in.

Illustration 3. *Betsy Wetsy* and Travel Case. *Women's World*, December 1937, advertisement.

Send Us a Name for This Doll
We will pay you $100.00 for the outstanding name

RIGHT: Illustration 4. The *Household Magazine*, January 1938, offered $100 for the outstanding name for *Betsy Wetsy*.

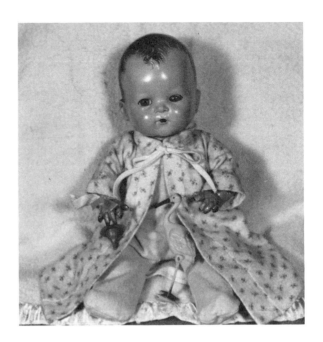

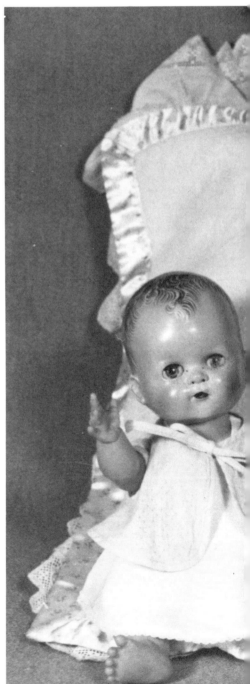

ABOVE LEFT: Illustration 5. *Betsy Wetsy* from a Christmas toy catalog advertisement, circa 1942.

ABOVE RIGHT: Illustration 6. This *Betsy Wetsy* from the late 1940s has a hard plastic head on a rubber body. She measures 12in (30.5cm) and is marked: "MADE IN U.S.A.//PAT. NO. 2252077" on her head and "IDEAL DOLL" on her back.

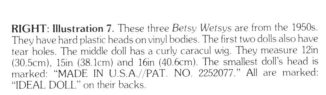

RIGHT: Illustration 7. These three *Betsy Wetsys* are from the 1950s. They have hard plastic heads on vinyl bodies. The first two dolls also have tear holes. The middle doll has a curly caracul wig. They measure 12in (30.5cm), 15in (38.1cm) and 16in (40.6cm). The smallest doll's head is marked: "MADE IN U.S.A.//PAT. NO. 2252077." All are marked: "IDEAL DOLL" on their backs.

threatening competition to the *Dy-Dee* came in 1950 when American Character Doll Company patented *Tiny Tears*. This patent, number 539-154, was registered on December 19, 1950. Their new innovation was a mechanism that enabled the dolls to cry "real tears" from two tiny tear holes near the inner eye openings.

The early *Tiny Tears* had hard plastic heads on rubber bodies and came in sizes 11½in (29.2cm), 13in (33cm), 16in (40.6cm) and 20in (50.8cm). One had the choice of painted molded hair in a straight style or the wigged version of curly lamb's wool hair. Later the hard plastic heads were given Saran hair rooted in an inset skull cap, and still later the rubber bodies were replaced by vinyl.

Tiny Tears could not only drink and wet and cry tears; she could also blow bubbles with her own tiny bubble pipe and even fall asleep realistically. This last feature was achieved by the "rockabye" eyes that gradually closed as *Tiny Tears* was rocked by her child mother.

The very popular NBC television program, "Ding Dong School," hosted by Miss Frances, claimed *Tiny Tears* as its star pupil. Miss Frances frequently used *Tiny Tears* as a teaching aid for her young television audience.

Tiny Tears came with a layette in a suitcase. These varied over the years, as did the style of the clothing articles the suitcases contained. The early dolls wore knit cotton panties and shirts, the later dolls wore white cotton plisse-crepe sunsuits trimmed in pink. The layettes included a dress and bonnet, flannel bathrobe, diapers, shoes and socks or machine knit booties, bottle, Kleenex, bubble pipe, pacifier, clothespins, sponge, washcloth, soap and instruction book.

Tiny Tears' popularity dwindled when the doll was redesigned in an all-vinyl version and issued in the 1960s. These dolls had rooted Saran straight hair and came in three sizes. *Teeny Weeny Tiny Tears* measured 9in (22.9cm); *Teeny Tiny Tears,* 12in (30.5cm); and *Tiny Tears,* 17in (43.2cm). The two smaller dolls have bodies with slender limbs and curved fingers imitative of young infants. The largest size has chubbier body, arms and legs. The baby faces closely resemble those of very young babies and have the mouth shape and receding chin of newborns. The dolls have no tear holes. These baby dolls were not the "pretty" type, but have an appeal all of their own. They were sold alone, in trunk sets or with additional packaged outfits. Prior to this, in 1962, Sears Roebuck and Company had sold a 20in (50.8cm) *Tiny Tears* with the chubby body style.

Illustration 8. This advertisement in a 1956 *Life* magazine introduced the *Campbell Kids* as *Betsy Wetsy*'s new playmates.

ABOVE: Illustration 9. McCall's pattern 2261 from 1958 was for *Tiny Tears*, *Betsy Wetsy* and *Dy-Dee* baby dolls.

LEFT: Illustration 10. All-vinyl *Betsy Wetsy* from about 1960 came with either rooted or molded hair. They measure 12in (35.5cm) and 16in (40.6cm) and are marked: "IDEAL DOLL//WC-1-1," (left), and "IDEAL DOLL//VW-3," (right).

BELOW: Illustration 11. These all-vinyl *Betsy Wetsys* date from the later 1960s. The smaller doll is dressed in her original seersucker play dress and panties, is 13in (33cm) tall and is marked: "IDEAL TOY CORP.//TD 12-W. PAT. PEND." on her head and "1965 IDEAL TOY CORP.//TD-12//2" on her body. Big sister, 25in (63.5cm), is marked: "IDEAL TOY CORP//OBW-20-5" on head and "BW-20" on the back. She is wearing real baby clothes.

Illustration 12. *Tiny Tears* by American Character Doll Company was keen competition for the *Dy-Dee* doll in the 1950s. Posing together are the 15in (38.1cm) *Dy-Dee Baby* on the left and the 16in (40.6cm) *Tiny Tears* on the right.

Illustration 13. The four sizes of *Tiny Tears* dolls with hard plastic heads on rubber bodies measure 19in (48.3cm), 16in (40.6cm), 13½in (34.3cm) and 11in (27.9cm). The largest and smallest are marked: "PAT. NO. 2, 675, 644" in addition to "AMERICAN CHARACTER" and are a little later issue. The 19in (48.3cm) *Tiny Tears* has the inset wig and rockabye eyes.

Illustration 14. These four *Tiny Tears* have hard plastic heads on vinyl bodies. The wigs are all inset in soft vinyl skull caps. The dolls carry both the company name and the patent number. The sizes are 11in (27.9cm), 13½in (34.3cm), 16in (40.6cm) and 19in (48.3cm).

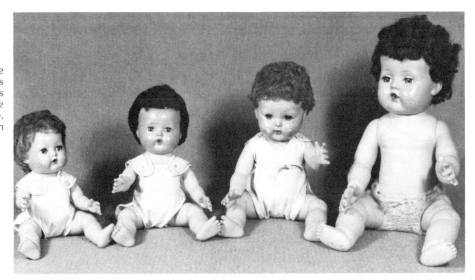

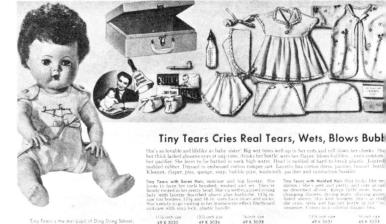

Tiny Tears Cries Real Tears, Wets, Blows Bubbl

She's as lovable and lifelike as baby sister! Big wet tears well up in her eyes and roll down her cheeks. She her thick lashed glassene eyes at nap time, drinks her bottle, wets her diaper, blows bubbles ... even comfort her pacifier. She loves to be bathed in neck high water. Head is molded of hard-to-break plastic. Jointe moldel rubber. Dressed in embossed cotton romper suit. Layette has cotton dress, panties, bonnet, bottl Kleenex, diaper, pins, sponge, soap, bubble pipe, washcloth, pacifier and instruction booklet.

Tiny Tears with Saran Hair, suitcase and big layette. She loves to have her curls brushed, washed and set. They're firmly rooted in her pretty head. She's a well equipped young lady with layette described above plus bathrobe 11½ in. size has bootees; 13½ and 16 in. sizes have shoes and socks. She's ready to go visiting in her leatherette-effect fiberboard suitcase with snap lock, plastic handle.

Tiny Tears with Molded Hair that looks like rea shown. She's pert and pretty and cute as can as described above. Keeps little mom busy changing diapers, drying tears, playing game listed above, plus knit bootees. She's as real she cries, wets and has her bottle at her con venience. Comes in a colorful diaper box.

Tiny Tears is the star-pupil of Ding Dong School, a National Broadcasting Co., Inc., Service and Trademark.

	11½-inch size	13½-inch size	16-inch size		13½-inch size	16-inch size
	49 K 3035	49 K 3036	49 K 3038		49 K 3031	49 K 3033
	Shpg. wt. 3 lbs.	Shpg. wt. 4 lbs.	Shpg. wt. 6 lbs.		Shpg. wt. 3 lbs.	Shpg. wt. 4 lbs.
	$9.37	$11.27	$13.90		$7.47	19.46

Illustration 16. *Tiny Tears* advertisement in the Sears, Roebuck and Company Spring · Summer catalog for 1957.

Illustration 15. Two 13½in (34.3cm) *Tiny Tears* perched atop an original pink suitcase model the two styles of pink and white dresses. *Tiny Tears* on the left wears the older version.

Illustration 17. McCall's pattern 1657 was specially issued for *Tiny Tears* in 1951.

This doll could wave its arm when its stomach was pressed.

When the American Character Doll Company went out of business in the late 1960s, Ideal purchased some of their molds and patent names. This explains why Ideal could produce a *Tiny Tears* doll in 1972 and then include it among their reissues of old favorites in 1981. The Ideal *Tiny Tears* has no resemblance whatsoever to the American Character *Tiny Tears*. The Ideal version is a 14in (45.6cm) all-vinyl doll with a one-piece, non-jointed body, large round glassene eyes and either molded or rooted blonde Saran hair. One innovation to this is the 1982 soft-bodied *Tiny Tears* in which, for the first time, a tearing mechanism has been put into a cloth bodied infant doll. The tear holes are absent.

The 1970 *Tiny Tears* came only in a disposable diaper. The 1980s version is packaged in attractive boxes, dressed in pretty baby dresses or flannel romper outfit or with additional layette. Both wigged and molded hair styles are offered. The latest dolls have a "bisque skin coloration" which is very lifelike in appearance, or come in a soft brown tone.

In 1951 McCall's issued pattern number 1657 of "Baby Doll Clothes to Fit the Tiny Tears Doll." Other patterns generally were designed for several baby dolls, listing the *Dy-Dee, Betsy Wetsy* and *Tiny Tears* among them.

A boxed set of paper dolls by Magic Wand of Charlestown, Massachusetts, in the 1960s was called "Tiny Tears with Rockabye Cradle." The 9in (22.9cm) doll and put-together cradle were of heavy cardboard. The clothing was the type that adhered to the doll simply by pressing it to the doll's body with the "magic wand."

Drink and wet baby dolls are a staple item in toy departments today. Nearly every American manufacturer of a full line of dolls includes drink and wet versions among its baby dolls. Some of these modern babies, such as Horsman's *Tynie Ruthie* and *Tynie David*, are even sexed dolls.

There is something sad about a doll from a bygone era that is found in pristine condition. Most likely that doll was not played with and loved. Most drink and wet babies show evidence that the opposite was true. They were fed and diapered, bathed and powdered, dressed and undressed, carried about and taken to bed. Very few turn up in "like new" condition. These beloved playthings gave an abundance of pleasure to their child mothers "yesterday" and continue to do so today for their collector mothers. □

ABOVE: Illustration 18. The new *Tiny Tears* in the 1960s came in all-vinyl and in three sizes: 12in (22.9cm) *Teeny Tiny Tears*, 17in (43.2cm) *Tiny Tears* and 9in (22.9cm) *Teeny Weeny Tiny Tears*. The largest doll has a chubbier body.

BELOW: Illustration 19. The 12in (22.9cm) *Teeny Tiny Tears* shows her slender "young infant" body modeling.

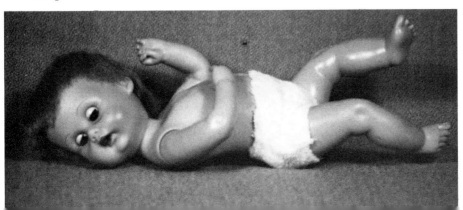

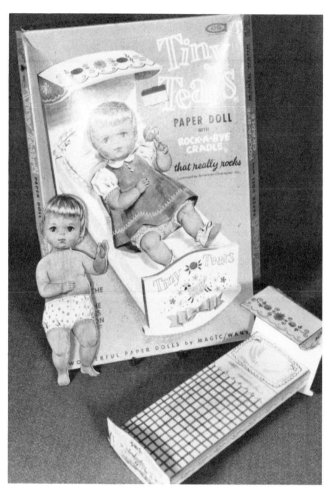

Illustration 20. A 1960s *Tiny Tears* paper doll set published by Magic Wand.

Illustration 21. Ideal's version of *Tiny Tears*, produced in 1972, measures 14in (35.6cm) and is an orangey vinyl with non-jointed body. The marks are (head): "© 1972//Ideal Toy Corp.//TNT-14-R-210" and (back): "© 1971//Ideal Toy Corp.//TNT-14-8-24."

BELOW: Illustration 23. Horsman's *Tynie Ruthie* and *Tynie David* are sexed drink and wet dolls. They are 7in (17.8cm) dolls with non-jointed bodies and turning heads are from 1980.

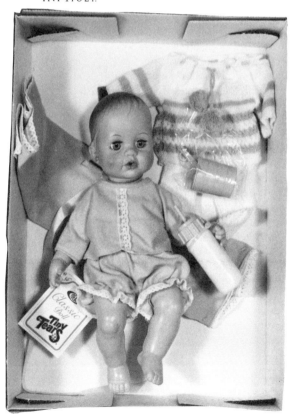

ABOVE: Illustration 22. Ideal's 1981 reissue of *Tiny Tears* is a paler vinyl, measures 14in (35.6cm) and comes with both molded hair or rooted hair. She is marked (head): "© 1971 IDEAL/TNT-14-H-370" and (body): "© 1971//IDEAL TOY CORP.//TNT-14-8-34." She is shown boxed with her layette. This doll does not sleep.

Kiddie Pal Dolly — A Doll in her Original Box

by **Ursula R. Mertz**

Photographs by **Otto J. Mertz**

Finding a doll in her original marked box is a special joy for any collector. When this box yields an unmarked doll, I feel like Sherlock Holmes in hot pursuit of a mystery about to be solved.

The doll that I am presenting here is unmarked and came in a box labeled only "Kiddie Pal Dolly." The Colemans' *Collector's Encyclopedia of Dolls* revealed that it is the trade name for a line of dolls registered in 1928 by the Regal Doll Manufacturing Co., New York City. This line was new in 1929, but still sold in the early 1930s. Regal produced a wide range of composition dolls. The Butler Brothers catalog of 1928 shows several versions of *Kiddie Pal Dollies* alone, ranging in price from $7.95 a dozen to $24.00 a dozen. (See *More Twentieth Century Dolls*, by J. G. Anderton, page 1053.)

Even though I am an avid collector of composition dolls, this is only the second *Kiddie Pal Dolly* I have been able to add to my collection. This is puzzling when one considers that in 1923, for example, the Regal Doll Manufacturing Co. produced 6000 dolls a day. It could be that many, like mine, are unmarked and waiting to be identified.

Illustration 1. 19in (48cm) all original *Kiddie Pal Dolly* girl. Her pink cotton dress has a matching combination and bonnet. The outfit is of simple construction and trimmed with cheap white cotton lace. The hem of the dress is decorated with two rows of white and blue lace in front and only one row in back. She is wearing white cotton socks and black oilcloth shoes.

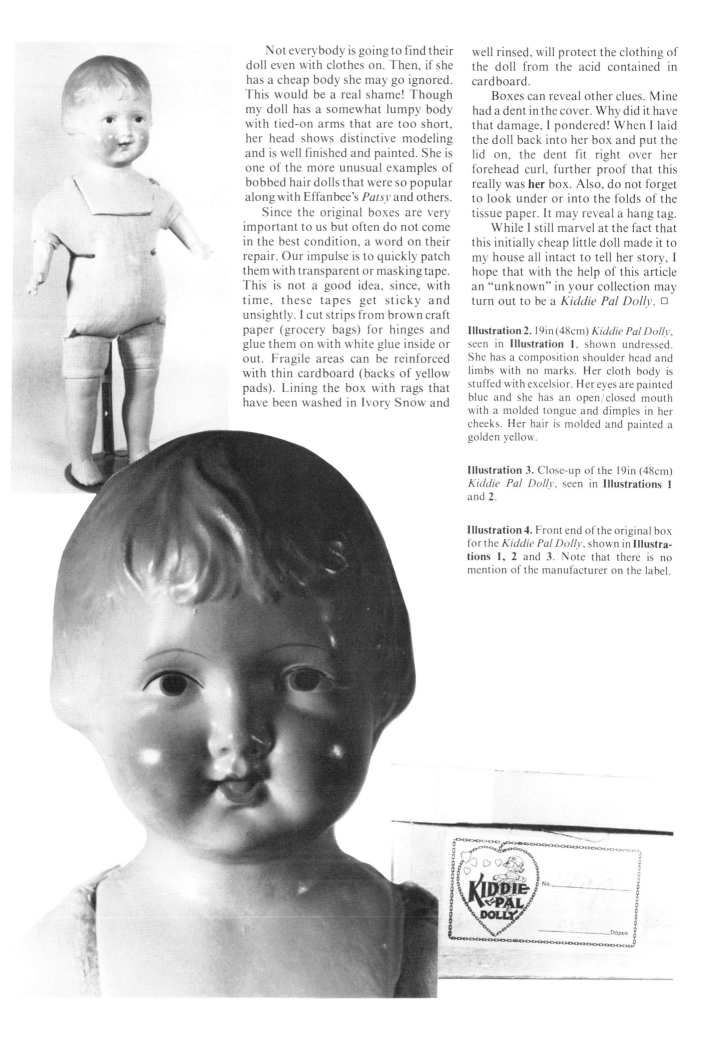

Not everybody is going to find their doll even with clothes on. Then, if she has a cheap body she may go ignored. This would be a real shame! Though my doll has a somewhat lumpy body with tied-on arms that are too short, her head shows distinctive modeling and is well finished and painted. She is one of the more unusual examples of bobbed hair dolls that were so popular along with Effanbee's *Patsy* and others.

Since the original boxes are very important to us but often do not come in the best condition, a word on their repair. Our impulse is to quickly patch them with transparent or masking tape. This is not a good idea, since, with time, these tapes get sticky and unsightly. I cut strips from brown craft paper (grocery bags) for hinges and glue them on with white glue inside or out. Fragile areas can be reinforced with thin cardboard (backs of yellow pads). Lining the box with rags that have been washed in Ivory Snow and well rinsed, will protect the clothing of the doll from the acid contained in cardboard.

Boxes can reveal other clues. Mine had a dent in the cover. Why did it have that damage, I pondered! When I laid the doll back into her box and put the lid on, the dent fit right over her forehead curl, further proof that this really was **her** box. Also, do not forget to look under or into the folds of the tissue paper. It may reveal a hang tag.

While I still marvel at the fact that this initially cheap little doll made it to my house all intact to tell her story, I hope that with the help of this article an "unknown" in your collection may turn out to be a *Kiddie Pal Dolly*. □

Illustration 2. 19in (48cm) *Kiddie Pal Dolly*, seen in **Illustration 1**, shown undressed. She has a composition shoulder head and limbs with no marks. Her cloth body is stuffed with excelsior. Her eyes are painted blue and she has an open/closed mouth with a molded tongue and dimples in her cheeks. Her hair is molded and painted a golden yellow.

Illustration 3. Close-up of the 19in (48cm) *Kiddie Pal Dolly*, seen in **Illustrations 1** and **2**.

Illustration 4. Front end of the original box for the *Kiddie Pal Dolly*, shown in **Illustrations 1, 2** and **3**. Note that there is no mention of the manufacturer on the label.

Unica Dolls of Belgium

by Polly & Pam Judd

Illustration 1. An early Unica doll dressed in an all-original beige velvet dress with beautiful Belgium lace trim. The cloche is made of straw trimmed with lace and flowers.

"Unica has been founded in 1921, and made from that time dolls in all sorts of materials. By 1940, it had become one of the most important manufacturers in Europe, occupying up to 400 people, and using the most advanced of techniques." So states a letter from J. Libeer, Managing Director of the Unica Company of Belgium. Libeer further stated:

"Its premises were destroyed twice during the war but by 1950 it again had become a prominent manufacturer. In the early sixties, its activities somehow slacked down, as it had failed to understand the growing demand for cheaper items, and did not cope with the ever growing competition of cheap labour countries.

"In 1971 a fire completely destroyed the manufacturing facilities and offices. Practically nothing was left of its collection, archives, etc. The owners decided not to reconstruct the plant, and converted their activities to wholesaling of general toys.

"Since then, we became the leading toy importers and distributors in Belgium, but do not have any manufacturing left. The dolls made by Unica, especially in the periods 1930-39 and 1947-65, are much in demand as collectors items, but very few are left."

Many of the Unica dolls of 1930 to 1939 have beautiful glass eyes in a composition or papier-mâché head. Often these dolls have a darker skin than we would see in the dolls from other countries. Usually well marked, they have a charm of their own and command attention. Despite the variety of materials, a Unica doll has a touch that separates it from the dolls of other manufacturers.

The flapper type doll, seen in **Illustration 1**, is from the early 1930s. It is 23in (58cm) tall. The socket head is made of a sturdy composition which some collectors have identified as papier-mâché. It is different from the usual composition known in the United States. She has a traditional strung composition ball-jointed body. The neck has a circle marking with "Verhoye Courtray Made in Belgium" around the outside of the circle, and "Unica//60//BR.//415.013" in the middle.

A later 1930s 21in (53cm) doll, seen in **Illustration 2**, has a shinier composition head and body with a very interesting walking mechanism. Her clothes are all original, and she still has her very sturdy original blue box with the Unica label which is shown in **Illustration 3**.

A much smaller 14in (36cm) doll, seen in **Illustration 4**, is painted bisque. She also has the deeper flesh tone of the composition dolls. Only her head is original with the original white earrings swinging merrily from her ears. The dress was made by York, England, doll club members.

Another small 8in (20cm) painted bisque doll, seen in **Illustration 5**, has the deep complexion. She is a lovely tourist-type doll dressed in Belgium lace.

Immediately after World War II Unica began to manufacture dolls with whatever material was available. A series of glazed bisque dolls on cloth bodies was made honoring the liberation. These were called rattle dolls because of the stones in their heads. There was a deep need for playthings for small children who had been deprived of toys for so many years. A tag on the doll in **Illustration 6**, says, "Liberated Holland//Unica patent Courtray Belgium." She is all original and came in a beautiful purple box with flowers and gold leaves. Inside the box was a handwritten note which said, "September 25, 1945 from Liberated Holland."

Another rattle doll of the series, seen in **Illustration 8**, has a tag from "Liberated Belgium." In keeping with tradition, the cloth has a similar deep flesh tone as had their earlier dolls.

Soon, as in other Western countries, hard plastic began to be used for dolls. Unica turned to this medium for an interesting 14in (36cm) doll, seen in **Illustration 9**, with a most unusual wig. It was a rubber cap which fits over the head and lower hair and has rooted hair. A small portion of the rubber can be seen in the illustration. It looks like a hair band. She has the brilliant blue

Illustration 2. A 1930s composition doll with an unusual wood walking mechanism, wearing a blue print ruffled cotton dress with organdy trim.

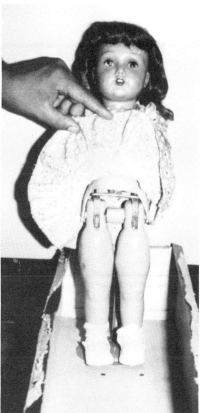

RIGHT: Illustration 3. The same walking doll seen in **Illustration 2**, all original with her box and showing her walking mechanism.

FAR RIGHT: Illustration 4. This 14in (36cm) painted bisque socket head doll has a pink print dress and hat.

Illustration 6. Within two months of the end of World War II this "Liberated" doll was purchased in Belgium. Although the company used a coarse glazed pottery for the head, the children could once more have toys. She is dressed in a Dutch costume of red, white and blue and has shiny red wooden shoes. *Pat Parton Collection.*

Illustration 5. Tourists could take home the beautiful Belgium lace when they purchased this 8in (20cm) Unica painted bisque doll. The dress is a beautiful rich brown.

Illustration 7. The beautiful box of Unica showed the pride of "Liberated Belgium." *Pat Parton Collection.*

ABOVE: Illustration 8. A "Liberated Belgium" doll, another in the series. She is dressed in bright yellow and orange stripes with a black apron. Her smile shows the happiness of the people.

RIGHT: Illustration 9. Soon Unica was using hard plastic for beautiful dolls for their eager customers. This 14in (36cm) one has an unusual rubber cap wig with an early type of rooted hair. *Private Collection.*

eyes that are typical of the company. There is a crier inside her body which so many European hard plastic dolls have. Many of the markings of Unica pertain to royalty and crown traditions.

Vinyl dolls appeared in the late 1950s and early 1960s, and Unica made these typical all-vinyl dolls for the mass market. The first of these dolls had a rigid vinyl body and unusual rigid vinyl head. The quality is excellent. The doll shown in **Illustration 11**, is 12½in (32cm) and has brown sleep eyes, rooted hair and a closed mouth. The clothes are not original.

The larger doll in the middle in **Illustration 12** is 15½in (39cm) and has a rigid vinyl body with a soft vinyl head and arms. She, too, has bright blue sleep eyes but unusually light skin for a Unica doll. The clothes are not original. She is marked: "Unica//Belgium" on the back of the neck.

The smaller dolls in **Illustration 12** are 12½in (32cm) and have rigid vinyl bodies and legs and soft vinyl head and arms. While their clothes may not be original, they did come from Belgium. They are also marked: "Unica// Belgium."

Today in Belgium, other parts of Europe and in the United States, these interesting dolls are beginning to attract attention and their value has risen in the past few years. Dealers and collectors in Belgium, especially, have begun to realize the importance of their heritage, and Unica dolls, which brought only a few francs three or four years ago, bring many times that amount today. □

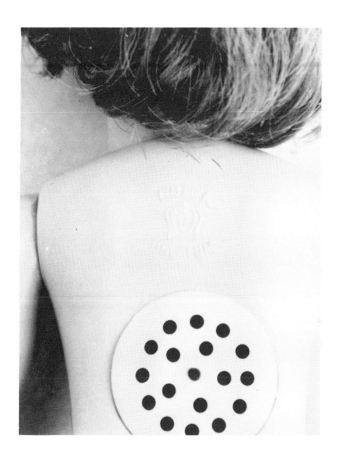

ABOVE LEFT: Illustration 10. The Unica Company used beautiful marks on their dolls. Often it was a crown or a royal symbol of some kind. *Private Collection.*

ABOVE RIGHT: Illustration 11. Although not in original clothes, this rooted hair doll with a rigid vinyl body and soft vinyl head was of excellent quality. *Private Collection.*

RIGHT: Illustration 12. As in other parts of the world, the cheaper vinyl dolls soon flooded the market. These three have rooted hair. The smaller dolls have Belgium-made clothes. *Private Collection.*

The Many Faces of *Ken*®, *Barbie's*® Boyfriend

by **Linda Poirier Holderbaum**

Ken® (number 750) introduced as "*Barbie's*® Boyfriend" in 1961, was 12in (30cm) tall and had a crew cut with flocked hair in blonde, brunette or brown. His eyes were painted looking straight ahead and he has a closed mouth and somewhat solemn expression, as seen in *Illustration 1*.

The flocked hair did not stand up well to child's play so changes were made a year later. A longer thinner face mold was used, with lighter eyes with no highlights. This *Ken* also had a molded painted crew cut available in either blonde or brunette coloring. Shown in *Illustration 2*, he still had the same series number (number 0750) and the same body mark as the previous *Ken*.

Ken (number 750) grew shorter in 1963. His new body was 1/4in (.65cm) shorter than the earlier dolls and had wider arms and more pronounced kneecaps. The face remained

ABOVE LEFT: Illustration 1. *12in (30cm) first edition* Ken® *(number 750), by Mattel, 1961, with a flocked blonde crew cut which was available in either blonde or brunette; manufactured of vinyl, he is jointed at the neck, shoulders and hips; has painted blue eyes looking straight ahead and a painted closed mouth. He is marked "Ken TM//PATD PEND//© MCMLX//BY//MATTEL//INC." A second issue* Ken *was also released with flocked hair.*

ABOVE CENTER: Illustration 2. *12in (30cm)* Ken® *(number 0750), by Mattel, 1962, with a molded blonde crew cut which was available in either blonde or brunette; manufactured of vinyl, he is jointed at the neck, shoulders and hips; have painted blue eyes looking straight ahead, a painted closed mouth and painted hair. He is marked: "Ken TM//PATD PEND//© MCMLX//BY//MATTEL//INC." This head mold was used from 1962 to 1968.* •

ABOVE RIGHT: Illustration 3. *12in (30cm) Hawaiian* Ken® *(number 2960), by Mattel, 1978, advertised as "Special! Includes Surfboard and Accessories;" has molded painted dark brown hair, painted eyes and an open/closed mouth; manufactured of vinyl;* Ken® *has a very wide leg stance and straight arms with palms facing back. He is marked on the back of his neck: "© 1968 MATTEL INC." and on his back: "1088-0500 2//© MATTEL//INC. 1968//HONG KONG."*

unchanged. He was marked: "Ken©//© 1960//by//Mattel, Inc.//Hawthorn//Calif. U.S.A."

"*Barbie's* Boyfriend" then proceeded to grow back to his original height (12in [30cm]) in 1964. Still sporting the 1962 hairdo and face mold, he had different body markings: "©1960//by//Mattel, Inc.//Hawthorn//Calif. U.S.A."

From 1965 to 1967 *Ken* was essentially unchanged but was available with bendable legs (number 1020) or with straight legs (number 0750).

Ken took a leave of absence during 1968 and returned in 1969 as *Neat Good-Looking Talking Ken* (number 1111), with a pinker toned skin color and a molded and painted brown "Edwardian" hairdo. Parted on the left, the slightly longer hair was more in fashion with the times and his

subtle smile lent a friendlier look. This head mold can be seen in *Illustration 3* on *Hawaiian Ken*. The same face mold was used for this *Ken* in the 1978 department store special. *Neat Good-Looking Talking Ken* was marked: "©1968//Mattel, Inc.//U.S. + For. Pat'd//Other Pat's//Pending//Mexico."

This model was used for *Spanish Talking Ken* (number 8372) in 1969 and the bendable leg *Ken* (number 1124), and also the *Talking Ken* and *Spanish Speaking Ken* produced in 1970.

Live Action Ken (number 1159), produced in Taiwan in "mod"est fashions in 1971, still used the same mold but with the addition of a jointed waist body section. He was marked: "© 1968//Mattel, Inc.//Taiwan//U.S. + For. Pat'd//Patented in//

Canada 1967//Other Pats.//Pending." His head was marked: "©1968 Mattel, Inc."

Ken appeared in 1971 with tanned skin and blonde molded hair instead of the brown color as *Malibu Ken* (number 1088). Again using the same face mold as seen in *Illustration 3*, he was produced in Hong Kong and marked: "©1968//Mattel, Inc.//U.S. + For. Pat'd//Other Pats.//Pending//Hong Kong." *Malibu Ken* remained essentially the same through 1974.

Ken became more flexible in 1972 with *Walk Lively Ken* (number 1184). All the "Walk Lively" dolls, which included *Barbie*, *Ken*, *Steffie* and *Miss America*, had arms and heads that turned as their legs were moved. *Walk Lively Ken's* hair was painted brown, using the same face mold as before and his mark was:

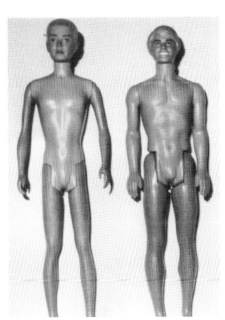

ABOVE LEFT: Illustration 4. *12in (30cm) Now Look Ken* (number 9342), by Mattel, 1976, with rooted brown shoulder-length hair; manufactured of vinyl, jointed at the neck, shoulders and hips; painted eyes, feathered eyebrows and open/closed mouth. This doll was issued twice with slight changes in the arm molding and the hair length. The first issue was marked: "©1968//MATTEL, INC//U.S. + FOR. PATD//OTHER PATS//PENDING//TAIWAN." The second issue was marked: "1088-0500 3//© MATTEL//INC. 1968//HONG KONG." Rosemary Deal Collection.*

ABOVE CENTER: Illustration 5. *A comparison of the Ken bodies. Left to right: first edition Ken (number 750), 1962; Sunsational Malibu Ken (number 3849), 1982. Note the muscle structure to the body which is developed in the Malibu Ken that is lacking in the first edition Ken. Also note the change in position of Ken's hands in relation to his body — this varies with the particular doll.*

ABOVE RIGHT: Illustration 6. *12in (30cm) Sport N' Shave Ken (number 1294), by Mattel, 1980, with rooted brown hair; manufactured of vinyl, he is jointed at the neck, shoulders, waist and hips; has painted blue eyes looking straight ahead, a painted open/closed mouth showing teeth and molded dimples. He is marked on the back of his neck: "MATTEL, INC." and on the back: "© MATTEL INC. 1968//TAIWAN."*

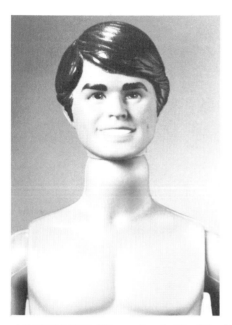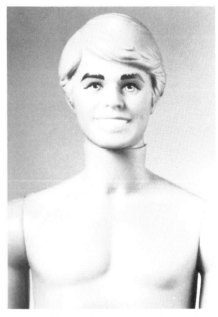

ABOVE LEFT: Illustration 7. *12in (30cm) Western Ken® (number 3600), by Mattel, 1981, with molded and painted dark brown hair; manufactured of vinyl, he is jointed at the neck, shoulders, waist and hips; has painted blue eyes looking straight ahead, a painted open/closed mouth showing teeth and molded dimples. He is marked on the back: "© MATTEL INC. 1968//TAIWAN" (the same mark as on the* Sport N' Shave Ken®*).*

ABOVE CENTER: Illustration 8. *A comparison of the Ken® bodies. Left to right:* Sport N' Shave Ken® *(number 1294), 1980 and* Western Ken® *(number 3600), 1981. With these dolls the muscle structure is highly developed. Note the differences in the arms. The doll on the left has straight arms with jointed wrists while the doll on the right has curved unjointed arms.*

ABOVE RIGHT: Illustration 9. *12in (30cm) Sunsational Malibu Ken® (number 3849), by Mattel, 1982, with molded and painted blonde hair; manufactured of vinyl, he is jointed at the neck, shoulders and hips; has painted blue eyes looking straight ahead, a painted open/closed mouth showing teeth and molded dimples. His straight arms are molded with the palms facing back. He is marked: "1088-0500 5//© MATTEL//INC. 1968//HONG KONG."*

"© 1968 Mattel, Inc.//U.S. Pat. Pend.// Taiwan." His neck was marked: "® 1968 Mattel, Inc."

Busy Ken® (number 3314), produced in 1972, was equipped with a new type of hand — the "busy" hand. This enabled *Ken* to grip and hold the 25 toys he came with. He also, for the first time, had bendable elbows. Manufactured in Hong Kong, he also was available as *Talking Busy Ken*® (number 1196), again with no changes to the face of *Ken*.

Another first for *Ken* occurred in 1973 with *Mod Hair Ken*® (number 4224), produced with rooted brunette hair and four other hair pieces: a beard, two moustaches and a pair of sideburns. *Mod Hair Ken* carries the mark: "© 1968//MATTEL, Inc.//U.S. + For. Pat'd//Other Pat's//Pending// Hong Kong."

Mod Hair Ken received a name change in 1976 to *Now Look Ken*® (number 9342), though the same face mold was used for both dolls. Two issues were made of this series, the first issue being produced in Taiwan, the second in Hong Kong. Both *Kens* had open/closed mouths with teeth which formed a smile, feathered eyebrows and came dressed in tan leisure suits, the men's fashion of the times, and was labeled "More handsome than ever!" The first issue *Mod Hair Ken* had longer brown rooted hair than the second issue. The first issue *Ken* also had bendable knees, while the second did not. The first issue was marked: "©1968//MATTEL, INC.// U.S. + For. Pat'd//Other Pats//Pending//Taiwan." The second issue *Mod Hair Ken* is marked: "1088-0500 3//©MATTEL//INC. 1968//Hong Kong."

Hawaiian Ken® (number 2960) used the same face mold as the *Live*

Action Ken® and *Busy Ken*®. Shown in *Illustration 3*, he was a department store "special" which included in his box "Surfboard and Accessories." *Hawaiian Ken* had a very wide leg stance and his palms were flat, facing back. He is marked on the neck: "1968 MATTEL INC." His body mark is: "1088-0500 2//© MATTEL// INC. 1968//HONG KONG."

Let us take a moment to note the change in *Ken's* physical appearance over the years. *Illustration 5* shows us two *Kens*, the first edition *Ken* (number 750) and the *Sunsational Malibu Ken*® (number 3849). Note the muscle structure to the body which has developed with the *Malibu Ken* and is completely lacking with the first edition *Ken*. You will also note that over the years the positioning of *Ken's* hands in relation to his body have changed with the various

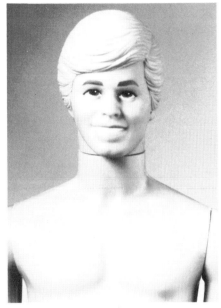  

ABOVE LEFT: Illustration 10. *12in (30cm) Sun Gold Malibu Ken® (number 1088), by Mattel, 1984, with molded and painted blonde hair parted to the right (note the* Sunsational Malibu Ken® *has hair parted to the left); manufactured of vinyl, he is jointed at the shoulders and hips; has painted blue eyes looking straight ahead, a painted open/closed mouth showing teeth and a molded cleft in the chin. His straight arms are molded with the palms facing back. He is marked: "©1968//MATTEL INC.//HONG KONG."*

ABOVE CENTER: Illustration 11. *12in (30cm) Sunsational Malibu Hispanic Ken® (number 4971), by Mattel, 1984, with molded and painted dark brown curly hair; manufactured of vinyl, he is jointed at the neck, shoulders and hips; has painted brown eyes looking straight ahead, a painted open/closed mouth showing teeth and a molded cleft in the chin. His straight arms are molded with the palms facing back. He is marked: "1088-0500 6//© MATTEL//INC. 1968//HONG KONG."*

ABOVE RIGHT: Illustration 12. *12in (30cm) Sunsational Malibu Black Ken® (number 3849), by Mattel, 1982, with rooted curly black hair; manufactured of vinyl, he is jointed at the neck, shoulders and hips; has painted brown eyes looking straight ahead and a painted closed mouth. He is marked: "1088-0500 6//© MATTEL//INC. 1968//HONG KONG."*

versions of *Ken* released. In some cases his palms face his sides, in other cases, as with this *Malibu Ken*, the hands face back. Because of the change in *Ken's* body over the years the newer *Ken* dolls cannot wear the clothing produced for the first *Kens*.

Ken's smile grew wider and dimples even deeper with *Malibu Ken* (number 1088). His blonde hair was molded and parted to the right. That style was reversed in 1979 with *Sun Lovin' Ken®* (number 1088) with the bangs swept to the left. This version was used for the *Roller Skating Ken®* (number 1881), produced in 1980, *Fashion Jeans Ken®* (number 5316) produced in 1982 and *Sunsational Malibu Ken* (number 3849) shown in *Illustration 9*.

One *Ken* produced which allowed you to take part in his grooming was *Sport N' Shave Ken®* (number 1294) seen in *Illustration 6*. Produced in 1980, he came with a "beard marker" which could be used to apply a beard which was than "wet-shaved" off with his shaver and shaving mug. He also had rooted brunette hair and jointed wrists and neck.

Western Ken® (number 3600), seen in *Illustration 7*, had the same molded hair, this time brunette, parted to the left. He also had a more muscled torso and molded bent arms with side movement.

Let us take another look at the body structure of the *Kens* shown in *Illustration 8*. The *Sport N' Shave Ken* (number 1294) and the *Western Ken* (number 3600) have essentially the same body torso and legs, but the arms are different. *Sport N' Shave Ken* has straight arms, jointed at the shoulders so they can be moved up from the side, and jointed wrists. The

Western Ken has curved arms, also jointed to move up from the side. Comparing this illustration with *Illustration 5* we see that these *Kens* have more muscles then the *Mailbu Ken* and have an extra joint at the waist for more flexibility.

The mold used for *Western Ken* was also used for *Sunsational Malibu Ken* (number 3849) shown in *Illustration 9*, and in 1982 was used for *Dream Date Ken®* (number 5868), *Horse Lovin' Ken®* (number 3600) and on the *Barbie and Friends Gift Set®*.

Ken's hairdo was parted again on the opposite side for the *Sun Gold Malibu Ken®* (number 1088) produced in 1984. His eyes were painted a darker shade of blue and he had a very subtle molded cleft to his chin and no dimples, as shown in *Illustration 10*.

ABOVE LEFT: Illustration 13. *12in (30cm)* Tropical Black Ken® *(number 1023), by Mattel, 1986, with molded and painted curly black hair; manufactured of vinyl, he is jointed at the neck, shoulders and hips; has painted brown eyes looking straight ahead, feathered eyebrows, a painted open/closed mouth with a smile and dimples. He is marked: "©1968//MATTEL INC.//US + FOR. PA'D//OTHER PATS.//PENDING//MALAYSIA."*

ABOVE RIGHT: Illustration 14. *12in (30cm)* Rocker Ken® *(number 3131), by Mattel, 1986, with rooted blonde hair (the only* Ken® *manufactured with rooted blonde hair); manufactured of vinyl, he is jointed at the neck, shoulders, waist and hips; has painted blue eyes looking straight ahead and a painted closed mouth. He is marked on the neck: "MATTEL INC." and on the back: "® MATTEL INC. 1968//TAIWAN."*

The "Hispanic" version of the *Sunsational Malibu Ken* (number 4971), produced in 1984, has very dark brown hair and (number 4971), produced in 1984, has very dark brown hair and eyes and the molded chin cleft and dimples. Shown in *Illustration 11*, *Ken* is marked: "1088-0500 5//© MATTEL//INC. 1968//HONG KONG."

The black *Kens* have achieved a strong ethnic appearance over the years. The 1981 *Sunsational Malibu Ken* (number 3849) was given a rooted Afro style and solemn molded black features as shown in *Illustration 12*. His body mark is: "1088-05006//©

MATTEL//INC. 1968//HONG KONG."

He received a happier expression with the face used for the 1985 *Day-To-Night Black Ken®* (number 9018), *Dream Glow Black Ken®* (number 2421) and the *Black Tropical Ken®* (number 1023) shown in *Illustration 13*. He has a more typical *Ken* smile — though his nose is molded slightly wider and he has the molded black Afro hairdo.

The newest *Ken* face available can be seen in *Illustration 14* as *Rocker Ken®* (number 3131). With rooted hair used for *Ken* only four times, this present-day *Ken* has long blonde "combable" hair. *Ken* was produced

as part of the second *Barbie and the Rockers®* sets.

We can see by taking a look at *Ken* over the years the changes which have occurred in men's fashions and looks. These dolls by Mattel truly represent history in progress, a history which we can see and often laugh at. □

Peggy — A Walking Doll by the Paris Doll Company

by **Ursula R. Mertz**

Photographs by **Linda K. Mertz**

LEFT: Illustration 1. This advertising page came with the all original brown-haired *Peggy* when she was bought from the primary owner. **BELOW: Illustration 2.** 28in (71cm) all composition walker with a brown mohair wig; blue sleep eyes with brown eye shadow, painted light brown lower eyelashes, black real upper eyelashes, one-stroke light brown eyebrows; open mouth with four upper teeth and a felt tongue. Her all original clothes consist of a pink nylon organdy dress with attached white cotton slip and separate white teddy. The dress bodice is made of pink taffeta. The bodice and skirt are trimmed with white lace. Her white rayon socks and thin white oilcloth shoes complete the outfit, along with a pink hair ribbon.

Unmarked dolls are often treated as stepchildren by collectors. We seem to prefer the ones with pedigrees. There are all kinds of reasons for this. Or maybe we just feel more secure with a marked doll. Therefore, it is always very gratifying when another doll, such as our *Peggy* in question, can join the ranks as a known specimen. Additional rewards accrue when, in the process of identification, a doll's name and a heretofore unknown company are found. Chance had it that two *Peggies* became available to be examined and a comparison study could be done as well.

Our brown-haired *Peggy* came with the original piece of advertising shown in **Illustration 1**, which lists the name of the Paris Doll Company, New York, N.Y. When the blonde *Peggy* surfaced, I noted that her dress was the same as that of the *Peggy* shown in the original ad. The two rows of printed ribbon trim on the front bodice are clearly identifiable. There is no mention of the Paris firm in any of the doll reference books I have consulted nor could I find

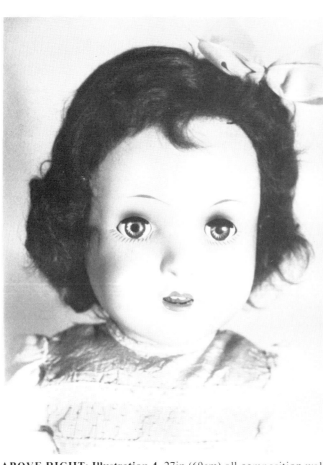

FAR LEFT: Illustration 3.
Close-up of the 28in (71cm)
doll shown in **Illustration 2.**
Note the one-stroke eyebrows
as opposed to the multi-
stroke eyebrows on the
blonde-haired doll.

ABOVE RIGHT: Illustration 4. 27in (69cm) all composition walker with a blonde mohair wig; blue sleep eyes with gray eye shadow, painted black lower eyelashes, real black upper eyelashes, multi-stroke light brown eyebrows; open mouth with four upper teeth and a felt tongue. Her original dress is made of light blue taffeta trimmed with pink printed 1in (2cm) wide ribbon. In the front, the bodice is trimmed with two rows of this ribbon. It is these two rows of ribbon that one can recognize in the original advertising reproduced in **Illustration 1.** She wears replaced shoes, socks and underwear.

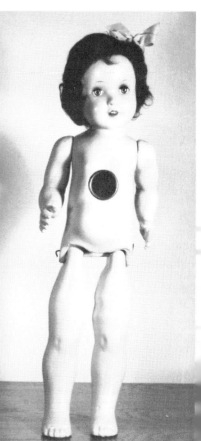

RIGHT: Illustration 5. Close-up of the 27in (69cm) doll shown in **Illustration 4.** Note the multi-stroke eyebrows on this doll, as opposed to the one-stroke eyebrows on the brown-haired doll.

FAR RIGHT: Illustration 6. Undressed brown-haired doll showing the body. Both dolls have identical bodies. Note the crier box inserted in the front. The crier box on the blonde-haired doll still works and emits distinctive "mama" sounds.

any information on *Peggy* or the company in question in other available literature. No patent date or "patent pending" label was found on the doll. They may not have made their own dolls but only constructed the walker mechanism and done the dressing. Another possibility is that this firm was small and did not exist long. The author would appreciate hearing from readers who can add information about this company.

Peggy was probably made in the 1940s, since she has eye shadow similar to other late composition dolls. Also, I have seen one example of her made of hard plastic. While mechanical walkers were all the rage in the 1950s, they were not common during the composition era. *Peggy* is an all composition fully-jointed doll with sleep eyes and a mohair wig. Like all composition dolls, she still has nicely hand-painted features with black lower eyelashes for the blonde-haired doll and light brown ones for the brown-haired doll.

Peggy's walking mechanism is of simple construction. A rod is mounted vertically inside the body and connects to a horizontal wire structure which is attached to the top of the legs. Holding her by the shoulders or under the arms, weight is put on the doll's foot and pressure applied in a forward direction. This propels the other leg ahead.

At first glance, there seemed to be only obvious differences between the two *Peggies*, such as wig color and clothes. The garments on both dolls are of good quality and well constructed, with finished seams at the neck, sleeves and hems. Little by little, I noted that the blonde-haired doll had all kinds of subtle quality differences. While the body seams on both dolls were finished well, our blonde had smoother composition and multi-stroke eyebrows instead of one-stroke ones. Her legs are held apart by a coil instead of a wooden dowel. This may be the reason why the blonde *Peggy* walks more smoothly. Her dress has hook and loop closures instead of punched-in snaps. Unfortunately, underwear, shoes and socks are replaced. The original ones might have shown further variations. One wonders if the blonde *Peggy* was made on special order for a better store.

Finding the original advertising and dolls in original clothes has led to new discoveries. Many questions remain unanswered. I, for one, would like to know more about the Paris Doll Company. I also have more questions about *Peggy* herself. Why is she seen so infrequently? Was she too cumbersome to operate, too large or too expensive? We hope that more information will eventually become available. It is these puzzles, I am sure, that keep us doll collectors interested. □

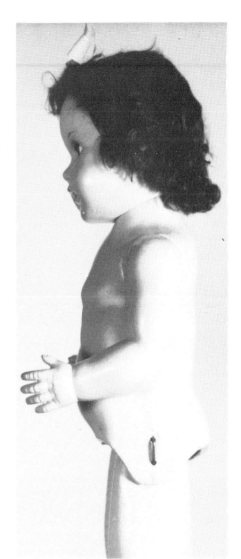

RIGHT: Illustration 7. Side view of the undressed brown-haired doll, seen in **Illustration 6**, showing the attachment of the legs. The arms are strung with elastic.

BELOW: Illustration 8. Close-up of the lower part of the undressed brown-haired doll, seen in **Illustrations 6** and **7**. Note the cut out area which accommodates the specially formed legs. They are mounted with a metal rod and wooden dowel which keeps the legs separated. On the blonde-haired doll there is no wooden dowel but a metal coil. Above the legs can be seen part of the wire mechanism inside the body.

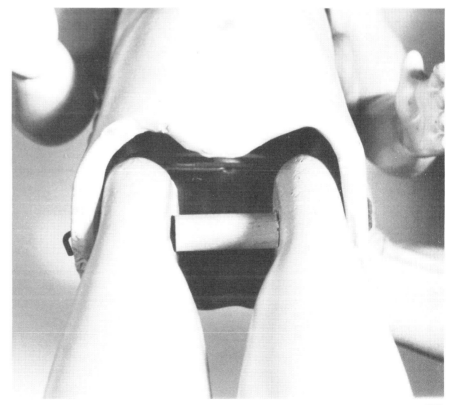

INDEX

AUTHORS

The Best Of The
DOLL READER®

Volume IV

A selection of 52 of the most interesting and well-researched articles from past issues of **Doll Reader**® magazine have been compiled for your reading enjoyment into **The Best of the Doll Reader**®, **Volume IV**. With topics ranging from some of the earliest antique dolls to those being debuted at recent Toy Fairs in New York City, the reader is introduced to doll collecting at its finest.

Dolls of china, bisque, papier-mâché, metal and wood are covered in the antique section, as well as automata and dolls with unusual hair styles. In the collectible section there are articles about composition, celluloid, cloth and vinyl dolls, and types of dolls from babies to the fashion dolls. In addition, the dolls which debuted at the 1986 through 1988 Toy Fairs are also featured.

The variety of the topics covered in these articles are sure to please the most discriminate doll collector. 192 pages. 48 pages of color.

ISBN 0-87588-374-5

51495

EAN

9 780875 883748

$14.95